Video Editing

A Postproduction Primer
Third Edition

Steven E. Browne

Focal Press
Boston Oxford Johannesburg Melbourne New Dehli Singapore

Focal Press is an imprint of Butterworth–Heinemann.

 A member of the Reed Elsevier group

Recognizing the importance of preserving what has been written, Butterworth–Heinemann prints its books on acid-free paper whenever possible.

Library of Congress Cataloging-in-Publication Data
Browne, Steven E.
  Video editing : a postproduction primer / Steven E. Browne. — 3rd ed.
    p.   cm.
  Rev. ed. of: Videotape editing. 2nd ed. c1993.
  Includes bibliographical references and index.
  ISBN 0-240-80269-1 (pbk. : alk. paper)
  1. Video tapes—Editing. I. Browne, Steven E. Videotape editing. II. Title.
  TR899.B725   1996
  778.59—dc20   96-17887
                                                   CIP

British Library Cataloguing-in-Publication Data
A catalogue record for this book is available from the British Library.

The publisher offers special discounts on bulk orders of this book.
For information, please contact:
Manager of Special Sales
Butterworth–Heinemann
313 Washington Street
Newton, MA 02158–1626
Tel: 617-928-2500
Fax: 617-928-2620

For information on all Focal Press publications available, contact our World Wide Web home page at: http://www.bh.com/fp

10 9 8 7 6 5 4 3 2

Printed in the United States of America

To Michele, the best friend and wife imaginable.

Contents

IV Working at the Keyboard   159

Preface

Video technology is constantly changing, but even though new video formats and dazzling effects devices are being announced almost every year, none of these advances has altered the overall concepts of video editing. Control track, insert and assemble recordings, time code, off-line editors, edit decision lists (EDLs), switchers—whatever the equipment or technique, the basics of video editing are still the same.

The ability to understand these concepts and how they relate to each other is the key to using different types of equipment. An individual who knows the principles of videotape editing can apply that information to any production or postproduction challenge.

Understanding the video postproduction process is, therefore, vital not only to the editor, but also to anyone planning to work in the video or film world. The purpose of this text is to provide the reader with a basic understanding of this process.

Introduction

Since the first edition of *Videotape Editing*, digital videotape, random-access editing, digital audio workstations, and digital audio tape have been accepted as standard hardware in the postproduction world. Magnetic film is disappearing, just as two-inch video did years ago. Hundreds of films have been edited on random-access systems. Video assist is a requirement on most film sets.

More and more feature films use electronic equipment for postproduction audio and picture. Though most of the basic editing concepts remain sound, digital video is reshaping the film and video world. In Japan, High Definition Television (HDTV) is already a broadcasting reality. And the transformations continue. But the process is not changing drastically; only the tools used within the process are changing. Assemble recordings, time code, dissolves, wipes, edit decision lists, and control track all exist and continue to be used on a daily basis.

One conceptual aspect of this text should be explained. This book is designed to build knowledge, not flood the reader with information. At first glance this process may seem slightly redundant, but it makes difficult ideas much easier to understand.

As new technology presents challenges and opportunities, the basics of videotape editing remain valid. This edition addresses the new technology, but remains dedicated to providing the reader with a basic understanding of the video postproduction process.

Acknowledgments

In any endeavor, there are people who provide support, advice, and guidance. I would like to take this opportunity to thank a few of the friends and peers who have helped make this book possible. Mitch Winit, Warren Hunt, and Barton Durfee for their impeccable technical advice; Dale Carroll, Scott Brown, and Celine Jackson for their help with the photography shoots. Finally, special thanks go to Richard Kaufman, Paul Apel, and Allen Haines for providing steady friendship, support, and advice.

PART I
Technical Aspects of Videotape

A Brief History of Videotape

Although videotape has been in existence for a relatively short time, the growth of its use has been astonishing. After capturing the television industry, video-tape invaded the home and, after much resistance, has moved into the world of filmmaking. A powerful new force entered the postproduction playing field in the late 1990s. Computerized storage and retrieval of picture and audio changed the editing room environment. The following is a brief history of the rapid growth of this technology along with the arrival of random-access editing.

AMPEX AND QUAD

In 1956, Ampex® announced that it had developed a new device: the videotape machine. A team of six men (see Figure 1-1), including Ray Dolby (who later created the Dolby sound system), had invented what is now referred to as *quad*. These large tape machines used four record heads (hence the name *quad*) and two-inch-wide tape. On November 30, 1956, CBS broadcast the first program using videotape. The live New York show, *Douglas Edwards and the News*, was recorded, then rebroadcast three hours later on the West Coast.

At first, quad videotape machines were used to record live programs for broadcast at a later time, but soon producers wanted to edit these programs. In late 1958, Ampex began marketing a videotape splicer. By sprinkling a small amount of magnetically active tracing powder on the tape, an editor could locate the video frame line with the aid of a microscope. The tape could then be cut at this line and new material spliced onto the tail of the original tape.

Figure 1-1 The Ampex team that created the original quad tape machine. Pictured from left to right: Fred Pfost, Shelby Henderson, Ray Dolby, Alex Maxey, Charles E. Anderson, and Charles Ginsburg. Photo courtesy of Ampex Corporation.

Five years later, Ampex introduced an editing device called Editec. An audio cue tone on a secondary audio track of the quad tape signaled Editec to make the quad machine go into edit. The engineers placed the cue tone at the beginning and at the end of the edit. The engineers would manually back up the playback and record machines, and put the machines into play mode simultaneously. Editec would electronically perform the edit.

TIME CODE EDITING

NASA provided the next big advance in video editing. The space agency was using a time code system based on Greenwich Mean Time (hours, minutes, and seconds recorded on their telemetry tapes) to track the vast amounts of data from their instruments. EECO, formerly the Electronic Engineering Company of America, modified this system to accommodate the 30-frames-per-second playing speed needed for videotape. In 1967, EECO introduced the time code technique to the video industry and began marketing editing devices based on this highly accurate coding system.

The popularity of the time code editing concept caused several other manufacturers to follow suit, each with its own type of code. In 1972, the Society of Motion Picture and Television Engineers (SMPTE) standardized the format for time code.

In 1971, a company named CMX® was created as a joint venture by CBS Laboratories and the Memorex Corporation. That year, CMX introduced the CMX 600, the first random-access video editing system (see Figure 1-2). The system worked by copying original pictures onto huge mechanical computer disks. The CMX 600 could then randomly access any frame from the disks. Because the CMX 600 was very expensive and prone to failure, it was not a financial success.

A year later, the same company introduced the CMX 300. Although the CMX 300 was limited in its functions and speed compared to today's editors, it was frame accurate, and it became the industry standard for computerized video editing.

Figure 1-2 The CMX 600, the first random-access editor. Instead of using a keyboard, the operator controlled the machine by placing a light pen on the screen. Photo courtesy of CMX Corporation.

TAPE FORMATS

During 1962 and 1963, manufacturers introduced a variety of helical-scan video machines, none of which followed any universal standard. Whereas quad machines record video frames perpendicularly to the edge of the videotape, the helical-scan format records video on a slant. This made cutting the tape on the frame line impossible. The early helical-scan machines were not accepted in the broadcast industry because engineers were unwilling to replace their expensive quad machines with these low-quality, nonstandardized units.

In the late 1960s, the Japanese formed the Electronics Industries Association of Japan (EIAJ) to standardize these new formats. In 1969, Sony™ introduced its EIAJ-standard three-quarter-inch U-Matic® series, which proved extremely popular in the United States, both in the industrial market and for broadcast editing. In 1974, Sony announced its VO-2850 three-quarter-inch editing deck, which was capable of recording both insert and assemble edits. CMX incorporated the VO-2850 into its next product, the CMX 50 (see Figure 1-3).

The CMX 50 used 3 three-quarter-inch U-Matic cassette machines: one record machine and two playbacks (the minimum number of decks required to

Figure 1-3 The CMX 50, the original off-line editing system. Photo courtesy of CMX Corporation.

create a dissolve or a wipe). CMX also marketed the CMX 40, a version of the unit used for electronic news gathering (ENG).

Both the CMX 50 and the CMX 40 used three-quarter-inch tape copies of the original two-inch quad videotape, with identical video and audio and matching time code. The off-line computer logged all edits performed on the three-quarter-inch work print and printed out a list on paper tape. When this list was fed into the CMX 300 the computer repeated the edits that had been performed on the CMX 50, using the camera-original two-inch quad tapes as playbacks.

What made the CMX 50 and 40 such successes was that the creative editing process was done on a less expensive system. If a punch tape containing all the edits was brought from a CMX 50 to an on-line editing session, the costly CMX 300 and quad tape machines were needed only for final editing chores. Using the CMX 50 saved producers thousands of dollars per show.

In 1974, CMX also introduced the CMX 340X, which enhanced computerized time code editing. The 340X simplified keyboard instructions and was easier to operate than the CMX 300. The 340X could be used for either off-line or on-line editing.

ONE-INCH TAPE

In 1975, Bosch-Fernseh℗ introduced its BCN one-inch videotape format. The next year, Sony and Ampex brought out their broadcast-quality one-inch machines. The problem of machine incompatibility stopped broadcasters from parting with their two-inch quad machines. During an SMPTE conference in 1977, ABC and CBS executives said that they would not adopt one-inch tape until some standard was established.

As a result of that meeting, two committees were formed. One committee focused on nonsegmented (one drum revolution per video field) recordings and the other group concentrated on segmented (more than one drum revolution per video field) recordings. The committees eventually defined three categories of one-inch recording: *Type A* was the original Ampex recording; *Type B* was the Bosch-Fernseh segmented standard; and *Type C* was the compromise standard to which Ampex and Sony agreed. In 1979, Ampex stopped manufacturing its original one-inch machines, and the Type A designation was formally dropped.

The standardization of the one-inch formats left broadcasters with two format choices. Each had its advantages and disadvantages. The Bosch-Fernseh format produced a better picture but could not be seen in fast-shuttle or still-frame editing modes. The Ampex/Sony format, Type C, did not produce as clear a recording, but it was less expensive and could be viewed in still-frame mode or at speeds other than play.

No independent production or editing company was willing to invest a large sum of money in a format that might quickly become obsolete. When ABC ordered its first batch of Type C machines, word spread quickly, and Type C became the standard for broadcast-quality one-inch machines.

CONTROL TRACK EDITING

In the 1970s, the sitcom became the king of American television. Many of these shows were recorded and edited on videotape. This increased use of video for production created a substantial market for videotape editing machines, inspiring other manufacturers to compete with CMX.

During the same period, the control track editor came into its own. Control track editors used the electronic frame pulses on the tape to keep track of tape location and edit points, rather than time code. By the late 1970s, many producers had purchased their own editing systems.

At the end of the decade, television news departments began to switch from film to videotape production to bypass the time-consuming process of developing film footage. The cuts-only control track editors were used on location to edit tape as it was shot. During this period, several prime-time network and syndicated programs increased the reputation of three-quarter-inch editing by using the format for show segments. The mass movement toward video as a medium had begun.

HALF-INCH VIDEOTAPE AND RANDOM-ACCESS EDITING

By 1984, broadcast-quality half-inch videotape had been accepted by the broadcasting industry. The picture quality of the half-inch tape was far superior to that of three-quarter-inch and incredibly close to that of one-inch, thanks to the technique of composite recording. An added advantage was that the recorder could be built into the camera, eliminating a crew member as well as the cumbersome wires that ran from the camera to the record deck.

Newer editing systems, including those from CMX, began mixing two-inch quad with one-inch videotape, three-quarter-inch cassettes, and half-inch tape. Video, which had once been a very expensive, quad-only process used almost exclusively by the networks, was becoming a flexible, fast, and relatively inexpensive production medium.

In the mid-1980s, several companies began to take advantage of microcomputers in the editing process. One company modified an IBM PC to control videocassette recorders (VCRs) and switchers (see the Glossary). To meet the growing pressure to provide low-cost editing systems, some manufacturers created less expensive units that could be upgraded. As a result of this technological innovation, editing videotape became less and less expensive. Now postproduction companies could build more editing bays. Corporations could afford to establish their own video departments to produce newsletters and public service programs.

As the cost of video editing dropped, the rate of technological change increased. By the middle of the 1980's, much of the film industry's resistance to videotape had evaporated. VCRs were becoming a common household appliance, and the marriage of the video and film industries appeared to be a lasting one. Television shows were shot on film, then edited and delivered on videotape.

The 1980s also brought the rebirth and growth of random-access video editing. *Random access* means that specific segments of tape, dispersed through one or more reels, can be defined and accessed independently and almost immediately.

Random-access video editing became popular because of its speed and reediting ease. In addition, the high-end random-access systems could provide film key numbers in order to conform the film negative. Random-access systems began to capture television film business and in the 1990s major feature films were being edited on this type of system. Thousands of filmed commercials have been edited on random-access systems, then conformed on video for broadcast (see Figure 1-4).

Figure 1-4   D-Vision is one of several popular brands of random-access editors. Random-access editors are now widely accepted in both feature film and television broadcast postproduction. Photo courtesy of D-Vision Systems.™

There are several popular brands of random-access systems. Each has its own particular strengths and is used more in one area than another. By the mid-nineties, tape-based linear off-line editors were considered obsolete. Computer prices had dropped and systems had been upgraded to allow the ability to hold hours of picture and audio information.

THE MTV/AMERICAN HOME VIDEO IMPACT

As the cost of video editing equipment dropped, increasing numbers of consumers bought their own cameras and editing systems. Music videos were shot on VHS, Hi-8®, or eight-millimeter film. In the latter part of the 1980s, complete shows built around home videos premiered. ABC's *America's Funniest Home Videos* revealed that the entire country was taping and editing everything that moved.

As the introduction of digital video into the commercial arena stretched the high end of editing, Super-VHS (S-VHS) and Hi-8 became the choice of the sophisticated consumer and budget-conscious professional. Videotape had strengthened its hold on both sides of the economic equation.

DIGITAL VIDEO

A growth pattern similar to the earlier one-inch standards problem emerged as digital video entered the marketplace. *Digital video,* which defines images by a representative series of electronic pulses, rather than voltage levels, offered superior image quality over traditional analog formats, such as one-inch, and Betacam™. However, because of its high cost, digital video did not offer an economically advantageous format; thus, its acceptance by the production and editing community was selective.

One-inch tape machines had replaced two-inch machines because the former were cheaper and provided a higher quality signal. Digital videotape was technically superior to one-inch tape, but more expensive to purchase and maintain. The competition between the digital formats, D1 and D2, each of which offered distinct strengths and weaknesses, further divided the potential users of digital videotape.

The split between these two formats segmented the high-end video market. One-inch tape, already firmly entrenched, continued to be the workhorse of tape production and postproduction. D1, an expensive, extremely high-end product, captured the effects and graphics portions of editing. D2, a less expensive digital medium, made inroads into the postproduction environment as a film-to-tape mastering format, and also as a high-budget production format.

Of course these formats crossed over from one use to another. Some expensive productions used D1 as their recording medium. D1 is also used for mastering home video products, while D2 is used for some graphic and animation product creation. One-inch tape remained the economical standard for delivery to networks and television stations.

In the 1990s, additional digital formats came onto the editing scene. D3, a Panasonic™ product, is a digital video format on a half-inch-wide tape, designed to compete in the digital domain as an economically feasible alternative to D1 or D2. The Ampex DCT® also gained a foothold in the postproduction environment. DCT is a component system with the advantages of being cheaper than D1 but more expensive and higher quality than D2. It has an incredibly quick lock-up time and excellent picture quality.

At the same time that digital video was changing video postproduction, a further fragmentation of formats was created by component-versus-composite recording techniques. *Composite* video combines the luminance (black and white) and chrominance (color) portions of the video signal. *Component* video separates the luminance and chrominance portions of the signal, which results in superior image quality.

Composite recording and editing had been the standard method of video production. However, the introduction of the component formats D1, DCT, and Betacam SP® made component recording and editing viable. The disadvantage of component recording is that it needs an entire system designed around the component signal to take advantage of the signal's strengths. In the late 1980s and early 1990s many component editing bays found uses ranging from graphics to feature film effects to show postproduction, often combining digital and analog signals in a component environment.

Both manufacturers and editing companies made a concerted effort to entice producers to explore and use these new formats. With no clear winner in the format wars, no one tape or recording format dominated. With High Definition Television (HDTV) and random-access on-line on the horizon, either of which could change or eliminate the new and old tape formats, there was no obvious choice as there had been with one-inch tape.

From a few farsighted people at Ampex, to computerized editing pioneered by CMX, to the smaller formats of one-inch, three-quarter-inch, and now digital videotape, video has come a long way in only three decades. And since videotape is an electronic medium, even more exciting developments are on tap as progress in electronic and computer technologies continues unabated.

2

Videotape, Control Track, and Time Code

WHAT IS VIDEOTAPE?

Videotape consists of a Mylar® backing covered with a thin layer of ferrous oxide (see Figure 2-1). Mylar is a strong, flexible plastic material that provides a base for the oxide. This oxide is easily magnetized and is the substance that stores the video and audio information. Metal tape is a highly refined videotape that uses metal particles instead of ferrous oxide to enhance recording sensitivity. Metal tape is used in D1, D2, DCT, Betacam SP, S-VHS®, and Hi-8. Videotape is very similar in composition to audio tape.

When videotape is purchased, whether by a production company, an editing facility, or a home user, it is usually blank. (A prerecorded tape has a signal on it.) When a blank tape is played on a video machine, the viewer sees either snow or nothing. The same condition exists after the viewer erases a recorded tape by putting it next to a very strong magnetic field, which destroys the video signal on the tape. The machine that does this is called a *bulk eraser.*

Tape can be bought, both new and used, from a number of sources. You should be very careful when buying used or off-brand tape. Videotape, like any manufactured material, can be created under various conditions and still perform the task of recording signals. Cheaper tape tends to have more *dropouts*, minute

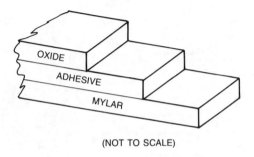

(NOT TO SCALE)

Figure 2-1   Cross section of videotape.

spots that have a lack of oxide attached to the base. These dropouts, which look like white horizontal scratches, are easy to spot on lower grades of VHS tape. Professional-quality tapes are manufactured under more stringent procedures than consumer tapes.

High-quality tape is not that expensive. Since it is the medium on which original pictures and audio are stored, buying quality tape is worth the extra expense. For off-line editing (see the Glossary), an editor might consider using recycled tape or a cheaper brand.

CONTROL TRACK

The *control track* is a pulse recorded onto a track of the videotape. Because the pulse, which is only created during an assemble recording, marks each revolution of the record drum and the beginning of each frame, it is called the *frame pulse.* The control track could be called the electronic sprocket holes of video, since its purpose is to act as a guide for the playback of the video signal (see Figure 2-2).

Since the pulses on the control track are recorded in evenly spaced intervals at each revolution of the recording drum, the playback machine must maintain the same relationship to play the signal properly. If the spacing of the control track pulses is altered, the picture will roll until the spacing becomes even again. During this roll, the playback machine will change the tape speed and drum rotation in an attempt to keep the control track pulses constant.

All video formats use different but similar control track signals. Some video machines are capable of playing videotape that has a damaged control track. This is accomplished by locking to the video signal rather than the control track pulses.

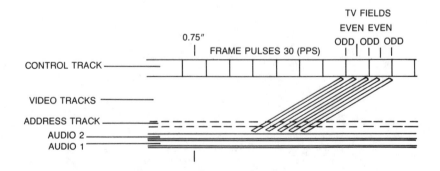

Figure 2-2   Diagram of three-quarter-inch recording tracks.

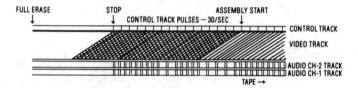

FULL ERASE STOP ASSEMBLY START
CONTROL TRACK PULSES — 30/SEC
CONTROL TRACK
VIDEO TRACK
AUDIO CH-2 TRACK
AUDIO CH-1 TRACK
TAPE →

Figure 2-3 Diagram of an assemble edit.

TAPE RECORDING AND EDITING

Two basic types of video recording are used: assemble and insert.

Assemble Recording

Assemble recording erases everything on the tape from the beginning of the assemble edit, replacing it with the new picture, audio, and control track (see Figure 2-3). This method is not very useful if you want to record audio from sources other than your picture. It is, however, a very effective way to make a direct copy of another videotape or to create a control track in preparation for an insert editing session.

Another disadvantage of assemble recording is that the control track pulses at the edit can occur either earlier or later than the previous control track pulses (if the tape already has a recorded signal on it). This difference in spacing will cause the picture to break up or roll, as mentioned earlier. Newer machines have the ability to lock to the previous control track, producing a stable assemble edit. However, the end of the edit will not have precisely the same spacing as the video that follows.

These two major technical disadvantages of assemble editing and recording explain why most professional editing is done using insert recording.

Insert Recording

Insert recording offers the advantage of clean edits and the option of performing audio or video-only edits. The editor can replace video, audio, or both without disturbing the tape's control track (see Figure 2-4).

Videotape is blank when purchased, so before an insert recording can be made, the tape must have a control track recorded on it. To do this, an assemble recording is made for the length of the videotape; this recording lays down a continuous, unbroken control track. An insert recording made on blank tape will not play back properly because the tape has no reference as to how to play the video.

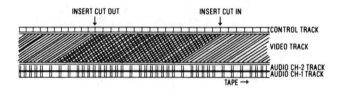

Figure 2-4   Diagram of an insert recording.

Professional editing houses buy new videotape and have night-shift employees assemble record them to prepare them for use. The assemble recording is usually a black picture with no audio, but it does have time code on it. This *black and coded* tape is used as a record tape for insert recordings. Therefore, when buying a record tape from a professional editing house, you will usually find that it already has the control track and time code on it.

To repeat, an assemble recording erases everything—all video, audio, and control track—and replaces it with totally new signals. An insert recording replaces only those tracks (video, audio, or both video and audio) selected. Insert recording is the method used by most professional editing companies.

Recording versus Editing

The words *insert* and *assemble* are used in several ways in the video vocabulary. An *insert recording* is done according to the method described above. To insert an edit, however, means to place an edit between two other edits or to erase part of a previously recorded edit by inserting a new edit. The *insert edit* is made using an insert recording.

An *assemble recording* erases all signals on a tape and records new signals on it. *Assembly* is a term referring to an on-line editing session using either an edit log or a computer-generated edit decision list (EDL); assembly is accomplished using insert recordings. An *A mode* or *B mode assembly* refers to one of two different approaches to assembling an EDL (see the Glossary). A mode and B mode assemblies also are accomplished using insert recordings. To *auto assemble* means to have the computer editor automatically perform a series of edits in an EDL list.

VIDEO FRAMES AND FIELDS

Recorded video signals are rather complex, and thus are tightly structured. The standard unit of video is a *frame*. Similar to film, motion video is created by displaying progressive frames at a rate fast enough for the human eye and brain to perceive continuous motion. Standard broadcast video in the United States, the rest of North America, and certain other countries records and displays approximately 30 frames per second (29.97 frames to be exact).

However, a frame of video is composed of two *fields*. These are recorded adjacent to each other on videotape and are interlaced during the playback process to display a full frame of video.

The basic means by which video images are recorded and displayed is a *scanning* process. When a video image is recorded by a camera, a beam of electrons sweeps across the recording surface in a progressive series of lines (think of the fine lines running horizontally across the face of an image on a TV set). National Television Standards Committee (NTSC) video, the North American standard, defines a frame as containing 525 scan lines. Each field contains 262.5 lines. One of the two fields in each frame contains the odd-numbered scan lines, and the other contains the even-numbered scan lines. When they are interlaced, they create a full frame. Blank videotape has no frames, fields, or control track.

INTERNATIONAL TELEVISION STANDARDS

As described in the previous section, NTSC is the video standard chosen by the United States and a number of other countries. PAL (phase alternate line) and SECAM (sequential color with memory) are the two other major worldwide television standards. PAL specifies a different means of encoding and transmitting color video. Both PAL and SECAM scan 625 lines per frame versus NTSC's 525 and have a rate of 25 frames per second. They also both operate at a 50-Hz frequency versus NTSC's 60 Hz. Finally, PAL defines the black level (see the Glossary) as 0, the same as the reference level for sync. In NTSC, 7.5 is the stated black level, and 0 is the sync reference level.

NTSC, PAL, and SECAM are incompatible with each other. Standards converters can convert video from one standard to another. Productions intended to be broadcast or released in different video standards are often shot on film, which can be converted to any video standard with little or no loss of resolution.

TIME CODE

The development of time code made frame-accurate, repeatable video editing possible. *Time code* is a labeling system that specifically identifies video frames and audio signals by referencing a 24-hour clock (see Figure 2-5). Each video frame is identified by an eight-digit number in the format hours:minutes:seconds:frames; for example, 05:15:18:23. Time code enables each frame to be identified and accessed for editing or reference. The time code can be recorded on videotape in several places: on one of the audio tracks (called *longitudinal*

Figure 2-5 The time code format.

time code), in the vertical interval portion of the video signal (*vertical interval time code*, abbreviated VITC and pronounced *vit-see*), or on the address track of the tape (a special area located in certain tape formats).

In concept, time code is very similar to the edge numbers on film. It is an arbitrary number assigned to each frame of video. Time code is arbitrary because the important portion of the tape is not the number but the picture that the code identifies. Time code is always read (by humans) in the same format. When recorded properly, time code is synchronized to the beginning of each frame. If time code is recorded by a code generator without being locked to a video source, the code may drift across the video frame, rendering it useless.

Time code has other data embedded in it: user information and sync information. Time code is divided into 80 digital bits recorded across the video frame. Groups of four bits create a decimal number from zero to nine. There are 32 bits reserved in the code for user information. With 32 bits, only the numbers zero through nine can be used in simple systems, or the letters A through F in more complicated systems. Four binary numbers are used to represent 16 characters (0–9 and A–F). This encoding method is called *hexadecimal notation*. User bits might indicate reels in a show; for example, reel 15 shot on September 20 at location 11 could be encoded 15 09 20 11. The coding equipment can be set to record the user information on each frame of video. The sync information defines the end of the frame of time code, which allows time code readers to determine the direction in which the tape is traveling.

In a composite video signal, the phase relationship of the color burst inverts every frame. (Component video does not require this phase reversal.) If an editor connects two frames with the same phase relationship, a horizontal picture shift occurs. When cutting to a completely new picture, this shift is unnoticeable. When cutting to the same image (to extend a freeze frame or graphic), this shift is very obvious. Color phase information is included in the time code signal, aiding computerized video editing systems in keeping the phase relationship of edited tapes consistent.

There are two kinds of time code: drop frame time code and non–drop frame time code. *Drop frame time code* is time accurate, meaning that one hour of time code equals one hour of videotape running in play mode. *Non–drop frame time code* is not time accurate. An hour of non–drop frame time code is equal to one hour and 3.6 seconds of videotape running in play mode (see Figure 2-6).

The difference between the two types of time code occurred because the NTSC decided that color television signals would run at 29.97 frames per

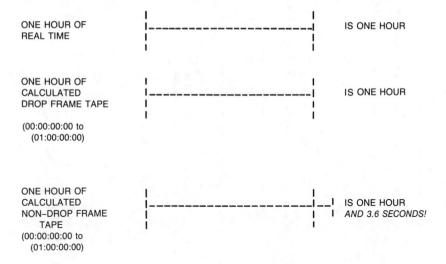

Figure 2-6 A comparison of timings between drop frame and non–drop frame time code.

second rather than 30 frames per second. When time code was first introduced, however, the code was designated with 30 frames per second. Over one hour, the 0.03-frame-per-second error adds up to 3.6 seconds. To compensate for this error, a system was devised to drop certain numbers from the counting.

The :00 and :01 frames are dropped at every new minute except at the 10-minute marks—10 minutes, 20 minutes, 30 minutes, etc. (see Figure 2-7). This amounts to 108 dropped numbers (3.6 seconds), which allows drop frame time code to keep accurate time and also gives it its name. Dropping these numbers does not change any video content.

Drop frame time code is often used for television programs that must be edited to meet certain time requirements. These shows must be edited to the second. Since drop frame time code is time accurate, it is used in these cases.

Non–drop frame time code is most often used to edit commercials and promotional tapes. Since commercials are usually no longer than one minute, there is no need to worry about the two frames dropped at the top of the minute. Similarly, promotional tapes are usually cut according to their content and pacing, without much concern for to-the-second timing.

Types of Time Code Recording

There are three types of time code recording, all of which originate with a time code generator. The three types are audio (or longitudinal) time code, address track time code, and vertical interval time code.

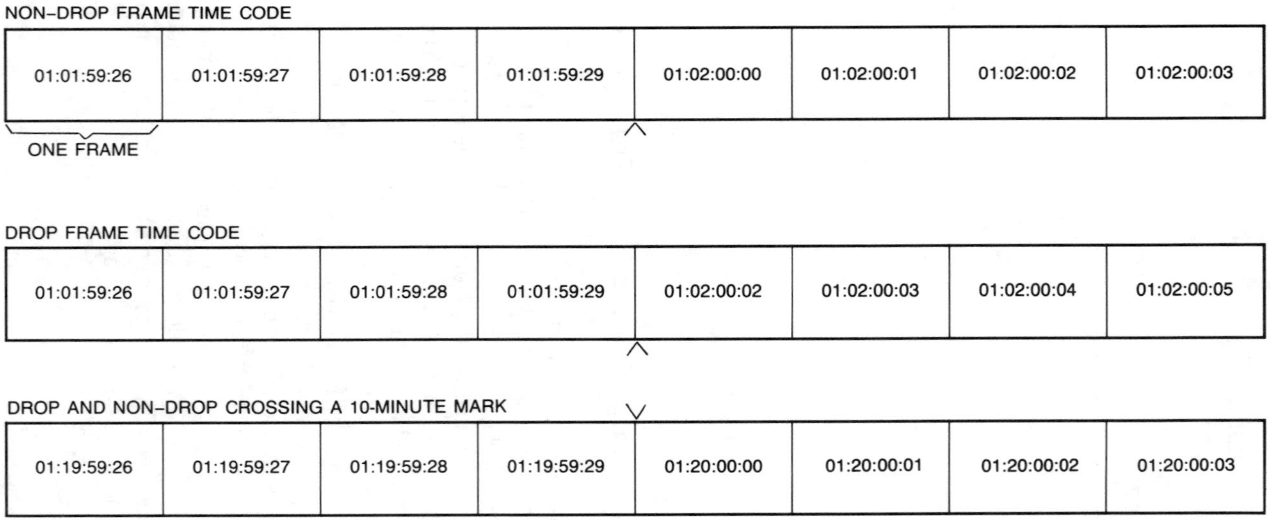

NON–DROP FRAME TIME CODE

| 01:01:59:26 | 01:01:59:27 | 01:01:59:28 | 01:01:59:29 | 01:02:00:00 | 01:02:00:01 | 01:02:00:02 | 01:02:00:03 |

ONE FRAME

DROP FRAME TIME CODE

| 01:01:59:26 | 01:01:59:27 | 01:01:59:28 | 01:01:59:29 | 01:02:00:02 | 01:02:00:03 | 01:02:00:04 | 01:02:00:05 |

DROP AND NON–DROP CROSSING A 10-MINUTE MARK

| 01:19:59:26 | 01:19:59:27 | 01:19:59:28 | 01:19:59:29 | 01:20:00:00 | 01:20:00:01 | 01:20:00:02 | 01:20:00:03 |

Figure 2-7 A comparison between drop frame and non–drop frame time code crossing a minute mark. Note that in the drop frame time code, the :00 and :01 are dropped. The exception occurs when crossing a ten-minute mark.

Audio or *longitudinal time code* is digitally encoded by a time code generator and recorded onto an audio track of a tape. It can be erased or regenerated (duplicated) and then recorded onto another tape. Audio time code can be recorded during the production phase of a show or after shooting has been completed. It can be recorded on any available audio channel. One-inch video-tape has a specific audio track (track 3) designed for time code. When using three-quarter-inch videotape audio time code, editing systems use audio track 1 or 2 for time code. Before coding the original production tape, the editor should check which track the system uses. (See **Ping-pong** in the Glossary for details about correcting time code recorded on the wrong channel.)

Address track time code is used only on three-quarter-inch professional broadcast videotape formats. Address track time code can be recorded only on decks specifically designed to record and read address track. Address track recording occurs during the shooting phase in an assemble recording—that is, at the same time that the video and audio are recorded. Although address track time code is recorded in the same location as the video, it is recorded at a different frequency (see Figure 2-8). The advantage of address track time code is that it does not occupy a production audio channel.

Vertical interval time code (VITC) is a picture signal recorded in the vertical interval. The advantage of this type of time code is that, unlike audio and address track time code, it is readable even when the tape is not moving. Since VITC is recorded in the vertical interval using a video channel, it does not occupy an audio channel. VITC can also indicate the particular field on which the videotape is parked.

VITC must be recorded at the same time as the picture. Recording and decoding the code requires special equipment. More expensive decks, such as D2s, come with VITC decoders built into them. You should check the availability of this equipment before planning to use this type of time code.

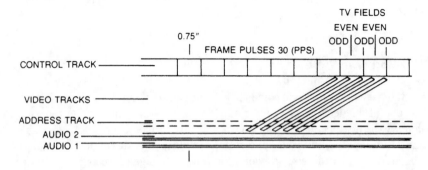

Figure 2-8 Placement of address track time code on three-quarter-inch recordings. The address track time code is recorded in the same location as the video signal, but at a different frequency.

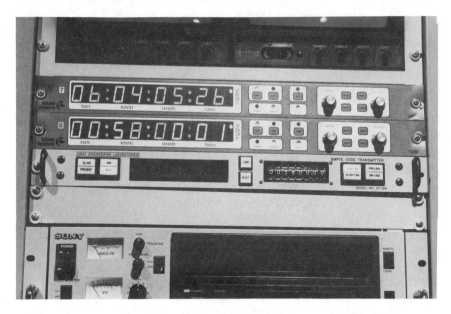

Figure 2-9   A time code generator, manufactured by Gray Engineering Laboratories, mounted in an equipment rack. Above the time code generator are two character inserters, used to display time code in video.

Time code should not be copied directly from tape to tape because time code is a digital signal that degrades with a straight transfer, and tape noise can render the code useless. Time code is regenerated by feeding the original time code signal into a regenerator, which creates a clean, new signal that can be recorded onto the same tape or used to create a window dub (a copy of a tape with time code "burned" into the picture) or submaster (a copy of an original show for protection).

Working with Time Code

As stated earlier, time code comes from a time code generator (see Figure 2-9). The operator selects drop frame or non–drop frame time code on the generator, along with the specific starting point (hour, minute, second, and frame). The time code must be in exact sync with the video, thus the generator must be locked to the record deck or a common reference signal. Recording unlocked time code will result in nonsynchronous code, meaning that the code for one field will fall across two video fields, making the code impossible to use in editing situations.

Some producers prefer to label videotape reels with code. For instance, reel 1 would have a one-hour time code, reel 2 a two-hour time code, and so on. If a shot is logged with a four-hour time code but the log indicates reel 3, there must be an error.

Another way to use time code is to record the time-of-day code on the tape. This is done by setting the time code generator to a clock and having it run in drop frame. For instance, time code 04:00:00:00 would indicate that the shot was made at four o'clock. If the producer wants to find something that happened at a particular time of day, he or she can just search the tape for that time code.

A potential problem with the time-of-day method is that the code generator switches from twenty-three o'clock to zero o'clock at midnight. If the operator has not put up a new reel before going home for the day, the time code at the end of the reel will have a lower number than the time code at the beginning. Since the computer editor will always look for the lowest number toward the beginning of the reel, one solution is to change the reels at midnight. Using time-of-day code also means that different reels could have the same numbers. A shot at time code 10:00:00:00 could be on any reel that was recording at ten o'clock.

For edit master stock, most professionals start their time code at 00:58:00:00 or 09:58:00:00, both of which allow for two minutes of code for bars and tone, slates, and any other visual or audio information. The program would start at either 01:00:00:00 or 10:00:00:00 (see Figure 2-10).

Most producers record time code on their production footage as they shoot. Others wait and code their footage after the production phase is over. Since address track time code and vertical interval time code must be recorded with the video, only audio time code can be used when the footage is coded after production.

It is generally cheaper to rent a time code generator and record the code during the production. This method also allows the producer to record identical time code on multiple videotape recorders (VTRs) during complex camera setups.

Adding and subtracting time code takes a little practice, but is not terribly difficult (see Figure 2-11). There are 30 frames of video to the second, 60 seconds

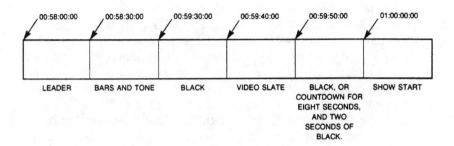

Figure 2-10 One method of placing the bars and tone, video slate, and countdown on a record tape.

```
        10:13
      + 55:16
        65:29 = 1:05:29

     00:01:15
   + 01:59:16
      1:60:31 = 2:00:31

   1:00:00:01
 + 4:59:59:29
   5:59:59:30 = 5:59:60:00 = 5:60:00:00 = 6:00:00:00

    1:02:17 =     61:77
   - :58:19 =   - 58:19
                  3:58

   5:01:10:08 =    5:01:09:38 =    5:00:69:38 =    4:60:69:38
 - 4:59:20:09 =  - 4:59:20:09 =  - 4:59:20:09 =  - 4:59:20:09
                         :29          49:29         1:49:29
```

Figure 2-11   Several examples of adding and subtracting time code.

to the minute, and 60 minutes to the hour. When calculating time code, an editor usually ignores the difference between drop frame and non–drop frame time code. Whichever numbering system the producer chooses, the most important consideration is finding the picture that each time code number represents.

THE COLOR VIDEO SIGNAL: COMPOSITE, COMPONENT, AND Y/C

The color video signal comprises four basic elements: the luminance or brightness (white) values within the picture, and the three chrominance or color values (red, green, and blue). These four elements combine to create the color signal.

As noted in Chapter 1, there are several methods of recording color, two of which are the component and composite formats. Composite video integrates both the luminance and the chrominance portions of the signal, and thus can be transmitted from point to point along one wire.

Standard component video divides the signal into three parts, and thus requires three wires to travel through switchers or other electronic gear. The three signals that travel in the standard component environment are the luminance signal (denoted by the symbol Y), the red signal minus the luminance (R-Y), and the blue signal minus the luminance (B-Y). With these three signals, the color green also can be represented (see Figure 2-12).

Since color information is not embedded in the component luminance signal as it is in the composite signal, the component path and recording signal are superior to those of the composite signal. However, the added cost of

COMPOSITE, COMPONENT AND COLOR UNDER

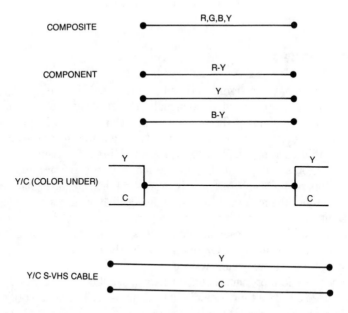

Figure 2-12 Composite video encodes the chrominance and luminance signals and sends them down one wire. Component video uses three wires to transmit the video signal. The green component of color is mathematically extracted from the information on three wires. Color under is a composite signal that is encoded and decoded at the recording and playback deck. Digital composite video is a digital signal using one wire; digital component video is a digital signal that uses three wires.

re-wiring and purchasing component equipment deters some postproduction companies from committing to component video. As a result, component editing bays are not very common. Five tape formats use component video: D1, MII℠, Betacam SP, Betacam, and DCT.

There is a third type of color recording, called *Y/C*, which is used to record the video signal. Also called *color under*, Y/C is used in VHS, S-VHS, 8mm, and Hi-8 recordings. Some edit systems have specific inputs to accept the separate luminance and chrominance signals. By separating the luminance from the chroma (the red, green, and blue signal), the two signals maintain a distinctness that helps to recreate the picture information during playback.

RGB (Red, Green, Blue) is another type of video signal that provides a separate channel for output from paint systems (computer used for picture creation and/or animation) and computers. This type of signal is of extremely high quality, and in many cases carries much more information than a component signal. However, to record the output of a paint system or computer, the

RGB signal moves with its accompanying luminance signal into a converter, where its information is transformed into a composite or component signal.

DIGITAL VIDEO

Digital technology has significantly altered the way video is shot, processed, and edited. Standard analog video signals consist of smoothly varying voltage levels that closely mirror the original image. Digital technology, on the other hand, divides a signal into tiny segments of time and measures the quality of the signal within each segment. The segments and their measurements are expressed in binary digits, a complex series of positive (one) and null (zero) values. Binary digits are more easily processed than analog signals and can be copied without the generational loss of quality that occurs with analog signals.

Digital technology in video often depends on converting analog signals to digital signals. Analog-to-digital converters and digital-to-analog converters accomplish these functions. Graphics may thus be created in the digital domain and integrated into an analog system.

There are four primary digital formats in use. Like analog video recording, digital video can be either component or composite. The D1 recording format, developed by Sony, and Ampex digital format, called DCT, both have separate Y, R-Y, and B-Y portions (component recordings). The D2 and D3 formats, developed respectively by Ampex and Panasonic, feature composite recording. Since the composite signal requires less processing, D2 and D3 are less expensive than D1, but D1 offers superior quality and is ideal for effects and graphics work. If all the editing equipment is kept in the Dl digital domain, hundreds of generations of copying can be performed with little signal degradation.

SUMMARY

Videotape is composed of a strong Mylar backing covered with a thin layer of ferrous oxide. The oxide, which is easily magnetized, is the substance that stores the video and audio information. Metal tape is a highly refined videotape using metal particles to enhance recording sensitivity.

Blank tape has nothing recorded on it. You can either buy blank tape or erase previously used stock.

Control track is a pulse, recorded on the videotape in an assemble recording, that marks each revolution of the record drum and the beginning of each frame (called the frame pulse). The control track acts as a guide for the playback of the video signal. If there is an alteration in the spacing of the control track, the picture will roll until the spacing becomes even again. All video formats use different, yet similar, control track signals.

Two types of video recording are available: assemble and insert. An assemble recording erases everything that was originally on that tape and totally replaces the video, audio, and control track. An insert recording can replace video, audio, or both video and audio, but it does not disturb the tape's control track. Before an insert recording can be made, the tape must have a control track recorded on it. To lay down a continuous, unbroken control track, an assemble recording is made for the length of the videotape. Almost all professional editing situations require the use of insert recordings.

Most time code is a digitally encoded audio signal that numbers each frame of video. The only exception is the vertical interval time code (VITC), which is a video signal.

Drop frame time code is time accurate, meaning that one hour of time code equals one hour of videotape running in play mode. Non–drop frame time code is not time accurate. An hour of non–drop frame time code equals one hour and 3.6 seconds of videotape running in play mode. The numbers that are dropped in drop frame time code are the :00 and :01 frames at every new minute, except at the 10-minute marks (10 minutes, 20 minutes, 30 minutes, etc.).

There are three types of time code recordings: audio (longitudinal) time code, address track time code, and vertical interval time code. All three originate from a time code generator. Audio (longitudinal) time code is recorded on one of the tape's available audio tracks. Address track time code is used only on three-quarter-inch professional broadcast videotape formats. Address track time code is physically recorded in the same location as the video but at a different frequency. Vertical interval time code is a picture signal recorded in the vertical interval (the video frame line) and must be recorded at the same time as the picture.

Time code is a method of labeling frames of video. The actual time code number is not as important as the picture the time code represents.

Composite video is an encoded signal that travels along one wire. Component video requires three wires, one each for the luminance signal (Y), the red signal minus the luminance (R-Y), and the blue signal minus the luminance (B-Y). The component path and recording signal are superior to those of the composite signal.

Two other color recording formats are Y/C and RGB. Y/C recording separates the luminance from the chroma (the red, green, and blue signals). RGB often originates from paint systems and computers.

Digital video can use either component (D1, Digital Betacam, or DCT) or composite (D2 and D3) signals. Digital video takes the analog video information (varying voltages) and converts it to digital video (a series of ones and zeros).

3

Videotape Formats and Their Uses

As technology has advanced, more videotape formats have come into use and older ones have disappeared (see Figure 3-1). In the early stages of videotape, successive formats became less expensive and often smaller in size. In the late 1980s, this trend was reversed with the introduction of D1 and D2. Digital video proved more expensive than its precursors and thus did not rapidly replace older formats as did one-inch and professional half-inch tape.

With the exception of two-inch quad, all video formats discussed here are helical-scan recordings. Quad machines rotate the record heads perpendicularly to the tape, whereas *helical-scan* machines spin the record heads at an angle to the tape. Helical scanning allows the video and audio heads to reach more of the videotape, allowing the use of narrower tape.

Both two-inch quad and one-inch Type B format use segmented video recording, which requires more than one revolution of the video head to record a field of video. Segmented recordings cannot be viewed in still frame (also called freeze or pause) or slow motion without additional equipment.

TWO-INCH QUAD TAPE

Two-inch quad is the granddaddy of videotape (see Figure 3-2). The name comes from quadruplex, which indicates that the signal is created using four record heads. Since quad requires segmented recording, the picture can be seen only in play mode. Slow motion and freeze frames are not possible without using another device.

FORMAT	PURPOSE	AUDIO TRACKS	RECORDING FORMAT
Home formats 8MM VHS, BETAMAX	HOME RECORDING, VIEWING, WINDOW DUBS, DISTRIBUTION	ONE OR TWO	Y/C
Semi-pro consumer Super VHS Hi-8	LOCAL NEWS, MUSIC VIDEOS, HOME RECORDING, VIEWING, WINDOW DUBS, DISTRIBUTION	S-VHS - TWO Hi-8 - 5	Y/C
U-matic THREE-QUARTER INCH WITHOUT ADDRESS TRACK TIME CODE	VIEWING, LOCAL NEWS, OFF-LINE EDITING, DISTRIBUTION	TWO (ONLY ONE IF TIME CODE TO BE USED)	COMPOSITE
Advanced U-matic THREE-QUARTER INCH WITH ADDRESS TRACK TIME CODE	VIEWING, LOCAL NEWS, OFF-LINE EDITING, DISTRIBUTION	TWO	COMPOSITE
Quad TWO-INCH VIDEO	DUPLICATION, DISTRIBUTION	ONE, BUT THERE ARE A FEW STEREO QUAD MACHINES	TRANSVERSE

Figure 3-1 Video formats and their uses.

Format	Uses	Generations	Type
Professional half-inch BETACAM MII BETA SP	VIEWING, BROADCAST ORIGINAL, ON-LINE EDITING, VIEWING	BETACAM - TWO MII & BETA SP - FOUR	COMPONENT
ONE-INCH	BROADCAST ORIGINAL, ON-LINE EDITING, DISTRIBUTION, DUPLICATION MASTERS	TWO	COMPOSITE
Half-inch digital D3	BROADCAST ORIGINAL, ON-LINE EDITING	FOUR	DIGITAL COMPOSITE
Composite Digital D2	BROADCAST ORIGINAL, SOME GRAPHICS, TELECINE MASTER	FOUR	DIGITAL COMPOSITE
Component Digital D1	GRAPHICS, TAPE TO FILM, TELECINE MASTER, EFFECTS MASTERING	FOUR	DIGITAL COMPONENT

Figure 3-1 *continued*

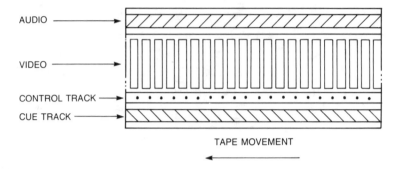

Figure 3-2 A quad (two-inch) recording.

Quad tape is capable of recording one picture (as are all tape formats) and two audio tracks. Unfortunately, the second track of audio is of such poor quality that it is generally used only for time code. In the early days, the second audio track was used to listen to the director's cues to the crew and was appropriately called the *cue track*.

In the commercial broadcast community, most quad machines have been replaced by one-inch or component digital machines.

ONE-INCH TAPE

One-inch tape comes in two formats: Type B and Type C. (Type A is obsolete.) Type B was developed by Bosch-Fernseh, while Type C was originally produced in a joint effort between Ampex and Sony. Neither the recordings nor the tape stocks of the two formats are compatible.

Both Type B and Type C tape are one-inch wide and have three channels of audio. The first two channels, or tracks, are designed for production audio and the third for time code. The two production audio tracks can be edited separately. Thus, music might be recorded on track 2 and voice or narration on track 1.

The major difference between the formats is that Type B (see Figure 3-3) is capable of recording a better quality video signal, but since it requires segmented recordings, the picture can be seen only in play mode. Slow motion and freeze frames are not possible without using an additional device. Type C (see Figure 3-4) uses unsegmented recordings, allowing slow-motion and still-frame playback.

DIGITAL TAPE

Digital videotape has brought several new formats into the production and postproduction arena. All have the advantages of little or no picture degradation

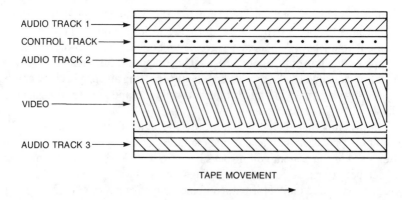

AUDIO TRACK 1
CONTROL TRACK
AUDIO TRACK 2
VIDEO
AUDIO TRACK 3

TAPE MOVEMENT

Figure 3-3 A Type B one-inch recording.

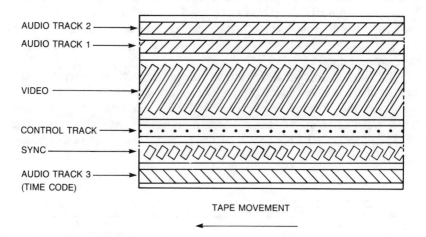

AUDIO TRACK 2
AUDIO TRACK 1
VIDEO
CONTROL TRACK
SYNC
AUDIO TRACK 3
(TIME CODE)

TAPE MOVEMENT

Figure 3-4 A Type C one-inch recording.

over multiple generations. This newfound power has furthered graphics and effects building. Where once the only digital machine in the edit room was a digital disk recorder (limited to 110 seconds of material), digital videotape and its associated support equipment (switchers, character generators, graphics computers, and digital effects generators) are creating a new and exciting picture arena.

The new digital formats are D1, D2, D3, DCT, and digital Betacam. D1 is a component format. Component formats transmit and record luminance and color separately. In a perfect video world, the ideal digital editing situation would provide a totally digital component path for the D1 signal. If the digital signal is not encoded into a composite signal, theoretically there is no limit to the number of generations you could create without signal degradation. However, because of the cost of the D1 format and its support equipment, full component digital bays do not exist in great numbers. D1 has become an effects and graphics medium (see Figure 3-5). Fast becoming an alternative to D1 is the Ampex format called DCT. Also a component recording and playback machine, it has long-playing tapes, incredibly quick preroll time, and a lower cost than D1. DCT has a growing number of users.

A third component digital format is the Sony digital Betacam. This deck has the ability to play back both analog and digital Betacam recording. This format is often used in component editing bays because of its lower cost and ability to play back both types of Betacam recordings.

D2, a composite digital format, combines the advantages of digital signals with the lower cost of composite circuitry. The D2 signal does degrade over multiple generations, but at about one-twentieth the rate of one-inch video. To keep this format at its highest potential, the video path should be totally digital. The composite digital machine can be used in an analog edit bay alongside one-inch and other composite formats; however, each time the digital signal is converted to and from analog, there is much greater signal loss than if the path were entirely digital.

D3 is also a composite tape format. Using half-inch tape, this Panasonic product offers low-cost digital composite production value.

Unlike the situation in which one-inch videotape totally replaced quad, digital video found specific areas where it performed better than traditional analog tape formats. D1 became an effects, telecine (film to videotape) master,

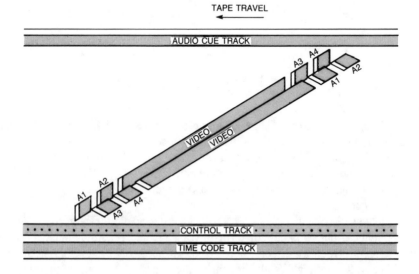

Figure 3-5 A D2 recording.

and graphics mastering medium. D2 became a premium show-editing format. D3 is used in sports and news production. Digital videotape is now being rapidly accepted at all levels of video production and postproduction.

THREE-QUARTER-INCH TAPE

In the late 1970s, the U-Matic three-quarter-inch format (see Figure 3-6) gained a great deal of popularity in both the broadcasting and industrial markets. With inexpensive editing controllers and two audio channels, this format is probably the most widely used videotape in the United States.

In the mid-1980s, Sony added address track code capability to the three-quarter-inch format, which allowed time code to be recorded on the tape and left both audio tracks available for production sound.

The three-quarter-inch format replaced 16mm film at most television news departments, as it made electronic news gathering much faster and easier. In addition, new three-quarter-inch machines offer improved picture quality, increased shuttle speeds, slow motion, and still-frame effects. The introduction of the Sony SP line improved this popular format still further, by using metal tape and more sophisticated recording methods.

Many industrial productions and locally produced television commercials are still made using three-quarter-inch playback and record machines. Occasionally, a producer will edit A and B rolls on three-quarter-inch tapes, then use an on-line facility to create special effects (wipes, dissolves, digital effects, and character-generated titles). Using the three-quarter masters as playbacks, the producer will then edit to a new one-inch master. You might also use A and B rolls to create a four-track audio mix (two tracks on the A roll, two on the B, then a combination of the four tracks on another tape).

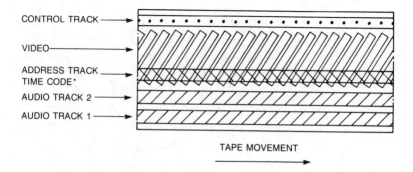

CONTROL TRACK

VIDEO

ADDRESS TRACK
TIME CODE*

AUDIO TRACK 2

AUDIO TRACK 1

TAPE MOVEMENT

Figure 3-6 A three-quarter-inch recording.

Three-quarter-inch, Betacam, 8mm, and VHS videotape are available in regular (ferrous oxide) and metal formats. Metal tape stores more information. Hi-8 and VHS, respectively the metallic formats for 8mm and VHS, provide greater resolution than regular tape. Consequently, many industrial producers and local news stations use Hi-8 or VHS for their programs.

The Sony three-quarter-inch metal SP format and the Betacam format both automatically engage the Dolby noise-reduction circuitry in their recording decks. However, while a non-SP recording can be played back on an SP deck, an SP recording can only be played back on an SP deck.

HALF-INCH PROFESSIONAL TAPE

The Sony Betacam

When professional video people heard that Sony was going to market a professional half-inch video format, many shook their heads and laughed. But upon seeing the picture quality of Betacam, these same people embraced half-inch tape as a valuable new production tool.

The reason that the Sony smaller size tape was capable of recording such a clean picture was the method of recording (see Figure 3-7). In the half-inch broadcast format, the luminance (white and black) is recorded separately from the chroma (color). This is called *component recording.* Compared to half-inch, one-inch and three-quarter-inch recordings are markedly different electronically. In most editing situations, the luminance and chroma are combined as the signal comes off the tape, before entering the switcher (see the Glossary). In an attempt to achieve the same quality produced with half-inch tape, some editing companies have purchased component switchers, which keep the signal separated. This method results in a higher-quality picture and produces cleaner keys, chroma keys, and other switcher effects. (See Chapter 9 for more information on keys and switcher effects.)

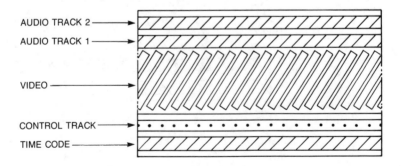

Figure 3-7   A Betacam recording.

News crews were among the first users of the half-inch broadcast format. Since the camera and recorder were contained in one unit, the camera operator could move around freely. In addition, Dolby noise encoders and decoders could be used with the new format.

Half-inch record decks have limiters (audio circuits that limit the peak of audio that will be recorded on tape) in the audio circuitry that can be turned on or off. In most cases, this option is not needed or wanted in production. Some early users of half-inch occasionally left the audio limiters on during a shoot and then regretted it when they listened to the results.

The MII Format

Panasonic unveiled its own professional half-inch format in 1986. The MII format (see Figure 3-8) records a cleaner picture than does the original Betacam system, and it has a built-in time code generator/reader and four audio channels with more than adequate recording capabilities. The studio version also has built-in slow-motion and still-frame modes and can record up to one hour of video per tape.

In early 1986, Sony announced that it would upgrade its Betacam with the Betacam SP line. This improvement was a direct result of the MII introduction that addressed many of the shortcomings of the original Betacam line.

The new format has established itself in the postproduction world since it takes longer loads (up to an hour), has improved picture quality, and has the ability to play Betacam SP, as well as the older Betacam recordings. Using the Betacam SP component recording, some producers are combining Betacam SP,

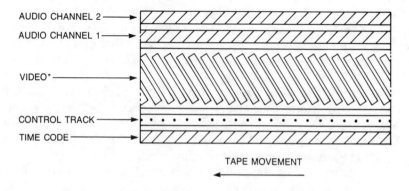

Figure 3-8 An MII recording.

DCT, and D1 to create a component editing environment. In component video, color accuracy is greater than in the composite environment.

SEMI-PROFESSIONAL HALF-INCH TAPE

In the late 1980s, with the advent of MTV and other alternative video outlets, Hi-8 and S-VHS (VHS format that uses improved recording methods on metal tape) became popular recording media for low-budget rock videos and video artists. With their small cameras, reasonable prices, editing systems that could be upgraded to use time code, and with the improved picture quality, both media could be edited or transferred to more professional formats during postproduction.

Hi-8 provides a higher quality picture than S-VHS. However, with massive numbers of VHS decks in the country, both choices have won converts, and they exist side by side in a cost-versus-quality continuum.

EDITING FACILITIES AND TAPE FORMAT CHOICES

Every editing room (see Figure 3-9a) is built in a modular fashion. Each piece of equipment is chosen and installed in accordance with the facility's demands (see Figure 3-9b). The design can allow for technological improvements and limited flexibility, but once determined, it is difficult to alter. For instance, some editing rooms lack the equipment needed to edit three-quarter-inch tape with time code on audio track 1. Others cannot read or use vertical interval time code, while still others do not offer digital videotape decks, digital effects, or character generators.

Despite such technical limitations, and in response to the introduction of so many new formats in recent years, many editing rooms can integrate a number of source formats. Composite and component signals can be edited in the same bay through the use of converters. The common edit configurations now in existence are analog composite, analog component (Betacam, MII), digital composite (D2, D3), and digital component (D1, DCT, digital Betacam) (see Figure 3-10).

There are fewer digital and component editing suites than composite suites. As a result, composite editing suites are easier to find, and most often are less expensive to rent or construct. In each case, however, the particular editing suite is unique to itself and may or may not have all the equipment necessary to perform a specific editing assignment.

The editing facilities, the available equipment, and the show's production requirements all influence the choice of video format. Following are some general rules for choosing the correct format.

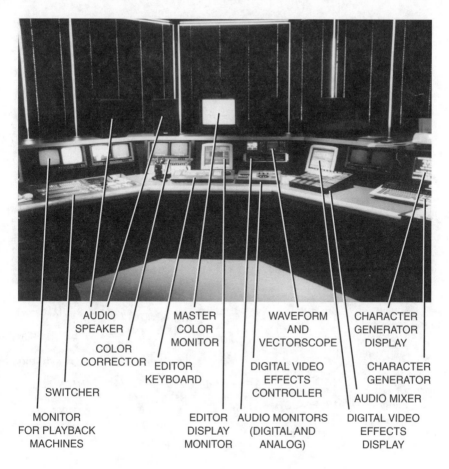

AUDIO
SPEAKER

MASTER
COLOR
MONITOR

WAVEFORM
AND
VECTORSCOPE

CHARACTER
GENERATOR
DISPLAY

COLOR
CORRECTOR EDITOR
KEYBOARD

DIGITAL VIDEO
EFFECTS
CONTROLLER

CHARACTER
GENERATOR

SWITCHER

AUDIO MIXER

MONITOR
FOR PLAYBACK
MACHINES

EDITOR
DISPLAY
MONITOR

AUDIO MONITORS
(DIGITAL AND
ANALOG)

DIGITAL VIDEO
EFFECTS
DISPLAY

Figure 3-9a An on-line editing bay.

PROFESSIONAL FORMATS

Digital Component

A high-end editing, effects, graphics and, when used with care, feature film medium. The specific sub-types of this format are: D1, DCT, and digital Betacam. The separate recording of luminance and chroma makes these machines ideal for blue screen or chroma keying.

Digital Composite

A great editing medium that is spreading throughout the industry, rapidly replacing one-inch as an editing standard. When kept in a digital path (switcher,

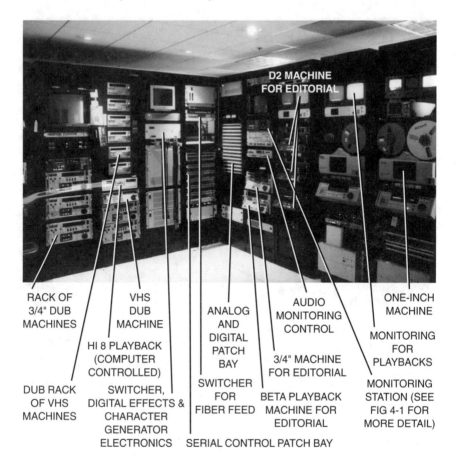

RACK OF 3/4" DUB MACHINES	VHS DUB MACHINE	ANALOG AND DIGITAL PATCH BAY	AUDIO MONITORING CONTROL	ONE-INCH MACHINE
	HI 8 PLAYBACK (COMPUTER CONTROLLED)		3/4" MACHINE FOR EDITORIAL	MONITORING FOR PLAYBACKS
DUB RACK OF VHS MACHINES	SWITCHER, DIGITAL EFFECTS & CHARACTER GENERATOR ELECTRONICS	SWITCHER FOR FIBER FEED SERIAL CONTROL PATCH BAY	BETA PLAYBACK MACHINE FOR EDITORIAL	MONITORING STATION (SEE FIG 4-1 FOR MORE DETAIL)

D2 MACHINE FOR EDITORIAL

Figure 3-9b   A typical machine room in an on-line facility. Photos courtesy of New Wave Entertainment, Burbank, California.

effects generator, character generator), the multiple generations are transparent (without discernable signal loss). Specific sub-types of this format are D2 and D3 (see Figures 3-10 and 3-11).

One-Inch

Many shows are shot, edited, and played back on one-inch tape (see Figure 3-12). Up to 90 minutes of tape can be loaded onto a machine, and two tracks of production audio are available. Most filmed shows and the majority of video programs shot on digital formats such as D1, D2, D3, DCT, and digital or analog Betacam can be delivered on one-inch video, if necessary.

Figure 3-10 The Sony D2 player/recorder. With four tracks of audio and both analog and digital outputs, this machine is becoming an industry standard. Photo courtesy of Sony Electronics, Inc.

Figure 3-11 A D3 studio videotape recorder (VTR), a composite digital format recording onto a half-inch-wide tape. Photo courtesy of Panasonic Broadcast Systems.

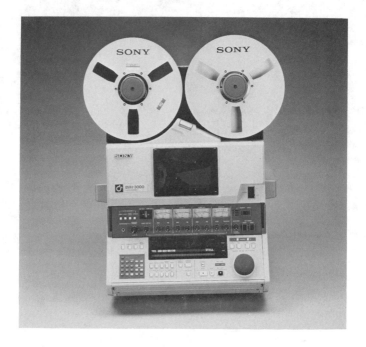

Figure 3-12 A one-inch video machine. Photo courtesy of Sony Corporation.

Quad

You would only use two-inch quad tape if it were the only tape format available for production or editing (see Figure 3-13). Even a show that must be delivered on two-inch tape can be shot and edited on another format, then transferred to quad for broadcasting. Quad is an outdated, rarely used format that should be avoided if possible.

Three-Quarter-Inch

This is an ideal format for documentaries or news productions that cannot afford to use professional half-inch formats. Three-quarter-inch editing and production equipment is common and has a history of performing well (see Figures 3-14 and 3-15). Ideally, the original footage should be edited to one-inch or professional half-inch, but this is not always possible or practical. News must be edited quickly, and documentary producers often do not have the financial resources to pay for one-inch or professional half-inch editing. Editing on three-quarter-inch tape is easily accomplished, although multiple generations will degrade the video quality.

Some local and cable television stations broadcast a portion of their programming on three-quarter-inch tape. It is also used to produce programs for

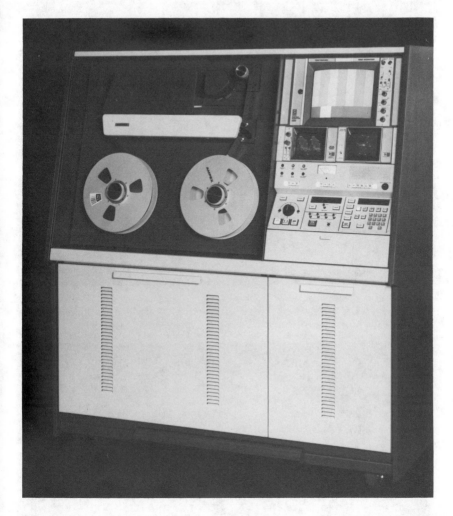

Figure 3-13 The Ampex AVR-3, a quad machine. Photo courtesy of Ampex Corporation.

schools or industrial users. Two primary professional uses of three-quarter-inch tape are approval/ screening copies and off-line editing.

Professional Analog Half-Inch

This format is excellent for on-location shooting, film transfers, and documentaries. Both MII and Betacam SP have superb cameras. In addition, in most major cities, one or both of these formats have been integrated into existing

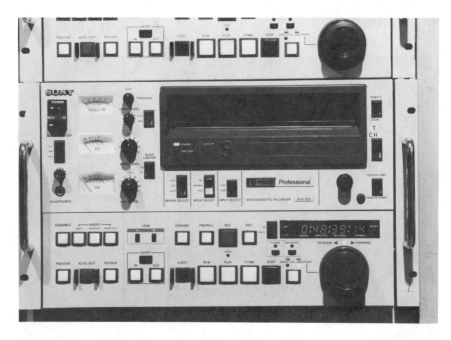

Figure 3-14 A professional three-quarter-inch U-Matic tape machine. Photo by Sean Sterling.

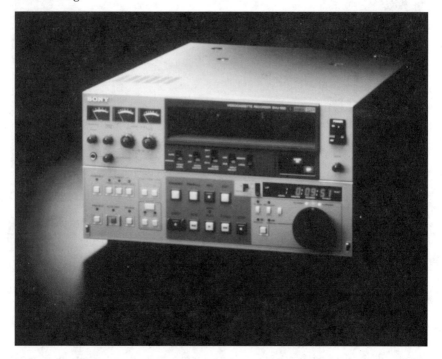

Figure 3-15 The Sony BVU-950, a three-quarter-inch U-Matic recorder/player. Photo courtesy of Sony Electronics, Inc.

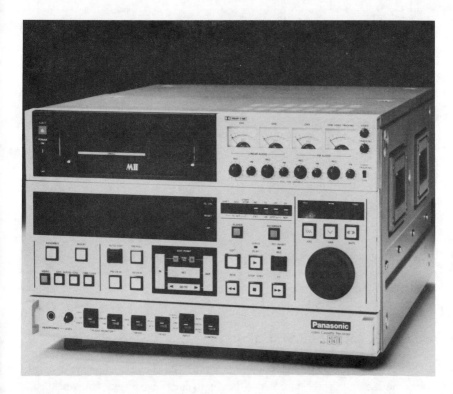

Figure 3-16 The Panasonic AU-650, a professional half-inch recorder/player using the MII format. Photo courtesy of Panasonic Industrial Company.

editing facilities because of their attractive cost coupled with their impressive image quality (see Figure 3-16). Now that component edit bays are being built with more regularity, there is more incentive to explore MII and SP. Several network television series, as well as numerous documentaries and news programs, are produced through the use of professional half-inch. Its combination of component signal processing, light weight, and high quality have ensured this format's future in the field and in the studio.

SEMI-PROFESSIONAL FORMATS

Both Hi-8 and S-VHS fall into the gray area between professional videotape and home consumer quality. Many music videos have been shot on these formats, then edited to Betacam SP, digital videotape, or one-inch. Hi-8 has the advantage of being smaller in camera size and higher in video quality; however, the cost of this system is greater than S-VHS. Both also offer the ability to edit because manufacturers have recognized the demand for editing with these formats. Both formats have editors that can be upgraded to read and use time code. Despite their similarities, S-VHS is not compatible with Hi-8, nor can it be played in a VHS machine. Likewise, Hi-8 cannot be played in an 8mm deck.

HOME FORMATS

For industrial or home distribution, half-inch VHS and 8mm tapes are widely accepted; however, these formats are not considered broadcast quality.

8mm

The 8mm format is currently being marketed for home use. The small size of the tape (and cassette) means that the camera-recorders are only slightly larger than a VHS cassette.

Half-Inch, 8mm, and VHS

VHS half-inch videotape and 8 mm (see Figure 3-17) were originally designed for home use, but professionals have begun to use these formats for workprints and preliminary viewing. Occasionally, a shot on 8mm or VHS tape might be edited into a broadcast video, but this rarely happens because the picture quality is poor compared to professional formats. This format also is susceptible to blanking problems (see Chapter 4).

There is one excellent, cost-effective use for half-inch home-format machines in the commercial world: window dubs (copies of original footage with visible time code). These tapes can be viewed quickly on 8mm or VHS machines, allowing editors to work at home using a tape machine and a television.

Half-inch home formats also can be used for demonstration or sales purposes. Keep in mind, however, that every video generation loses a great deal of picture quality. Thus, the only professional uses for home half-inch video are screening, off-line editing, and distribution of finished videos for home or industrial use.

SUMMARY

Videotape began as a two-inch format called quad. One-inch tape then offered broadcast quality with much less expense, while three-quarter-inch tape improved its recordings and added address track time code. Still later, half-inch

Figure 3-17 Panasonic VHS Hi-fi. The widespread use of VHS has allowed editing and playback decks to expand their capabilities. Photo courtesy of Panasonic Industrial Company.

professional broadcast recordings allowed ease of shooting as well as Dolby sound and better picture quality. All of these tape formats are still in use.

With the exception of quad, all video formats are helical-scan recordings. Both quad and Type B one-inch tape use segmented recording techniques, which do not allow slow motion, still frames, or viewing in fast forward or reverse without the use of additional equipment.

Digital video, when kept in a digital path, can be dubbed many times without generational loss. There are two types of digital tapes: component, in which the luminance is recorded separate from the chroma, and composite, in which the entire signal is mathematically combined, then recorded and played back using a single wire. Most digital formats have four channels of audio available, plus a time code channel.

One-inch Type B and Type C videotape have three audio channels available. The first two channels are designed for production audio, while the third is expressly for time code.

Digital Betacam, professional half-inch, DCT, and D1 digital formats record video using component recording, in which three distinct signals are recorded to determine the luminance, red, blue, and green values of the picture. D2 and D3 are digital formats using composite recording techniques. There are a limited number of composite editing bays. D1 and professional half-inch formats are being used in component edit situations. S-VHS and Hi-8 have been used for cable, local news, and artistic programming.

In half-inch professional video recording and digital Betacam, the camera and recorder can be one unit. Half-inch home formats can be used for commercial broadcasts with extreme caution (consult a professional editing facility). Window dubs on 8mm or VHS can be viewed quickly.

4

Video Scopes, Time Base Correctors, and Volume Unit Meters

When editing in a room with a single playback and a record machine, there is often no way to adjust the color and white values of the playback tape, since the record machine makes a direct copy of the playback image. Many facilities, however, have video scopes and time base correctors (TBCs) integrated into the editing system (see Figure 4-1). An understanding of the video signal, an ability to read video scopes, and the ability to operate the basic controls of a TBC are important skills to acquire.

THE VIDEO SIGNAL

Video first originates at a television tube or a charged coupled device (CCD—see the Glossary). These devices convert light into electrical pulses. The pulses include the luminance values of the image (white values), the red, green, and blue values (chroma), and synchronization pulses that keep the information together and allow the white and chroma information to be combined at a later date.

A composite signal mathematically combines this information into a single pulse that is sent out of the camera. A component signal is created by sending the video pulses out of the camera using three wires, one for the luminance signal (Y), one for the red signal minus the luminance (R-Y), and one for the blue signal minus the luminance (B-Y).

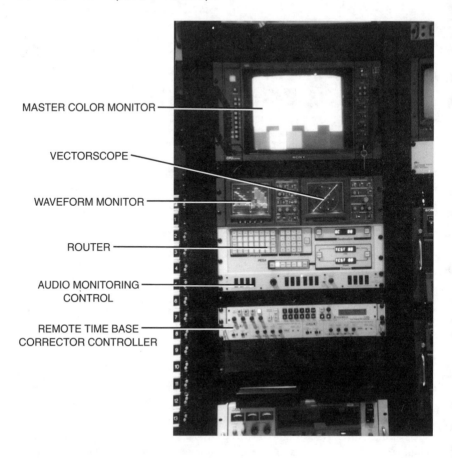

MASTER COLOR MONITOR

VECTORSCOPE

WAVEFORM MONITOR

ROUTER

AUDIO MONITORING CONTROL

REMOTE TIME BASE CORRECTOR CONTROLLER

Figure 4-1 Monitoring equipment in an on-line facility. Photo by Sean Sterling.

The video information can be displayed on a monitor, sent along a cable, broadcast, or stored on videotape. In recording or broadcasting the video in an analog format, the electronic pulses constituting the video information are modulated, or impressed onto a radio frequency signal. *Modulating* means altering a signal at a set amplitude or frequency so that its features conform to those of the original video information. This resulting, modulated signal can then be recorded to tape or videodisk or transmitted over the air.

Signals to be recorded in analog format are sent to an electromagnet within a recording head. The signals charge the electromagnet, which, in turn, charges the oxide on videotape as it passes across the top of the recording head during the recording process. Playing back a recorded tape reverses the process. The minute magnetization recorded on the tape charges an electromagnet inside a playback head. The resulting signal is amplified, and then the video information is decoded (demodulated) from the signal and sent from the playback deck.

In over-the-air broadcasting, the video signal is modulated onto a radio frequency signal. The video signal modifies an electromagnetic wave called a *carrier signal*. The carrier wave, normally a constant wave, is altered in a direct relationship to the video and audio signals. This modulated signal is amplified, then transmitted by a radio antenna. A television set tuned to the carrier frequency picks up this wave, demodulates it, and displays the picture on its screen. Instead of televisions decoding radio frequencies, in edit bays, monitors display video from an input source.

THE VIDEO PICTURE

As noted in Chapter 2, the image we see on a television screen is created by an electron beam sweeping across the back of the picture tube. The beam causes the phosphor on the tube to glow, creating a picture. The technical aspects of the U.S. television broadcast system are generically called NTSC. SECAM and PAL are two other television broadcast and recording formats (see the Appendix).

This beam sweeps across the tube 525 times for each video frame in a process called *interlace scanning*. The beam scans the odd lines in the first pass, then returns to the top of the frame and scans the even lines to complete the video frame. The beam shuts off for a brief time when it moves to the beginning of the next line or when it returns to the top of the screen after the field has been scanned. The time that the beam is blanked while moving to the beginning of the next line is called *horizontal blanking*. The time that the beam shuts off to go to the top of the next field is called *vertical blanking*.

Just because the electron beam has been turned off, however, does not mean that the television signal is blanked. During the time when the beam is retracing the field for the next horizontal line, information is sent concerning the color reference (*color burst*), and synchronizing pulses are sent to ensure that the beam is in the right place at the right time (*horizontal sync pulse*). When the beam returns to the top of the tube to prepare for scanning the next field, information is sent concerning which field this scan represents (*equalizing pulses*), and signals are sent to make sure the beam is in its proper place (*vertical synchronizing pulses*).

VIDEO SCOPES

Video scopes are used to monitor various aspects of the video signal. To a video editor, the most important of these scopes are the vectorscope, the waveform monitor, and the cross-pulse monitor, all of which display and measure the horizontal and vertical blanking. The *waveform monitor* (see Figure 4-2) exhibits the complete (composite) video signal while the *vectorscope* (see Figure 4-3a) displays the color component of the video signal. The *cross-pulse monitor* (see Figure 4-3b) is a television monitor with the ability to shift the picture horizontally and vertically. These shifts allow the horizontal and vertical blanking to be seen in the center of the screen.

On the face of the waveform monitor screen in Figure 4-2 are various markings. The left side has a series of numbers ranging from −40 to 100. These numbers represent *IRE* units. (IRE was a standard set by the Institute of Radio Engineers, now known as the Institute of Electrical and Electronics Engineers, abbreviated IEEE.) Horizontal markings are shown at zero, the baseline. The longer lines represent one microsecond, while the shorter lines are divisions of 0.2 microsecond.

When looking at one full line of video on the waveform and cross-pulse monitors (see Figures 4-3a and 4-3b), you can see that the video signal is

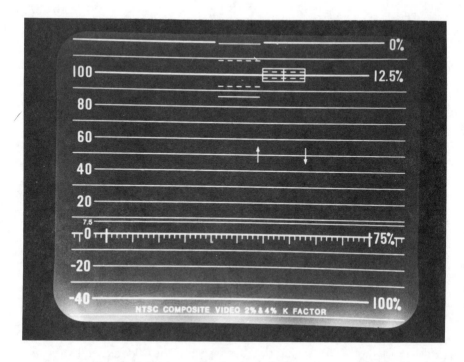

Figure 4-2   A waveform monitor. Photo by Sean Sterling.

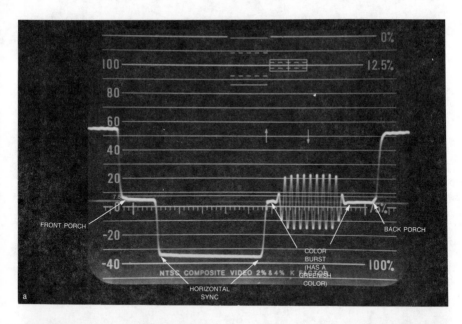

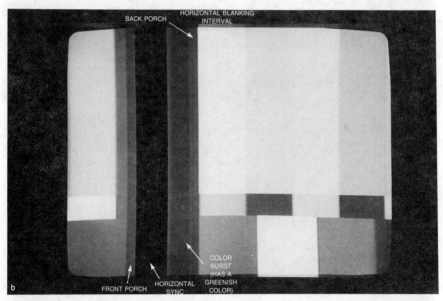

Figure 4-3 (a) A waveform monitor displaying the horizontal blanking interval. Note that the waveform portion of the display is expanded to show the horizontal blanking portion of the signal. (b) A picture of the horizontal blanking interval on a cross-pulse monitor. Photos by Sean Sterling.

140 units (– 40 to 100). Reading the signal from right to left, you find the end of the video picture. At this point, the electron beam is blanked out, and it returns to the beginning of the next line. Next comes what is called the *front porch*, which is the portion of the blanking from the end of a picture to the leading edge of the sync. The line then drops down to – 40 IRE units, indicating the leading edge of the horizontal sync pulse. The space between the end of the horizontal sync pulse and the next element, the color burst, is called the *breezeway*. After the color burst comes the beginning of the next video signal. The area from the end of the color burst to the beginning of the next video signal is called the *back porch*.

Looking at the vertical frame using the waveform and cross-pulse monitors (see Figures 4-4 and 4-5), you can see the bottom of the picture, the preequalizing pulses, the vertical sync pulse, the postequalizing pulses, and the beginning of the next field, at the top of the video picture.

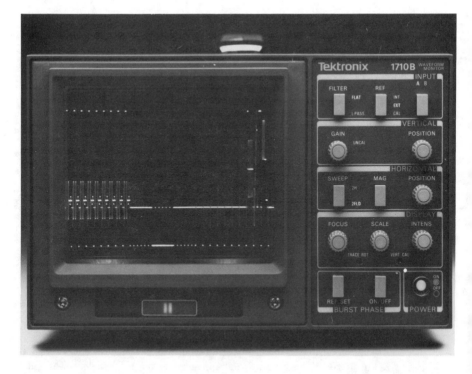

Figure 4-4 A waveform monitor displaying the vertical blanking interval. Photo courtesy of Tektronix Corporation.™

Figure 4-5   A picture of the vertical blanking interval on a cross-pulse monitor. Photo by Sean Sterling.

COLOR STANDARDS

The U.S. television standard is built around three primary colors (red, green, and blue) and three secondary colors (magenta, cyan, and yellow). A mathematical formula is used to encode the color information for broadcasting. To use the formula, however, you must have a standard reference point. This point is called the *color burst*, and it appears on the vectorscope, as can the other colors in the video picture.

Color bars are produced by a reference signal created by a camera or test signal generator. This signal is usually recorded at the beginning of a tape. When the tape is played back, the TBC is adjusted so that the reference signals correspond to the reference points on the vectorscope and waveform monitor.

UNSTABLE VIDEOTAPE SIGNALS

Since the wrap (the amount of tape) on the two sides of the videocassette or take-up reels is always changing, the video machine is continually altering the speed of the tape in an attempt to maintain a constant speed across the video heads. The result of this push-pull motion is a highly unstable signal. The TBC accepts this unstable information, delays and corrects the signal, then sends the signal out, in sync with the rest of the video system. In addition to correcting time base errors, most TBCs (including the one shown in Figure 4-6) also have controls for video and chroma levels.

The frame synchronizer is similar to the TBC in that it accepts unstable video signals (from tape or perhaps a remote truck), stores one frame of information, then releases the frame in sync with the rest of the system. The problem with the frame synchronizer is that the video is delayed for one whole frame. If this process is repeated several times, the picture gets out of sync with the audio.

ADJUSTING THE VIDEO AND CHROMA WITH A TBC

A TBC can alter the color of a television signal in four areas: hue, saturation, video, and setup. The operator checks hue and saturation by examining a vectorscope, and video and setup by using a waveform monitor.

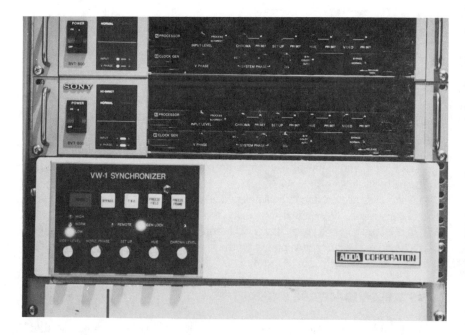

Figure 4-6 A Sony time base corrector and an Adda™ frame synchronizer. Photo by Sean Sterling.

Hue is the relative phase of color and is monitored using a vectorscope. As the operator moves the hue control, all colors of the tape (or television signal) are rotated.

Saturation is the amount of color and is also monitored using a vectorscope. Nonsaturated pictures are dull almost to the point of being black-and-white. An overly saturated picture blooms with color to the point of smearing.

Video refers to the amount of white in the picture and is monitored with a waveform monitor. By dropping the video, the operator can make the shot progressively darker; by raising the video, the operator can bring out more of the white.

Setup, or *pedestal*, refers to the amount of black in the picture and is monitored using a waveform monitor. A high level of setup raises the intensity of the dark and light areas, making the black areas appear gray. The NTSC definition of video black is 7.5 IRE units. Anything below that is considered part of the horizontal blanking.

Some clients prefer to adjust the chroma and luminance values of particular shots during the editing process. This is often necessary with material that has been shot under adverse or changing lighting conditions. The TBC is used to adjust these values. If more intense correction is required, a color corrector is employed to make additional changes in the picture. To ensure that the resulting signal remains technically acceptable, many editing facilities have clipping circuitry to ensure that the luminance values do not exceed the capacity of the video machines, or that the black levels do not fall below 7.5 IRE units.

A CAN OF VIDEO

You may imagine that the video signal is in an empty can (see Figure 4-7). Looking directly down on the can, all you see is a circle because the sides are not visible. This area contains the hue and saturation values of the picture. The sides of the can hold the video and setup portions.

Looking at the picture of a vectorscope in Figure 4-7, you can see that it is actually a circle, just like the top of the can. The center of the vectorscope corresponds to a stick going through the center of the can.

When you look directly at the front of a can, the top is not visible. It is a square, like the waveform monitor. Just as looking at a can from two different perspectives shows separate but related aspects of the can, the two video scopes show two separate but related portions of the picture.

Let us assume that the can is full of red paint. By raising the white level (video) of the paint, you get a "whiter" red, or pink. By raising the color value (chroma), you get a brighter, richer red. Shifting the phase (hue) of the paint changes the color. Shifting the phase in one direction makes the red appear more magenta, while shifting it in the other direction makes the red appear

THE VECTORSCOPE

WAVEFORM MONITOR

100 — 80 — 60 — 40 — 20 — — 20

HUE

SATURATION

VIDEO
SETUP

more yellow. By moving the black level (setup), you can raise or lower the contrast. A high contrast level results in a washed-out look. If the contrast is lower than 7.5 IRE units, it may look great, with deep dark blacks, but it is too low to be broadcast.

You can adjust a video signal by using these TBC controls, which are very similar to those on a television set. This is how the two sets of controls match up:

TBC Control	=	*Television Control*
hue	=	tint
saturation	=	color
video	=	brightness
setup	=	contrast

USING THE TBC AND SCOPES TO SET LEVELS

Color bars are a playback reference to what the camera or record machine originally recorded. Once a tape has been set to bars, additional adjustments to the TBC controls may be required to enhance a particular shot. (The following procedure assumes that the scopes have been properly calibrated.)

To set the TBC to bars, you load the tape into the playback machine and put it in play mode at the beginning of the color bar recording. Watching the waveform monitor (with the filter set on FLAT, so the scope only looks at the black-and-white portion of the signal, and on 2H, which shows two horizontal fields of video), you adjust the setup until the black level is at 7.5 IRE units. Then you move the video level to 100 units. Referring to the vectorscope (see Figure 4-8a) and waveform monitor (see Figure 4-8b), you increase or decrease the chroma so that the six dots are as far from the center as the small boxes. You should use the hue control to place the dots as close to the center of the boxes as possible.

You can play the bars back and move each knob to see how each adjustment works. Moving the hue knob rotates the dots on the vectorscope, first one way, then the other. You can see how the color shifts in the bars. Moving the chroma control moves the color level in and out on the vectorscope. Twisting the video control and watching the waveform shows the white level increasing and decreasing. Finally, adjusting the setup knob increases and decreases the white and black levels together.

In composite video, the luminance signal carries the mathematical equation for chroma. As a result, increasing the luminance (white) value of a shot will also increase the chroma values of that shot. In component video, luminance is separate from chroma. However, since the luminance and chroma will most likely be combined for broadcast, it is important to check these monitored

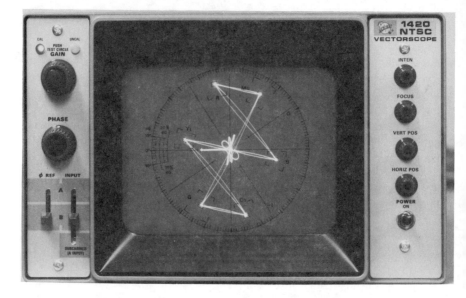

a

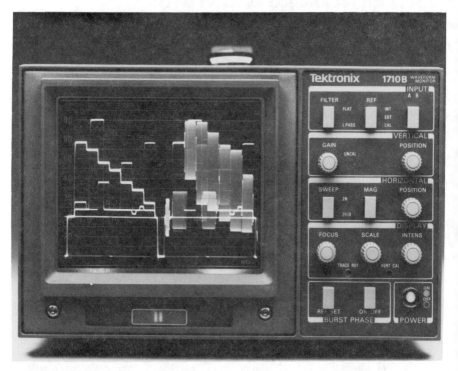

b

Figure 4-8 (a) Color bars displayed on a vectorscope. (b) Color bars viewed on a waveform monitor. The left side is the signal without color information (luminance and setup only); the right side includes the chroma portion of the signal. Photos courtesy of Tektronix Corporation.

values in a composite environment to ensure that the chroma values do not exceed the videotape's tolerance.

After you set TBC levels, the playback tape should be set to replay the picture that was originally recorded. But this might not always be the case. You should always check the four color aspects of the video if a waveform monitor (see Figure 4-9) is available so that you can make adjustments for technical or creative reasons. Many editors use skin tone to make subtle adjustments in the chroma and hue once the tape has been set up (see Figure 4-10). You must be very careful to ensure that a dark-skinned person does not appear green or red. A slight hue adjustment can make a world of difference in how a person looks.

PLAYING TAPES WITHOUT TBCS

You can view three-quarter-inch and other formats such as S-VHS, Hi-8, VHS, and 8mm without TBCs through the use of *heterodyne processing*. This method stabilizes the picture enough to view a color signal but not enough to allow a switcher to perform wipes, dissolves, and other multiple-playback effects.

EDITING WITHOUT TBCS

Systems using only one record and one playback often edit machine-to-machine without the use of TBCs or a switcher, which eliminates the need for system timing. This type of editing occurs in news production and many industrial applications. Many three-quarter-inch and professional half-inch video decks have an output and input for dub-mode recordings. By taking the dub-mode output of the playback deck and feeding it into the dub-in of the record machine, you can transfer the video signal from the playback deck directly to the record deck without converting the signal to video and back to radio frequency. As a result, the quality of the recorded signal is greatly improved over that of a video-to-video recording.

The same situation occurs in digital and S-VHS systems. If you use dedicated cables, digital to digital editing can be transparent. In S-VHS situations, you can avoid combining the luminance and chroma by using S-VHS dub cables.

TIMING

All video signals sent to a switcher must be in perfect synchronization with each other in terms of horizontal phase and subcarrier phase. A quick test of switcher timing is to perform a wipe between two sources. If the picture or color shifts at the end of the wipe, then the two signals are not properly timed to each other, and an adjustment must be made. You can check the timing by viewing the

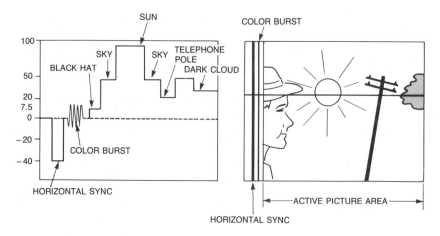

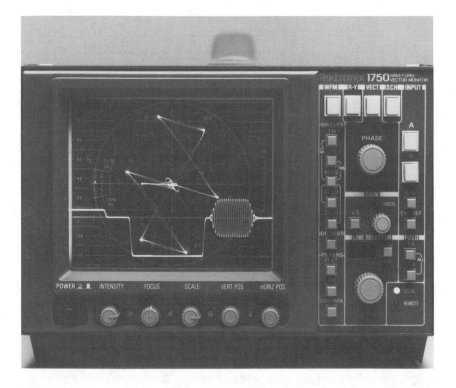

Figure 4-9 An example of reading a line of video on a waveform monitor. The waveform reading (left) corresponds to the video picture (right).

Figure 4-10 Color bars viewed on a combination waveform monitor/vectorscope. Note that the waveform portion of the display is expanded to show the horizontal blanking portion of the signal. Photo courtesy of Tektronix Corporation.

waveform monitor and vectorscope. The sync and subcarrier signals must be in the same positions and in the same phase relationship with each other, because all video signals feed the switcher. Although TBCs and most video equipment have timing controls, adjusting the timing is usually an engineering rather than an editing function. The following is an example of timing a machine using the vectorscope and waveform monitors. Usually the A side of these scopes is the standard operating side.

The purpose of timing a video device is to electronically align that device with a reference signal. Each edit bay uses one signal as a reference; in most instances, it is either color bars or black from the switcher. First, you select the reference signal on the switcher. Next, you set the waveform monitor to channel A, to a two-line display (magnified to 1 microsecond per division) to look at sync, and external (as opposed to internal) sync. Then you align the waveform using the horizontal adjustment, so that the leading edge of sync is on a specific hatchmark (so you can remember the setting). On the vectorscope, you should set external sync on channel A. Now, you align the scope using the phase to put color burst at the 0° mark (the 9 o'clock position; see Figure 4-8a).

You select the machine to be timed on the switcher, and return to the waveform monitor. You should adjust the H phase of the machine so that the leading edge of sync is in exactly the same place on the waveform as it was on the reference signal. Finally, you adjust the subcarrier at the new machine until the color burst is located at 0 on the vectorscope. The machine should now be in time with the reference signal.

Timing is easier in component editing situations because there is no color burst, thus no subcarrier timing. Component video has direct color information and is not encoded in the single video signal.

BLANKING

One major concern of on-line editing is video blanking. The Federal Communications Commission (FCC) has certain rules concerning video signals broadcast over the public airwaves. Most cable networks have similar specifications that closely follow the FCC guidelines. Blanking is one area addressed by these specifications.

Blanking is that portion of the picture that is blanked out while the electron beam is retracing either to scan another line (horizontal blanking) or to start another field (vertical blanking). Horizontal blanking is the area in which the information telling television receivers and monitors how to recreate the picture is stored. Other information, such as VITC and information needed for automatic color tuning, can be stored in vertical blanking areas.

The vertical frame line should be between 20 and 21.5 lines wide. Most video signals fall within this FCC specification. Horizontal blanking should not exceed 11.4 microseconds. Keeping the horizontal blanking within the FCC specifications is always a concern in commercial editing (see Figure 4-11).

Blanking is originally created by the video camera, which can be the matte camera in the editing bay, the electronics of the film-to-tape transfer system, a standards converter, or the original video camera in a studio or on location. At this stage, horizontal blanking is usually set at 10.9 microseconds.

If a camera is set up properly before a shoot, the horizontal blanking will be acceptable, but in an analog system, each time that signal is copied, the horizontal blanking gets a little bigger and the picture gets a little smaller. This is not a problem for one generation of video, but if a tape has been duplicated seven or eight times, perhaps to create a very complicated effect, or if the tape was not set up properly at the beginning of the editing session, the blanking can exceed the FCC specifications.

If a tape is being made for in-house use or for a demonstration, blanking is of no concern unless it is so wide that it can actually be seen on the screen. If, however, the program is to be broadcast on a commercial station, careful attention must be paid to the blanking of each shot. If a shot's blanking is so wide that it cannot be adjusted to meet FCC specifications, the image must be fixed before being included in a broadcast show.

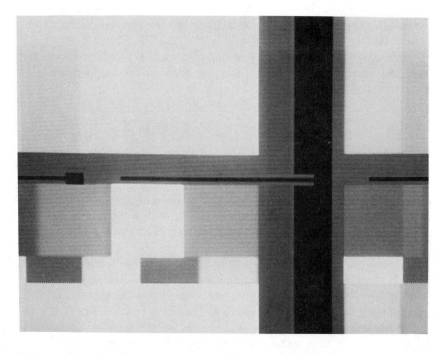

Figure 4-11 Vertical and horizontal blanking intervals as seen on a cross-pulse monitor. Photo by Sean Sterling.

One of the most common ways to correct such a problem is to use a digital effects generator to expand the picture. Increasing the size of the picture area reduces the width of the blanking. The disadvantage of a digital effects generator is that it degrades the quality of the picture. The amount of degradation depends on the effects generator being used and how well it has been maintained.

The new digital video formats have eliminated this expanded horizontal blanking problem—if dubs are completed within the digital domain. Since the picture comprises a series of ones and zeros, an exact replica of the picture can be made. Thus the horizontal blanking, if originally set properly, will not expand.

VOLUME UNIT METERS

Another important indicator in the editing bay is the volume unit (VU) meter. The VU meter measures the output of the audio signal in volume units. The goal is to keep the audio level strong enough to produce a good signal but not so strong that the sound becomes distorted.

Using Tone to Set the Record Levels

Tone is a reference signal for audio, just as color bars are a reference signal for video. Usually there is a source of audio tone in the editing bay.

The first step in using this tone is to set the tone level at zero on the mixer. Then, in E-to-E mode on the record machine (which lets the record machine electronically look at the incoming video and audio signals), adjust the record level of the record deck to zero. The audio level that comes out of the mixer will then be recorded at the same level on the video deck (see Figure 4-12).

At least a minute of video bars and audio tone should be recorded onto the record tape. After this edit, while playing back this section of the tape, you should set the playback level at 0 dB on the record machine through the use of the playback knobs. Now the playback audio correctly reflects the level at which you recorded the tone.

The only time you would not follow this procedure is when you are reediting into an edited master. If the tape was originally edited on the same machine, then the record levels will probably match. But if the tape was recorded on another machine, the new audio level must match the original tone.

To do this, you first set the playback level and the mixer's reference tone at zero, as before. Now, instead of recording a long segment of audio, you record a short segment over the original tone and replay the segment. If the tone drops at the edit point, you must raise the record level. If the tone level is too hot

Figure 4-12   A VU meter measuring audio tone at 0 dB. Photo by Sean Sterling.

(loud), you must lower the incoming tone on the record deck. This process continues until the short segment levels are the same as those of the original tone.

Riding Audio Levels

Proper levels must be maintained when recording production audio (see Figure 4-13). Sometimes tone is recorded on playback tapes for reference, but this is no guarantee that the recorded levels will be the same as the tone at the head of the tape. Riding (adjusting) audio levels during an edit keeps the meter moving and peaking at or just above 0 dB. It is acceptable for the audio to bounce into the red area of the VU meter, but the indicator should not stay there. Audio levels that remain in the red area for any length of time may become distorted.

Not only must the audio level remain consistent during an edit, but it also must be consistent from one edit to another. Nothing is more disconcerting than a sudden drop or rise in audio level.

Figure 4-13   A VU meter with the needle moving between − 7 dB and − 1 dB. Photo by Sean Sterling.

CONCLUSION

Although video scopes are not used very often during the off-line editing process, VU meters are. A poor audio edit can ruin a picture-perfect master. In the on-line editing process, both video scopes and audio meters are of vital importance.

SUMMARY

Video originates at a television tube or CCD. These devices convert light into electrical pulses.

A composite signal is a picture's entire video information combined into a single signal. A component signal is picture information that uses three separate video pulses: one for the luminance signal (Y), one for the red signal minus the luminance (R-Y), and one for the blue signal minus the luminance (B-Y).

In over-the-air broadcasting, a carrier wave, normally a constant wave, is altered in direct relationship to the video and audio signals. This modulated signal is amplified and transmitted by a radio antenna in all directions.

The image we see on a television screen is created by an electron beam scanning across a picture tube, causing the phosphor on the tube to glow. The beam sweeps across the tube 525 times for each video frame in a process called interlace scanning. There are two fields to every frame of video. The time that the electron beam is turned off is called blanking.

The vectorscope and waveform monitor are oscilloscopes used to monitor aspects of the video signal. The cross-pulse monitor is a television monitor with the ability to shift the picture horizontally and vertically. This shift allows the horizontal and vertical blanking to be viewed in the center of the screen.

In composite video, luminance carries the mathematical equation for chroma. As a result, increasing the luminance (white) value of a shot will also increase the chroma values of that shot. In component video, there is no color burst. The U.S. television standard uses three primary colors (red, green, and blue) and three secondary colors (magenta, cyan, and yellow). Color bars are a reference signal created by a camera or test signal generator for the purpose of setting up the playback of a video recording.

A time base corrector (TBC) accepts an unstable videotape signal, corrects it, then sends it out in sync with the rest of the video signals. In addition to correcting time base errors, TBCs have controls that can alter video and chroma levels.

A TBC has the ability to change the video signal in four areas: hue, saturation, video, and setup. Viewing three-quarter-inch and other formats such as VHS without TBCs is possible through the use of heterodyne processing.

Machine-to-machine dubbing can preserve video quality if you use specialized cables (S-VHS, dub cables, digital cables).

A frame synchronizer is a device that accepts unstable video, stores one whole frame of information, then releases the frame in sync with the rest of the video signals. All video sources entering a switcher must be in perfect time with each other in terms of horizontal phase and subcarrier phase.

Blanking is originally created by the video camera. Every time an analog signal is copied, the horizontal blanking gets a little bigger and the picture gets a little smaller (unless it is a digital-to-digital duplication). One of the most common ways to correct a blanking problem is to use a digital effects generator to expand the picture and decrease the blanking width. The FCC specification for vertical blanking is between 20 and 21.5 lines, and for horizontal blanking, not more than 11.4 microseconds.

A volume unit (VU) meter measures the output of the audio signal in volume units. The purpose of a VU meter is to keep the audio level strong enough to give a good signal but not so strong that the audio is distorted. Tone is a reference signal for audio.

5

The Video Edit

The remainder of this book deals with insert recordings—edits made after the record tape already has the control track and video recorded on it. Assemble recordings, as mentioned in Chapter 2, erase the control track, audio, and video.

On all editing systems, the record machine can only make a cut. Special effects, such as dissolves, fades, keys, and graphics, are created by some other machine. Nothing is physically cut during a video edit (see Figure 5-1). Instead, a section of video, audio, or both is copied from a source tape onto a record tape.

With the introduction of the D2 machine came the remarkable capability of playing back and recording on the same machine. In all other formats, to add visual information, you must put the program on a playback machine and record a new generation of tape, or rerecord the original edit, adding the new visual information. The D2 can play back and record at the same time. It has the unique ability to preread picture information before the record head erases the video on the tape. For example, a complicated graphic could be preread and you could add a disclaimer to the picture without rebuilding the effect or going to an additional video generation. Preread can also be used with audio, allowing you to make transitions using only one playback source. (Technically, the record machine becomes the second playback.) Since the video or audio being preread is subsequently erased, you must make sure that the system and edit are prepared before actually performing the edit. In addition, material being used from the record machine for effects must be recorded for the entire length of the effect.

DEFINING THE CUT

The following three points or locations define a simple cut on either analog or digital systems:

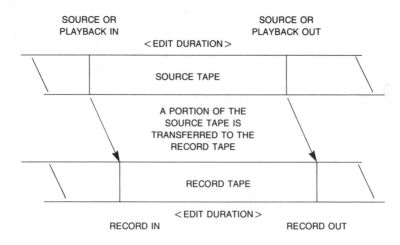

Figure 5-1 A diagram of a video edit.

1. The IN point on the record machine
2. The IN point on the source machine
3. The OUT point

The IN Point on the Record Machine

The point or location on the record tape where the image will change is the IN point on the record machine.

The IN Point on the Source Machine

The IN point on the playback or source machine is the beginning of the picture (and/or audio) that will be copied onto the record machine. This image will be recorded starting at the IN point of the record machine.

The OUT Point

The OUT point is where the edit ends. It defines the length or duration of the edit.

When an edit is performed, video and/or audio is transferred to the record tape. Without slow motion, freeze frames, or other special effects, it takes one frame of video on the record tape to copy one frame of video from the source tape. This means that the distance from the IN to the OUT point on the source tape is the same as the distance from the IN to the OUT point on the record tape.

Thus, there need be only one OUT point, since its purpose is to define the length of the edit. You can choose the OUT point of the edit on the record tape or the playback tape, depending on the editing requirements.

If you know the duration of an edit, the location of the OUT point on the record tape, and the location of the OUT point on the playback tape, you can *back time* the edit by subtracting the duration from the OUT points (see Figure 5-2). This will give the two IN points on the source and record tapes. Similarly, if you know the IN and OUT points on the record tape and the OUT point on the source tape, you can find the IN point by subtracting the duration of the edit (the record IN point from the record OUT point) from the playback OUT point.

OPEN-ENDED EDIT

An edit that does not have an OUT point before the recording begins is called an *open-ended edit*. In an open-ended edit, the OUT point is chosen during the recording process. When the open-ended edit has been completed, the edit will have the required OUT point.

If an IN point on both playback and record has been chosen, as well as an OUT point, then an edit has been defined. This edit is a cut because only one picture source is being transferred to the record tape. If an effect requires recording from multiple sources, more source IN points must be defined. A source IN point is required for every videotape source used in an edit.

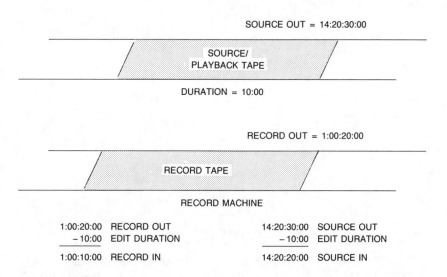

Figure 5-2 Calculation of a back-timed edit. Subtracting the edit duration from the OUT point produces the IN point.

MULTIPLE-SOURCE EDIT

If you had a tape of a clear blue sky and wanted to add a flying saucer over the sky, you would need three IN points: the IN point of the background (the sky), the IN point of the flying saucer footage, and the IN point on the record machine (see Figure 5-3).

If you wanted to make four digital effects boxes containing close-ups of players in a sporting event appear over the arena, you would need six IN points: one source IN point for each of the four players, a fifth source IN point for the arena background, and the final IN point on the record machine.

THE EDITING PROCESS

The video editing process is a straightforward use of materials and tools that vary from sheets of paper describing the original footage (the master log) to the on-line editing system (see Figure 5-4).

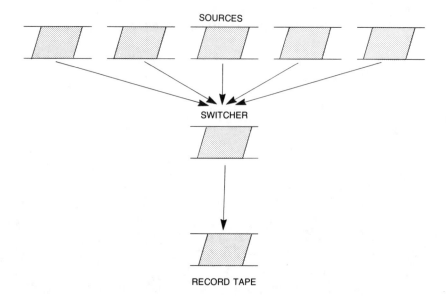

Figure 5-3   Diagram of several video signals being combined in the switcher. Multiple sources are transferred to the record tape after being combined into one video signal by the switcher.

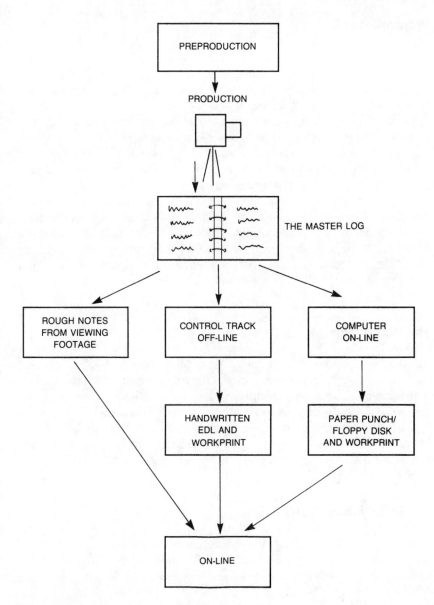

Figure 5-4 Flowchart of the video editing process and the three possible methods of preparing for the final on-line editing session.

Preproduction

The most important aspect of any visual show is preproduction. The crew must know where to be and at what time; the production manager must know what equipment has to be rented; the director should know where the editing will take place and who will be the editor.

Problems will always occur during production, but careful preproduction preparation is one of the best ways to avoid scheduling or editing difficulties. Shooting schedules, storyboards, and an editing plan should be determined before production begins. Ninety percent of all production and postproduction is actually accomplished during preproduction.

In large productions, commercial computer programs specifically designed to help in preproduction chores are often used. In those large productions, weeks and often months are taken to resolve as many potential problems as possible. Although production seems to be the most exciting and interesting aspect of any visual project, it is the preproduction that determines how smoothly the overall strategy will be accomplished.

The Master Log

The *master log* is an organized, legible list of all available footage on each reel, the location of each shot on that reel, and the reel number. This information is noted during the shoot, along with any special instructions from the director. Special comments pertaining to each shot (such as bad audio, an audio boom in the shot, a particularly good performance, excessive dropouts, great action, or bad camera movement) are also logged. Additional information is entered in the master log while viewing the footage, before the editing session begins.

The Edit Decision List

The next step is to prepare for the on-line, or final, editing of the show. There are three methods of preparing the *edit decision list* (EDL). (An EDL is a list that includes all the picture and audio edits, in sequential order, that will be in the show.) These methods are:

1. Making rough edit notes while viewing the footage
2. Making notes while viewing the control track off-line
3. Using a computer off-line to produce computer punch tape or a diskette of the edit

Rough Edit Notes

While viewing the footage, you can list all the shots, in the order in which they will be edited into the show, without actually cutting the shots together. The notes include where each shot and/or audio source is located, along with any other important information; for example, a general description of the shot, the time code and reel, or sound notes for the audio sweetening process. Many professionals use this method to prepare for off-line editing sessions. Some create their lists at home, viewing window dubs of their footage on VHS or three-quarter-inch decks.

Off-Line Editing

An *off-line* edit is a session in which a show is cut together to determine the exact order of the edits, using copies of the original footage. The end result of an off-line edit is an EDL and an edited workprint that can be reviewed during or after the session. The off-line session often uses window dubs for playback material. The EDL and edit workprint are used in the on-line session to create the final version of the program.

The Workprint

The *workprint*, or *rough cut*, is a videotape created as a result of an off-line editing session using a control track, computer, or random-access editor. Often the workprint includes effects.

If you find that additional changes are necessary after viewing the workprint, these changes might be made in another off-line editing session. If the modifications are not too complicated, they might be performed during the on-line edit.

The On-Line Edit

During the *on-line* editing session, the original footage is assembled for the final time. The EDL from the off-line session is used to re-create the edits made during the off-line session. Some programs, such as news shows, do not bother with the off-line editing process. The footage is viewed, logged, and edited on-line.

Organization

The key to any show's success is organization. A confusing, disorganized show will be unpleasant, difficult to shoot, and a challenge to edit.

SUMMARY

Video editing consists of copying a section of a source tape onto a record tape. On analog editing systems, the record machine can only make a cut. A composite digital machine can play back video or add video to the original picture. Once a video edit is performed on any record machine, the video that was originally there is completely erased. The following three points determine a cut on either analog or digital systems:

1. The IN point on the record machine
2. The IN point on the source machine
3. The OUT point

If an effect requires more than one playback, more source IN points must be defined. A source IN point is required for each videotape source used in an edit.

The most important aspect of any show is preproduction. You should try to avoid being distracted by the excitement to be experienced later during production. The master log is an organized, legible list of all available footage on each reel, the location of each shot on the reel, and the reel number.

The edit decision list (EDL) is used to prepare for the final, on-line edit. The list may be composed by making rough notes while viewing the footage or during an off-line edit session.

The workprint is a videotape created as a result of an off-line editing session. Changes in the workprint are made in another off-line edit or in the on-line, or final, edit.

PART II

Concepts of Videotape Editing

6

Creating and Using the Master Log

A master log should be used for every video production so that scenes and shots can be located quickly. With news editing, the master log usually consists of only the notes taken while viewing the footage. Since a news program is edited so quickly, there is no time to build an extensive shot list. In all other dramatic, documentary, and informative programs, including feature news stories, the master log is a larger, more complete reference guide to the show's components.

REEL NUMBERING

Before the master log is started, it is good practice to set up a reel numbering system in advance of the shoot. This system may be ordered in terms of location, shooting day, time code, or any method that is logical and informative.

Every reel to be used in the editing of a show should be numbered and have identifying labels that explain exactly what is inside the box. A label such as "9–15, Prebuild, hold for on-line" is useless to anyone but the original author. If the tape is a preedit reel, it should have a log describing the contents and an EDL inside the box. The reel also should be added to the reel summary and the footage log of the master log.

THREE DIVISIONS

There are three major divisions of the master log: the show script, the reel summary, and the footage notes. Professionals often use a three-ring binder as their master log. The show script, which can be in several formats, is an invaluable guide for the editor. Copies of the script should be given to the editor with director's and production notes. Time code and shot composition notes are written on many dramatic and comedy scripts during production to help speed the editing process.

Reel Summary

The *reel summary* (see Figure 6-1) is a page or two that encapsulates the material on each reel. Note that time code indications do not include frames, because the note refers to a general location on the tape.

Footage Notes

Footage notes (see Figure 6-2) are details of each shot on each reel. These notes include technical problems, the timing of each scene, the location on the reel, and/or the time code at the beginning of the shot. Specific shots that might work well in a certain area of the show are also noted in the show script.

Footage notes are made during the shoot and in a viewing session after the production. While viewing the footage, you can add additional notes that were not apparent or available during production to the footage log.

TIMINGS

It is important to keep track of where each shot is located on every reel so that it can be quickly found during editing. One method of making these *timings* is by viewing the tape with a watch. You can write the location of the shots and any notes concerning them in the master log. Using a watch or clock, however, does not allow you to stop the tape for more complete note-taking without ruining the timing. Using a stopwatch does allow you to stop the tape and the watch while making extensive log notes. A control track timer also allows you to stop the machine and make notes, then continue viewing the footage. Control track editors usually contain such a timer. Some VCRs also have control track timers built in.

Time code is the most accurate method of logging shot locations in the master log, but you need a machine that can read time code or a window dub. A *window dub* is an exact copy of the original footage with a visual representation of the time code burned into the picture. Because the time code appears on the

1″ SOURCE

REEL #

#50........00:58:00–01:25:00........(STOCK FOOTAGE)
#51........01:00:00–01:22:00........(CH. 4 CHROMA-KEYS)
#52........01:48:30–01:54:30........(GENERIC CHS. 1 & 4)
#53........00:58:00–01:50:00........(1810/1820 PRE-BUILD W/O TITLES)
#54........00:58:00–01:50:00........(1810/1820 PRE-BUILD W/TITLES)
#75........00:00:00–00:23:00........(GRAPHICS REEL)
#99........09:00:00–09:10:00........(MUSIC REEL)

BETA SOURCE

ON CAMERA & INSERT SHOTS

REEL #

#1..........01:00:00–01:17:00....... (CH. 2, CH. 6)
#2..........02:00:00–02:17:00........(CH. 3)
#3..........03:00:00–03:19:00........(CH. 3, CH. 7, CH. 2 & 3 VO)
#4..........04:00:00–04:19:30........(CH. 3 & 6 VO, CH. 7)
#5..........05:00:00–05:19:30........(CH. 7, CH. 8, CH. 3 VO)
#6..........06:00:00–06:19:00........(CH. 3 VO, CH. 8 VO, CH. 5)
#7..........07:00:00–07:19:30........(CH. 5, CH. 9)
#8..........08:00:00–08:18:30........(CH. 9)
#9..........09:00:00–09:19:00........(CH. 9, CH. 9 VO)
#10........10:00:00–10:18:30........(CH. 9 VO)
#11........11:00:00–11:19:00........(CH. 9 VO)
#12........12:00:00–12:20:00........(FDP/MEM PANEL CHS. 3, 5–9)
#13........13:00:00–13:21:00........(MEM. PANEL/FDP CHS. 9, 2, 3)
#14........14:00:00–14:19:30........(ECU MEM/FDP CHS. 3, 6, 7)
#15........15:00:00–15:19:00........(MEM. CHS. 7, 8/FDP ALL CHS.)
#16........16:00:00–16:18:30........(FDP CHS. 3, 5, 7, 8)
#17........17:00:00–17:21:00........(FDP CHS. 8, 2, 9/POWER CH. 2)
#18........18:00:00–18:20:00........(2ND CTRL CHS. 8, 9, 2, 3, 6)
#19........19:00:00–19:20:00........(ECU 2ND CTRL CHS. 3, 6, 9)
#20........20:00:00–20:20:00........(LOCK-OFFS CHS. 9, 5)
#21........21:00:00–21:19:00........(LOCK-OFF CH. 5/SWIVEL CHS. 2, 3)
#22........22:00:00–22:20:00........(REMOTE SHOTS ALL CHS.)
#23........23:00:00–23:10:00........((MON/VCR HK-UP CH. 9/ON-SCRN CH. 8)

VOICE OVER REELS

REEL #

#102......00:00:00–00:27:30........(CHS. 1–7)
#103......00:28:00–00:37:00........(CHS. 8, 9)

ADDITIONAL REELS

REEL #

#160......16:00:00–16:20:00........(1870 CAMERA MASTER-PLAYBACK)
#230......23:00:00–23:18:00........(1810/1820 CAMERA MASTER)
#240......01:30:00–01:49:30........(1810/1820 CAMERA MASTER)
#250......02:30:00–02:50:00........(1810/1820 CAMERA MASTER)

Figure 6-1 An example of a professional reel summary. This particular show demonstrates how to operate a Zenith™ VCR. Note that most of the reels have time code that corresponds to the reel number. Also note that this show uses other edited shows as playbacks, such as show 1810/1820. A lock-off is a series of shots with a camera firmly held in the same position, allowing for pop-on effects or dissolves (CH = chapter, VO = voice-over reel, ECU = extreme closeup, FDP = front display panel of the VCR, Mon-VCR Hk-Up = a recorded video playback through the VCR).

Project Title _"V.C.G 1820/1820"_   Project # _2860L_   Date _2/18/86_
Client _ZENITH_   Producer _ADAMS_   Director _NACZ_
Camera Op. _VACZ_   Camera _HL79E_   Reel # _16_   VTR _____
Location _entire filming_   INT ☒ EXT D N Notes _____

SCENE	PAGE	TAKE	AUDIO SLATE	TIME CODE	REMARKS	STATUS
				: :	Chapter 2 inserts	
12	6	1	Slote	16:01:02	right hand opening door, left hand pressing clock switch	
..	"	—	—	16:01:37		
"	"	—	—	16:01:55	ECU clock adjust switch	
"	"	—	—	16:02:17	" " " "	
"	"	—	—	16:02:23	finger pushing switch to clock (left hand)	
"	"	—	—	16:02:39	" " " " "	
"	"	—	—	16:02:47	" ↘ switch to clock adj	
"	"	— --	—	16:02:57	" " " to program	
"	"	—	-- --	16:03:02	" " " to clock	
"	"	1	SLATE	16:03:46	redo w/ right hand CU	
"	"	—	—	16:04:00	switching to clock position	

REEL 16   Page No. 45

Figure 6-2   An example of a professional footage log.

screen, there is no need for a clock, stopwatch, control track timer, or time code reader to log the timings. Some producers and editors have window dubs made on VHS or three-quarter-inch tape and screen the material on a VCR at home.

DIRECTOR'S NOTES

During the production, the director often gives verbal instructions concerning shots and angles, possible editing choices, and other information. The person responsible for keeping the master log should incorporate these notes into the show script. If no script is available during the shoot, as in the case of a documentary, these notes should be kept in a separate section of the master log.

SINGLE- VERSUS MULTIPLE-CAMERA PRODUCTION

There are two very different methods of video production: single-camera production and multiple-camera production. *Single-camera production* is used most often for location shots, while *multiple-camera production* is usually employed in the studio. Filmed location shows, including motion pictures, use single-camera production. The exception to this rule is when a complex effect is being performed. In this case multiple cameras are set up to film all angles of the action. Sitcoms, whether shot on film or video, are most often shot using multiple cameras.

Since the single camera records only one angle of the action, more footage notes are used in the master log. Multiple-camera productions usually rely on the script for production notations.

Single-Camera Production

The master log for a single-camera production is usually more detailed than the log for a multiple-camera production. This is because each scene requires more takes and more individual shots. Trying to fit all this information into the margins of the script is not practical. Brief notes concerning particular shots or scenes can be made in the script, with reference to the appropriate reel. The details are then recorded in the footage log.

The footage notes for a single-camera production are more detailed than those for a multiple-camera shoot. Each reel should be viewed and logged in a viewing session. The location and running time of each take should be logged. Additional technical information also should be included in the footage notes.

Finally, as mentioned above, the script for a single-camera production contains short notes referring to the more detailed footage log. The director's or other crew members' notes also can be written briefly in the script's margins.

Multiple-Camera Production

The script is the basis of the multiple-camera log (see Figure 6-3). Different-colored lines drawn down the side of the script indicate the camera or VTR source. Timings are written in the margins, along with technical notes. When viewing the footage, you can add more notes to the script. The reel summary is also updated at this time if necessary.

Productions that do not have a script are occasionally shot with multiple cameras. These are usually interviews for documentaries or special effects shots requiring the action to be covered by several cameras. In the case of interviews, it is good practice to transcribe the dialogue, then mark the transcription as if it were a script, using different-colored lines to indicate the camera or VTR source. Special effects shots should be logged in a viewing session after the footage has been shot. Careful attention must be paid to the angle of these shots because the action will be very similar from each angle.

3.

	CAM 1	CAM 2	CAM 3

CONTINUED:

12:15:01:00 | CU
NU

NU
We have heard otherwise.

WING
Mr. Maxwell, when you cashed our
check, you entered an agreement
with us. We are grateful for your
work, but there must be a change.
(beat.)
We want access to all your notes
and programming.

WS

Jake smiles and shakes his head in disbelief.

CU
JAKE

JAKE
He's kidding . . . You're all
kidding.

Thunder is HEARD in the background, but no one at
the table stops to notice.

NU
No one is kidding, Mr. Maxwell
12:15:25:00

JAKE
Then you gentlemen have a
problem.

Korin gets up from the table.

KORIN
I still don't think you understand . . .

JAKE
I understand perfectly, Jack. You're
not getting your paws on my
program. As far as I am concerned,
our agreement is terminated.

WS

2S
KORIN
JAKE

Jake rises and leaves the table. Korin grabs his jacket and
holds him in place.

12:15:48:00
(CONTINUED)

Figure 6-3   Multiple-camera productions often use the script to indicate the shots made by each camera at any particular time during taping. In this case, three cameras were being used, each having its own corresponding line on the script. The shots taken by each camera are labeled at the appropriate line. The time code also is indicated on the script (WS = wide shot, 2S = two shot, CU = close up).

KEEPING TRACK OF MATERIALS

Tracking all the source materials in a large production can be a major chore. Not only are there videotapes, but there are also quarter-inch audio reels, title cards, scripts, off-line diskettes, digital audio tapes (DATs), computer disks, credit lists, director's notes, and much, much more. Keeping track of every show's production elements requires an extra effort, but attempting to find a missing reel or shot during the on-line edit is even more time-consuming, frustrating, and extremely expensive.

USING THE MICROCOMPUTER

There are various ways to structure log programs using microcomputers. One method is to watch the production footage using a window dub and type notes into a data base. Then with a search function, you can find key words, character names, locations, and/or dialogue, along with the shot's corresponding time code. The data base can be cross-referenced. Information such as characters, locations, dialogue lines, even reel summaries can be called up and printed out. A laptop or portable computer could be brought to the on-line editing session to allow quick access to the material. As with all computer information, a backup file and printout of the material should be kept to avoid accidental data loss.

Other useful programs are available, like "Log Producer®" by Video Logic®. This program, running on a microcomputer and interfaced with a time-code-reading VCR, can log the time code and then store typed information about that location. In addition, the VCR can be controlled from the computer keyboard and an EDL can be created. The computer program's information can be recalled or printed out. More and more programs like Log Producer are being developed. Good sources for these types of programs are video supply distributors.

SUMMARY

A master log should be used for every video production. Before the master log is even started, it is good practice to set up a reel numbering system in advance of the actual shoot.

The master log consists of three parts: the script, reel summary, and footage notes. The reel summary is a page or two encapsulating what material is on each reel. Footage notes are details of each specific shot on each reel.

You must keep track of where each shot is located on every reel so that it can be found during editing. Director's notes are often written in the show script (see Figure 6-4) or kept in a special location in the master log. Single-camera productions rely heavily on footage notes. Multiple-camera shoots rely more on the script.

THE LAST FRONTIER

The Exploration of Central Brazil

VIDEO	AUDIO

REEL 7 5:06:15:00

The show opens with a wide
aerial shot of the rain
forest. Miles of untouched
land stretches for miles.

NARRATOR VO: IT IS A LAND OF *Helicopter sounds*
MYSTERY, A LAND TIME HAS
FORGOTTEN, A LAND THAT IS NOW
DISCOVERING IT HOLDS THE
FUTURE OF WESTERN
CIVILIZATION.

(15 ft)

Dissolve to massive waterfall
as we circle the swirling
mists. *Reel 11 - 11:15:01:00*

THERE IS ABUNDANT NATURAL *WATER Sounds*
ENERGY, WATER AND RICH SOIL
TO SUPPORT A VARIETY OF
COMMERCIAL ENTERPRISES.

(25 ft)

Dissolve to natives eating
around their ramshackle huts.
Poverty and filth are
everywhere. *REEL 7 5:22:00:00*

DOES CIVILIZATION OFFER HOPE
AND SALVATION TO THESE *Kidscrying*
IMPOVERISHED PEOPLES, OR
TOTAL ENSLAVEMENT TO THE
WESTERN WORLD?

Dissolve to World Issues
Graphic, key paint box title
over graphic. *Graphics Reel 1
1:02:00:00*

TONIGHT WORLD ISSUE EXAMINES
BRAZIL, ITS PEOPLE, ITS *MUSIC*
NATURAL RESOURCES. ARE
INTERNATIONAL CORPORATIONS
EXPLOTING THIS AREA? ARE
THERE REAL BENEFITS TO GIVE?

(Flip)

DVE effect to the studio, a
wide shot of Sterling in a
bookcase filled office. He
moves to a large globe as we
dolly in. Sterling swivels
the globe to reveal South
America as he motions to
Brazil. *TAKE 5
Prod Reel 6 6:22:01:00*

HELLO, I'M SEAN STERLING,
YOUR HOST FOR OUR PROGRAM,
BRAZIL THE BRIGHT LIGHT OF
SOUTH AMERICA. OUR
EXAMINATION OF BRAZIL'S
NEWFOUND POWER STARTS IN THE
MIDDLE OF THE RAIN FOREST,
AND ENDS IN A COSMOPOLITAN
CITY. THE PEOPLE OF BRAZIL
HAVE A COMMON FUTURE TIED TO
COMMERCIAL EXPLOITATION. BUT
CAN THEY CONTROL THEIR
DESTINY? OR WILL THEY BE USED
AND ABSORBED?

Figure 6-4 An example of notations on an audio-video formatted script.

7

Control Track, Time Code, Computer, and Random-Access Editors

In the late 1970s, only two types of video editors were available: those that read time code (*computer editors*) and those that did not (*control track editors*). Since then, dramatic improvements in the videotape deck have allowed time code use with every format. Of course, having a tape with time code on it does not ensure its readability on every deck. The hardware must be able to read the code. Nevertheless, the widespread use of time code has blurred these two categories. S-VHS, Hi-8, even VHS can be time coded, edited, and used for effects. The high-end Omni® editing controller from CMX is built with S-VHS control.

To keep clear the distinctions between the controllers, this text will refer to four types of machine editors: control track editors, machines that can only count control track; time code editors, machines that access time code but cannot remember more than two edits; computer editors, machines that can remember more than two edits; and random-access editors, computers that store video images, audio and time code, but can edit and access their images instantaneously.

CONTROL TRACK EDITORS

Control track editors use the tape's control track pulses to register tape location. In most editing situations, control track editors control either three-quarter-inch or half-inch videotape, although some control track systems can operate with one-inch tape. Control track and time code editing capabilities are built into newer three-quarter-inch tape machines.

There are three basic ways to use the control track editor. The first is to use the system for the final step in the editing process (the on-line edit). Second, the machine can be used to create an off-line EDL and workprint. Finally, you can use the control track editor to produce segments of a program prepared in A/B roll method, described later in this chapter. These tapes could then be brought to an on-line facility. During the on-line edit, the various segments are combined and sophisticated effects performed.

On-Line Editing

The control track editor (see Figure 7-1) is frequently found in news departments, corporate video departments, schools, and retail companies. Actors and actresses will have their scenes edited onto a cassette that they can use when trying to land a part.

Some upgraded control track systems read time code accurately. Some can fade up from black and back down again, but most systems just cut. This does not mean that less sophisticated systems are editorially less creative. The cut is the most powerful editing transition available (95% of the edits in motion pictures and television shows are cuts), and control track editors handle this task very well.

Most control track editing systems can perform either assemble or insert recordings. The problems with assemble recordings discussed in Chapter 2 also apply to the control track editor. To use the insert recording mode, the record tape must have continuous control track recorded on it for the length of the final show. This is accomplished by performing an assemble recording on the record tape before beginning the actual editing.

The great advantage of control track editing, besides the attractive price, is that the machines are easy to learn. This allows the editor to concentrate on the other important aspect of editing: cutting pictures and sound.

The disadvantage of these systems is that they rarely remember or store edits. It is good practice when editing on a control track editor to record the edits long. Erasing the unneeded tail portion of an edit is much easier than trying to re-create an edit to make it a second or two longer.

This lack of memory also means that you must consider all editorial changes carefully before going into record. Editing videotape is a linear process, and when you add (or delete) a shot in the middle of a scene, every edit after that will be affected. One solution is to put the record tape into the playback machine and make the necessary changes on a new record tape. Despite these problems, if edits are made with care, and if careful editorial judgment is exercised, a control track editor can be the perfect editing tool.

Off-Line Editing

When the control track editor is used with window dubs or careful editing notes, it can open the door to creative editing without the added expense of renting a time code editing system. After the workprint is completed, the off-line master can be shown to the client or potential purchaser. Once the show has been approved, the EDL is brought to the on-line session, where the control track edits are re-created. Graphics and effects are often added to visuals during the on-line edit. Many expensive broadcast shows have been off-line edited on control track editing systems, but most of these use window dubs for source material.

Figure 7-1 The Panasonic AG-A800 controller. This controller works with either control track or time code. This multi-event edit controller is time-code compatible. It can hold 128 edits in memory. On the left side of the controller are the keypad and external device controls. The center of the keyboard has the cue, edit enable, and mode selects. On the right side are the shuttle and machine-select controls. Photo courtesy of Panasonic Communications & Systems Company.

Preediting

The third way control track editing systems are used is to prepare an edited master for a second on-line session. Producers can edit on three-quarter-inch tape using a control track editor, then use that tape to create a new edited master in an on-line edit session. Effects and graphics are added in the on-line session.

A more complicated use of the control track editor would be to prepare edited segments on two different reels (A and B). The A reel would be edited by cuts only up to the point where an effect was needed. At this point, a proper tail would be added to the A reel to allow for the transition. On a separate record tape, the B reel, adequate head would be added for the effect. The editing would continue on the B reel until another effect was planned. The editor would go back and forth, alternating record tapes. During the on-line edit, both the A and B reels would be used as playbacks, with the effects creating the transitions from one reel to the other.

Another way of using a control track editor to preedit for an on-line edit would be to make a copy of the edited master, onto which you could edit audio effects and music. These two tapes offer a total of four audio tracks during the on-line session (two tracks from the edited master and two from the dub). The tapes can be played back in sync during the on-line session and the four audio tracks mixed down onto the edited master.

The edited master would be the final product except for the added video effects. Therefore, special care must be taken with the technical aspects of the video when using control track editors.

TIME CODE EDITORS

The late 1980s brought time code into the newsroom. The fast-paced world of information, exemplified by the O.J. Simpson trial, and reality shows like *Cops*, clearly requires the accuracy and efficiency offered by time code. Simple time code editing systems, as defined in this book, read time code and allow the editor to create simple video sequences with minimal special effects. Such systems are also relatively inexpensive and are easier to operate and maintain than the more complex computer editing systems. These time code editors are an excellent option for newsrooms and similar environments where speed and expense are primary concerns.

Basic time code editors are electronic, but do not match the processing power, speed, and memory of a full-fledged computer-based editing system. Unlike computers that possess extensive memories, time code editors retain only a few edits at a time. In other words, while entering an edit, you can only see and modify the previous edit or two. Linked to a nearby printer, such systems can display the edits that have been performed. This printout is useful for reference, as edits often are repeated exactly or approximately during an editing session. In the past, such repeatability was only available with an expensive controller.

The uses of the time code editing system are similar to those of the control track editor. With little memory, the time code system cannot auto-assemble an edit list, but can be used as an accurate off-line system or on-line editor. In most cases, control of a sophisticated switcher or other peripheral equipment is limited or nonexistent. However, although some effects can be made on-the-fly, using time code allows you to repeat an edit even if the effects device is being operated live.

Time code editors can be used to preedit segments, and like the control track editor, they are easy to operate. If a printer is attached to the editing system, each edit can be printed as it is performed. The resulting list could be typed into a list cleaning program. (These programs flag and resolve inconsistencies within the edit list—several are available for personal computers.) The list cleaning program cleans and generates a time-code-accurate EDL for an on-line session.

One element to remember when relying on the accurate repeatability of a time code editing system: When you are repeating an edit in the middle of a program, the tail of that edit may have been erased by the following edit, or by an edit performed in the middle of a cut. Careful attention must be paid in complicated editing situations when returning to a previously edited section. Audio edits are not readily apparent, so you must check meticulously before repeating an edit to avoid erasing a carefully built sequence.

The time code system has all the advantages of the control track system. In addition, it can be used for building A/B rolls for an on-line effects session, and for creating separate audio tracks. It is an excellent choice for news, documentary, off-line, or industrial program editing. With its ability to repeat edits accurately, a time code system can be a powerful editing tool when used with forethought.

COMPUTER EDITORS

Time code made it possible to perform edits repeatedly and accurately. The computer editor added speed and flexibility, enabling editors to focus more on aesthetics and less on technology. Computer editors also introduced the need for the abstract generalization of the video edit itself and the different electronic devices that make up the editing system. Eight-digit numbers represent video frames, and lines of computer information represent edits.

The pulse or control track editor is a simple machine to operate, with only a few buttons and options, but the computer editor requires extensive experience in controlling multiple machines while reading, analyzing, and utilizing a complex cathode-ray tube (CRT) screen. The most complicated of these systems can control over ten video machines, five digital effects machines, several character generators, an audio tape recorder (ATR), and sometimes more.

In the early days of computer editing, human operators were more technicians than editors. Making computer edits required a combination of engineer, computer programmer, and maintenance person. Long sessions of typing and staring at the CRT screen were punctuated only occasionally by edits. As the computer became more powerful, video edits could be made faster and more often. With the dropping prices of videotape machines and other postproduction equipment, advertising agencies, large corporations, and production companies bought their own computer editors, designed their own on-line bays, and built sophisticated graphics departments.

Accuracy and Repeatability

With a computer editor, edits can be performed again and again with frame accuracy. This repeatability is due to the computer editor remembering the time codes of the source and record tapes of each edit. Newer, more sophisticated computer editors can store switcher effects, digital video effects, and TBC settings for each edit. Although most special effects are created for each individual show or edit, many of the effects' specifics can be stored and subsequently retrieved.

By instructing the computer to save the EDL to a recording medium, usually a 3½-inch diskette (see Figure 7-2), you can store the list for future use or load it into another computer.

For example, an off-line workprint can be created using inexpensive three-quarter-inch machines, or a random-access editor. The EDL can then be transferred to a computer on-line editing system, and the original edits can be performed during the on-line edit.

Computer diskettes have become a common method of transferring EDLs. There are several standard EDL formats. However, many computer editors will accept or translate other computers' diskettes. There are also computer programs that convert diskettes. Punch tape, and large 8-inch floppy disks have gone the way of the dinosaur. Even 5¼-inch floppies are rarely used anymore.

Computer Editing Room

The computer editing room can be designed in many different ways (see Figure 7-3). It can be built to edit three-quarter-inch cassette video in an off-line fashion or to create cassette masters. Editing rooms can handle conversions from three-quarter-inch to one-inch tape, one-inch to Beta cam, one-inch to D2,

Figure 7-2 The keyboard of the Sony BVE-9100, a large, powerful on-line editor. Photo courtesy of Sony Electronics, Inc.

and so on. A room that allows editing from, or to, more than one tape format is called an *interformat editing suite*. An interformat editing suite handles several types of video formats; however, the tapes must be of the same standard. For instance, a suite may not accept both PAL and NTSC signals. There are edit bays that can edit in either PAL or NTSC, but not both at the same time. There are also composite analog as well as composite digital bays. The concern with so many types of configurations is that if the bay is digital, the digital signal should stay digital though the entire edit path, through patch bays and switcher, preserving the digital signal. Converting back and forth from digital defeats the formats' strengths.

Most computer editing rooms are equipped with several video playback machines, a record machine, a switcher, an audio mixer, monitors, and some optional equipment that the client can rent by the hour. The more elaborate the editing suite, the more varied and expensive the optional equipment will be. Chapter 9 deals with this optional equipment and explains how it relates to the computer editing room.

Random-Access Editor

Random-access editors have drastically changed the post production world. Random-access is not only an editor, it can also perform complicated effects. In

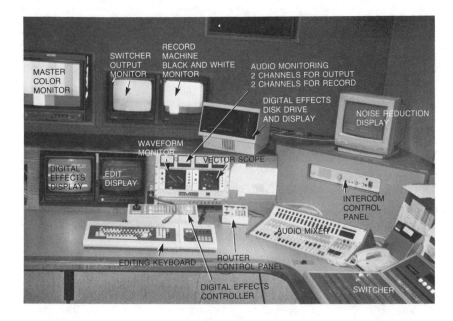

Figure 7-3 An on-line editing console. Photo by Sean Sterling.

larger cities, clients have become accustomed to being able to change an off-line program quickly and to see digital effects in their off-line programs. Since the random-access editor is more a software-driven machine than hardware, changes and improvement come rapidly. In addition, the random-access editor can keep track of time code, correlate film key numbers, edit in 30 or 24 frames per second, and create an accurate, clean EDL.

These systems are extremely flexible and user friendly, and foster creativity, allowing editors to make changes without dealing with the tape's linearity. The random-access editor is also capable of producing on-line quality output at about the level of half-inch professional video quality. Though this type of signal demands huge amounts of memory, random-access on-line is a reality. More than a few shows have been edited and then broadcast using a random-access editor. Soon videotape will only be used as a storage medium, replaced in edit bays by RMAGS (removable magnetic memory modules).

Each random-access system is unique to itself, although many share similarities in operation and user interface. Most employ computer images or icons to simplify their operation for users, and thus time code is not as important a part of editing. The computer keeps track of original time code and outputs a list at the end of the session. Random-access editors can read time code and recall many complicated edits. Random-access editors are usually "platformed" on either Macintosh® computers or IBM® clones.

Figure 7-4 The Avid Media Composer™, one of several random-access editors marketed by the Avid Corporation™. Visuals are stored on large digital hard disks, and are retrievable instantaneously.

The incredible power of the random-access editor lies in its ability to retrieve audio and/or video instantaneously. This eliminates the "linear" aspect of editing. Shots can be moved here or there without reediting or dubbing entire programs. Instead of waiting for a tape to shuttle, any shot, time code, or sequence can be accessed immediately. Random-access editors are becoming less expensive, and are definitely a part of the professional creative process.

The random-access edit bay differs from the traditional computer edit bay. There is a console with a computer; however, there is usually only a single playback deck, and that machine's purpose is to input video into the computer. Older random-access editors that used banks of VCRs or laser disks, have rapidly been replaced by those using gigabytes of computer memory. A full discussion of the major random-access systems can be found in Chapter 20.

The only way to find out about a particular editing room and the equipment it offers is to take a tour, talk to the staff, watch a demo reel, and contact some of the facility's clients; then you can make the proper choice based on the program's requirements and the editing equipment available. With so many corporate and in-house editing systems, it's worth asking around. Often an expensive editing system can be used very inexpensively during off-hours.

THE HUMAN FACTOR

No matter what type of system is used, the individuals actually performing the editing are as important as the technology, if not more so. Editors are the creative translators for the producer or director. They combine information from the production company with their own talent to create a show. Some directors will work only with certain editors or companies. Video is a highly technical and creative medium. Whoever edits the tape should have a well-balanced blend of technical and creative expertise.

SUMMARY

There are three basic ways to use a control track or simple time code editor:

1. As a final step in the editing process.
2. As an off-line or workprint editor.
3. As a step before an on-line edit.

The computer editor remembers the time codes of each edit it performs. This allows the computer editing system to perform edits over and over with frame accuracy. An EDL generated on punch tape or diskette by the computer can be loaded into another computer.

With computer editing you can:

1. Edit a workprint creatively at a cheaper rate than with on-line editing.
2. Edit directly in an on-line session.
3. Conform original material from a cuts-only listing (a handwritten EDL), computer punch tape, or a diskette. Diskettes for different computer editing systems might not be compatible, but are the standard method of transferring EDLs.

Most video computer editing rooms come equipped with several video playback machines, a record machine, a switcher, an audio mixer, monitors, and certain optional equipment that the client can rent by the hour. An interformat editing suite handles several types of video formats; however, they must be of the same standard. You should examine and test an unfamiliar editing system before using it for an important project. As a general rule, conversion from digital to analog degrades the picture quality.

Random-access editing has changed the editing world. More effects and quick changes during the off-line process have become standard in every major video market.

On-line random-access editors are a reality and are changing the post-production environment again.

8

Off-Line versus On-Line Editing

The purpose of an *off-line* edit is to create an EDL and an edited workprint of a program. Usually the off-line edit is accomplished using three-quarter-inch U-Matic tapes or half-inch VHS or 8mm. Random-access footage also originates from these sources. In the past, few video effects were available in an off-line editing session. With the advent of less expensive editing equipment and random-access editors, more often than not, effects and graphics are incorporated in the off-line workprint. Source tapes are usually copies of the original videotapes (window dubs).

On-line refers to the final editing process of production—picture and sound. An on-line session could be a cassette-to-cassette edit using a control track editing system, or it could be a month-long random-access editing session costing tens of thousands of dollars. In most cases, an off-line session precedes the on-line session, but often an off-line session is not necessary or possible. In the reverse order, a *prebuild* on-line session precedes an off-line session so that graphics and complicated effects can be created.

Even when a program goes directly to on-line, the session should be preceded by some planning. Using the master log, the editor organizes a rough list of the edits before the on-line session begins. It might take a few minutes during the session to decide in which order the shots will be edited, but preedit planning can help the editing session flow smoothly.

OFF-LINE EDITING

Quality Control

Since the off-line master is a reference to what will be created in the on-line session, the focus is on the editorial aspect of the show, not the technical quality of the off-line master. However, because the off-line master is often used for client approval, consideration should be made as to how the tape looks and sounds. Taking a moment or two to adjust a video or chroma level would not hurt the project unless there were terrible time constraints. Finessing a music edit can make the difference between a good program and a great one. When apparent tape damage or technical problems appear on the off-line source tapes, the location and type of each problem must be noted, and that same area must be checked on the master tape as soon as possible.

Control Track Editing

The control track editor can be used as an inexpensive off-line editor, but this necessitates taking detailed notes each time an edit is recorded.

A control track or time code off-line edit results in (1) a copy of the off-line record master and (2) a handwritten or printer-generated EDL. These documents should include the reel number from which the edit came, the approximate location of the shot on that reel, and any other information that might facilitate the search for the shot during the on-line edit.

When a control track off-line edit uses window dubs, the off-line edit master will have the time code source number of each video edit recorded on the picture (see Figure 8-1). These numbers, and the reel from which they came, are written in the EDL as each edit is recorded.

When the off-line session is over, many of the original edits will be erased, and the EDL will have to be rewritten to prepare for the on-line session. It is still a good idea to note all the edits performed, especially the audio edits. Since there are no numbers in the audio portion of window dubs, these edits must be carefully noted as they are made. Later, if a video edit covers a portion of a previously recorded audio-video edit, the time code number of the audio-video edit will be erased and replaced by a new number from the video edit. This new number will bear no relation to the audio.

The simple time code editor, if used properly, should have a printer attached to it. The printer records the time code of each edit. This printout eliminates much of the disadvantage of using the control track editor. Also, the printed record is vital in on-line editing because the audio edits are available for reference when it is time to assemble the final show.

The edits can be loaded into a list cleaning program and a computerized EDL created. Notes should be made on the printer's output, for example, when time code is duplicated on different tapes.

To save money, some producers edit off-line using their original videotapes. This method can be dangerous. Any machine is capable of damaging tape and off-line editing often requires tapes to be shuttled back and forth numerous times. The more a tape is played, the greater the chance of damage.

Figure 8-1   A frame of a window dub with the time code burned into the picture. Photo by Sean Sterling.

Refer to the workprint if there are questions about the EDL. Bring the tape to the on-line session. It is easier, and more accurate, to check the workprint than to try to remember how a sequence was built.

Computer Editing

A computer editing system is more expensive than a control track editor and an experienced editor is often required to operate it. The computer editor uses time code on the source and record tapes. It remembers which reel each edit came from and at what time code. Computer off-line editing results in (1) a copy of the off-line record master, (2) a paper printout of all the edits, and (3) a paper punch tape and/or computer disk of those edits.

In most computer off-line editing, the source material has the time code burned into the picture (a window dub). The time code can be "burned" into the edited master also. This creates an easy reference to the code on the program and helps when reviewing and making notes from the off-line master.

Figure 8-2 The Sony BVE-910, a small computer editor capable of performing on-line and off-line chores. Courtesy of Sony Electronics, Inc.

With the rapid acceptance of random-access editors, you might consider random-access editing rather than conventional off-line editing. Random-access systems can be rented by the day, week, or month, and if time is an important consideration, editing on this type of system can be advantageous. The object is still the same as video-based off-line editing: to create a viewable product along with an EDL and printout (see Chapter 20 for more on random-access editing).

The EDL is usually printed out on paper and also stored on a diskette. At the on-line edit, the diskette is loaded into the on-line computer, telling it the exact edits that were performed during the off-line session.

When to Use an Off-Line Edit

An off-line editing session should be considered if the program is complicated. Most news stories are not off-lined because there is little time for experimentation. A two-edit commercial is not off-lined because there are few choices to be made. Most network dramas, sitcoms, commercials, and specials use the off-line process. These shows go through so many changes during the editing process that an off-line session is a necessity.

The choice between a control track or time code editor and a computer editor often depends on the show's budget. Most shows that are edited on a computer system have larger budgets and are fairly elaborate in their post-production needs.

ON-LINE EDITING

Whether a show has been off-line edited or not, the most important aspect of a successful on-line edit is preparation. Planning for the on-line edit might include reviewing the footage and making a rough EDL, or it might be as involved as spending several days in an off-line session.

Many news stories, magazine shows, and industrial programs go directly on-line once an editing plan has been approved. Occasionally, for more complicated programs, prebuild on-line sessions precede the final on-line edit. A prebuild session is on-line because the video is being prepared for a final viewing. This footage will be used as a playback source when the entire program is edited together. The purpose of a prebuild on-line edit might be to create a complicated effects sequence or to edit segments that will be added to a studio show. The session often occurs at a different facility from the one where the actual show will be assembled because the editorial requirements are different from the program. Sometimes a prebuild on-line edit is performed because a show requires so many expensive machines that it is cost-effective to do all the complicated editing at one time.

Dealing with Sources Not Originally on Video

Many picture and audio sources begin not on video but on 35mm slides, home movies, quarter-inch audio tape, 16mm film, 35mm film, photos from magazines and books, computer-generated images, title cards, and so on. These source materials must be transferred to video in order to be edited (see Figure 8-3). Some of these sources should be transferred to tape before the on-line edit, while others can be used during the edit session. The design of the particular edit bay will often determine whether the transfer occurs before or during the session.

Control Track, Time Code, or Computer Editors

The choice of editors is usually determined by availability and cost. The larger the budget of a show, the more likely that a computer editor will be used for the on-line edit. When cost is not a factor, as when a corporation owns the editing

ORIGINAL SOURCE MATERIAL	EQUIPMENT NEEDED TO TRANSFER TO VIDEO	WHEN TRANSFER SHOULD TAKE PLACE
35 mm film	Telecine	Transfer before edit session
16 mm film	Telecine	Transfer before edit session
8 mm film	Telecine	Transfer before edit session
Slides	Film chain or Telecine	Transfer before edit session
1/4-inch audiotape	Reel to reel	Live in edit session or transfer before edit session
Audio cassette	Cassette player	Live in edit session or transfer before edit session
DAT audio	Make sure facility has DAT	Before or duing edit session
Mag (film audio)	Dummy or television driven Mag (telecine is used to keep audio running at same speed as film transfer)	Before edit session
Animation	Paint box for original telecine	Before edit session
	Telecine for film animation	Before edit session
Title cards*	Matte camera	Live in edit session or transfer before edit session
Electronic titles	Character generator	Live in edit session or before loa CG memory session edit sessior
Slow motion effects	Film chain, disk, or slow-motion tape machine	Live in edit session or transfer before edit

Note: You need to check with the edit facility to determine the availability of these machines. Usually there will be an additional charge for them.

*Not only will you have to order the matte camera in advance of the edit, you will need to have th title cards made in advance of the edit session.

Figure 8-3   Routine methods of transferring non-video materials to video.

system, larger, more complicated productions will be edited on the computer editor, and less important projects will be edited on the time code or control track editors.

SUMMARY

There are two types of editing sessions: off-line and on-line. The off-line edit is a practice session designed to create an EDL and an edited workprint. On-line refers to the final editing process of a production's picture and sound. An editing strategy must be determined before the editing begins.

A control track off-line edit requires that detailed notes be taken after each edit is recorded. When a control track off-line session uses window dubs, the off-line edit master should have the time code source numbers of each video edit recorded on the picture. You should always use copies of the original video in the off-line session to avoid damage to the master tapes. A control track off-line edit results in (1) a copy of the off-line record master and (2) a hand-written EDL of all edits.

A time code off-line edit results in (1) a copy of the off-line record master, and (2) a printout of the edits made (if a printer is included in the system). If no printer is available, a handwritten list should be made for later reference.

A computer off-line system requires an experienced operator and normally uses time code on the source and record tapes. A computer off-line edit results in (1) a copy of the off-line record master, (2) a paper printout of all the edits, and (3) a paper punch tape and/or computer disk of those edits.

An off-line editing session is considered if the program is extremely complicated and many different editing combinations will be tried. Whether a show has been off-line edited or not, the most important aspect of a successful on-line edit is preparation.

In a prebuild on-line session, a master tape is made of a show segment or graphic. This tape will be used as a playback source when the whole program is edited together.

Many picture and audio sources do not begin on video, and must be transferred to video before being edited.

In the final analysis, the larger the budget of a show, the more likely it is that a computer editor will be used for the on-line edit.

9

Creating Video Effects

Video effects are fun to watch and exciting to create. When used properly, they can improve the entire look of a show.

In the early stages of computerized video editing, effects were limited to wipes, dissolves, and keys. Words that were to appear on the video picture (lower thirds and graphics) had to be hot-pressed or typeset, shot with a video camera, then keyed over a background video. (*Lower thirds* are graphics keyed over an image that describe a location or state a person's name and title. These graphics are usually placed in the bottom third of the frame. Lower thirds are commonly used during news broadcasts and documentaries.)

With two-inch editing, there was no way to produce slow motion on tape. The first video effect, other than those created in the switcher, was the slow-motion disk. The video image was recorded on a metal disk that could hold a limited number of video frames. The disk was then able to play back the images at varying speeds. Not until the introduction of one-inch tape could slow-motion be used directly from the videotape.

The next machine that expanded the horizon of video effects was the character generator. A *character generator* is a video typewriter that creates letters and symbols, thus allowing an editor to design a person's name or a credit roll, store it, and then play it back in an editing bay or during a production.

Before the digital video effect was introduced in the 1980s, an image that was shot in the center of the screen remained in the center of the screen. Pictures that were going to be used in quad splits or split screens had to be composed and recorded in the proper position. With the digital effect, zooming images on or off the screen and placing them in a box (for instance, beside a newscaster) became commonplace.

Shortly after the introduction of digital effects came computer animation. At first, computer animation was extremely expensive and was used only by producers with large budgets. With the ever-decreasing cost of computers, this type of animation has come within the reach of more and more producers.

Currently, even less expensive machines are available to create single-frame (nonanimated) graphics. These machines are used instead of hand-drawn artwork for illustrations. Two advances brought the microcomputer into the video postproduction world. The Apple® Macintosh®, with its impressive capabilities, has opened the area of effects to everyone. IBM clones have come into their own for creating two-dimensional (2D) and three-dimensional (3D) effects. In the fast-paced, high-gloss broadcast world, these inexpensive devices are finding a great deal of use.

At the high end of graphics, film effects are being created in the digital computer. In 1995, Walt Disney Pictures released an entirely computer-animated feature—*Toy Story*. Harry, Cineon, Harriet, Domino, Flint, and Flame are just a few of the dedicated graphics and effects devices in use today.

THREE TYPES OF VIDEO EFFECTS

Three types of effects are used in the video editing process: switcher effects, external effects, and computer digital effects.

Switcher Effects

A videotape machine can only make a cut. A *switcher* creates effects such as wipes, dissolves, and keys. The purpose of a switcher is to mix many sources of video into a single video signal, to which the record machine cuts. The number of video signals that the switcher can access is determined by the number of inputs into the switcher. For instance, a switcher could be mixing sources such as a tape machine, a camera, a digital effects generator, a character generator, a color bar generator, or a safe-title generator. (A *safe-title generator* is a white box placed in a monitor to indicate the acceptable areas where titles can be placed and still be seen on a home television. Since a portion of the video picture is not visible on many home receivers, this equipment sets boundaries for title placement.)

The switcher can create background colors and matte colors but not video images. The video images that the switcher mixes always come from a source other than the switcher itself. A magazine picture, for instance, must be transferred to video by a camera before the switcher can deal with it.

A switcher can be a tiny box with only a few inputs, or it can be six feet long and require two operators (see Figures 9-1a and 9-1b). Some switchers have a built-in computer that allows you to program the effects, while others must be operated by hand. However it is used, the switcher's purpose is the same: to mix sources of video into one signal.

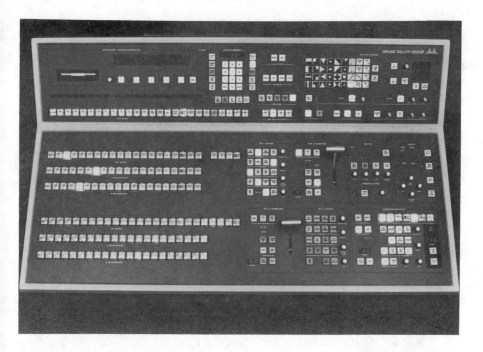

Figure 9-1a The Grass Valley 200™. The two fader bars control two key levels in addition to dissolves and wipes. The wipe patterns are at the top right, a disk drive for storing complicated switcher set-ups is on the left, and the downstream keyer is at the bottom right.

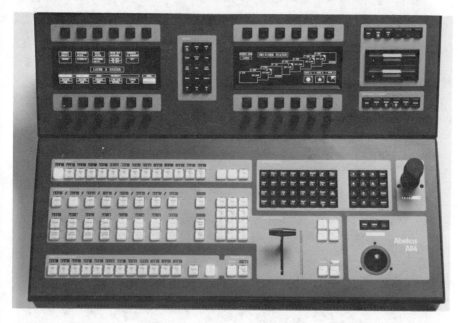

Figure 9-1b An Abekas™ A84 component digital switcher. Note the graphic display of the switcher's status in the top center portion of the device. Switchers such as the A84 prove the widespread acceptance of the digital formats. Photo courtesy of Abekas.

Wipes

A *wipe* is a transition from one picture to another using a pattern, such as a vertical bar that moves across the screen. The pattern reveals the new picture as the old one is wiped away. Some switchers have options concerning these wipe patterns. The edges of the wipe can be hard or soft. The wipe can have a colored border. A very soft-edged wipe looks almost like a dissolve.

Wipes come in many shapes and sizes, from stars to squares to diamonds. Not all switchers produce the same patterns. Some switchers can modulate or electronically distort these wipe shapes (see Figure 9-2). Using modulation, a circle, for instance, can become an undulating, wavy line.

Dissolves

A *dissolve* is a fade from one source to another. A dissolve to, or from, black or a dissolve to a key is called a *fade*. For instance, the director might instruct the editor to "dissolve to reel 2, fade in the end title, and then fade to black."

Figure 9-2 A modulated circle wipe with border. Photo by Sean Sterling.

Keys

A *key* is an electronic hole cut into a picture and filled with a video source. One example of a key is in the credit sequence at the end of a television show. The switcher cuts a hole for the words using a video source (a character generator, videotape, or artwork) and then fills the hole with the video signal. Another example of a key is the digital effects box over a newscaster's shoulder. In this case, the switcher cuts a hole in the studio camera's video signal and fills it with the video from the digital video effects generator.

The four types of keys are luminance keys, chroma keys, key cuts from external sources, and matte keys.

Luminance keys.   *Luminance keys* are electronic holes cut by using the white or black portion of a source and then filling in with video (see Figures 9-3a, 9-3b, and 9-3c). An example is white letters on a black graphics card shot by a video camera. The luminance key cuts a hole in the background picture in the shape of the letters and then fills the hole with the same video signal.

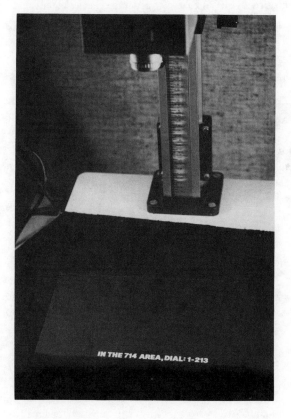

IN THE 714 AREA, DIAL: 1-213

a

Figure 9-3a   An art card under a matte camera.

Figure 9-3b A character generator and its monitor.

Figure 9-3c A luminance key from the character generator and matte camera over a beach scene. Photos by Sean Sterling.

If the switcher has enough capability, the video that fills the key can come from a source other than the key itself. The key could cut a hole using a graphics card, then fill the hole with another image, perhaps a close-up of running water. This use of the luminance key can produce very interesting effects.

Chroma keys. A *chroma key* is an electronic hole that cuts out a specific color in a video signal (see Figure 9-4). The hole is then filled with another video source. Chroma keys are often used during the weather segment of news broadcasts. The weather reporter stands in front of a blue screen. The maps are then chroma-keyed "behind" him or her. The reporter often seems to be looking off to the side of the screen because an off-screen monitor shows the switcher output of the chroma key. In reality, the reporter is pointing at an empty blue wall, and he or she must coordinate action with the map on the monitor.

Key cuts from external sources. In this case, the key is a separate video signal sent to the switcher by another machine, such as a character generator or a digital effects machine (see Figure 9-5). The switcher cuts a hole in the

Figure 9-4 A beach scene chroma-keyed into color bars. A specific color was eliminated by the chroma key, and the beach scene was inserted in that opening. Photo by Sean Sterling.

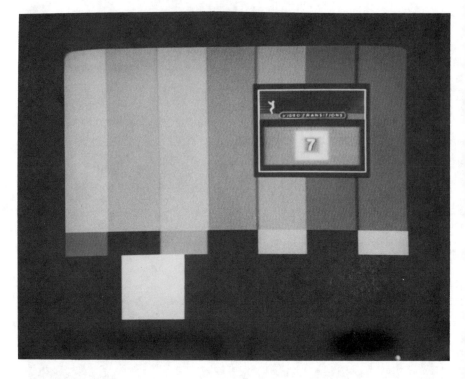

Figure 9-5 A key cut from a digital effects generator over color bars. Photo by Sean Sterling.

background video, using the key cut signal, and fills that hole with the video from the external source.

Again using the news as an example, the digital effects box over the announcer's shoulder is created by cutting the hole with the key cut signal from a digital effects machine, then filling the hole with the video from the digital effect. This creates a clean, defined cut in the background. If the video in the digital effects device contains both low and high luminance values, then the switcher will not be able to cut an accurate hole in the background material using a luminance key or a chroma key. A high-contrast image can be used in the switcher or in a digital effects device to cut a clearly defined hole in the background. This is the most common use of the external key cut.

Matte keys. A *matte key* is made by cutting a hole in the background source using a luminance key, a chroma key, or a key from an external source and filling the hole with a switcher-generated color. For example, when shooting white letters on a black art card, a matte key could color the holes created by the white letters.

Other Effects

The *nonadditive mix* is an option on some switchers that allows two video sources to be combined with full video levels from each source at the mid-point of the transition. A normal mix (dissolve) allows only 50% of each video source at the mid-point of the transition. The spotlight (see Figure 9-6) is an option that lowers the intensity of a portion of the image, while retaining the full video level in the remaining part of the picture. The spotlight is created with the switcher's wipe patterns.

Two Examples of Switcher Use

All switchers can create wipes, dissolves, and keys. Although these effects might seem limited, switchers can offer hundreds of ways to use them. Here is one example: A sportscaster is shown in a broadcasting booth. Keyed behind him is the stadium; in front of him, on his lower third, is his name. The background wipes to a blimp, the announcer fades out, and the game's statistics are

Figure 9-6 A spotlight effect. Photo by Sean Sterling.

dissolved in over the shot of the blimp. In this example, the character generator would be used twice to produce luminance or matte keys, the announcer would be chroma-keyed over the stadium, and the stadium shot would use a wipe effect to transition to the blimp.

Another simple example is the end of a football play. The scores fly in, then as a block the scores rotate and fall below the screen. This effect uses a paint system or frame store to input the picture into a two-channel digital effects device. The digital effects device "flies" the score over the background, the switcher uses the effects devices' external key cut to make the hole, and the video also comes from the digital effects device. The digital effects device (DVE) has to be two channels, because the side of the slab (two-sided rectangular image) is another channel, moving in exact cadence with the front portion of the image.

External Effects

The second type of effect is the external effect, which is created when another machine's video is fed into the switcher. External effects are often used in conjunction with switcher effects.

Character Generators

Character generators create video words. Most of these machines offer several fonts (boldface, roman, italic, etc.). In the more expensive models, words can be manipulated in much the same way that they are manipulated with a digital effects machine. Character generators can also create designs or capture images from a camera source and manipulate or store those images on a floppy disk. The character generator's signal is often keyed over other video sources.

Slow-Motion Devices

Most slow-motion effects are made using videotape machines, or in the case of film, an optical printer or high-speed camera. *Slow-motion* is a generic term that indicates an alteration of the original speed of a moving image. Each slow-motion deck has its own limitations of the speed variation in both forward and reverse. As a general rule, the limitations of video decks are −100% in reverse, and +300% in forward motion. To make a 600% effect, you would have to record a tape going forward at 300%, then play that recording back at 200%.

Computer Digital Effects

The computer digital effect can be broken down into two categories: digital video effects, which are created by a digital effects generator (see Figure 9-7), and computer-generated graphics. Both types of effects require very sophisticated computers.

Digital Video Effects

The digital video effect is accomplished by taking an existing video source (a video image, a moving shot, a still shot from a camera, a wipe, or another effect created by a switcher) and manipulating its position within the video frame. This effect can be seen on almost any network newscast. The DVE can flip a picture upside down or mirror-reverse the image; they can take a full-frame image and shrink it to infinity (nothing) or blow it up from infinity to full size. Most of these electronic devices can expand video past full frame, eliminating the possibility of a microphone's creeping into the shot or an accidental pan off the edge of the set.

Newer devices have the ability to bend the video frame into a ball or a cylinder, make a page turn, or create ripples and other distortions. Digital video effects devices are often used in compositing commercials or music videos.

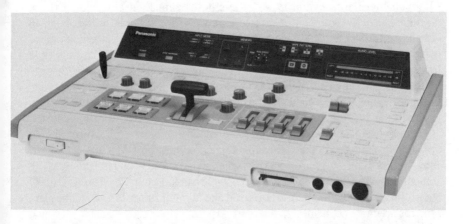

Figure 9-7   The Panasonic WJ-MX12 is an ideal example of the integration of video systems. This audio-video mixer has a variety of picture and audio capabilities, including fades, strobes (alternating a freeze, then release of moving footage), mosaic (turning a picture into a series of small rectangles), posterization (accenting and distorting the chroma portion of an image), and wipes. The mixer is S-VHS compatible. Photo courtesy of Panasonic Communications & Systems Company.

When a performer is shot in front of a blue screen and then chroma-keyed into the scene, the digital video effects device is often used to position the performer and even move the artist during the shot.

One of the most effective uses of the digital video effect is to build a story from still pictures. Static, full-frame pictures are boring, but a picture that zooms out from a colored background, spinning until it reaches full frame, then slides off to reveal another picture, is much more interesting.

Digital video effects are created by a *digital effects generator*, which converts the video signal into digital form. Using complex mathematical formulas, the generator changes the image's size, aspect, and position, converts it back to video, and sends the new video signal, along with a high-contrast key signal, to the switcher.

Each channel of the digital effects generator can handle only one video signal. If, for example, an editor needed 10 digital effects on the screen at one time, he or she would need a 10-channel digital effects device, 2 five-channel devices, 5 two-channel devices, or 10 one-channel devices. Alternatively, the editor could build successive generations of effects by recording one group, then playing that tape back and adding another group, repeating the process until the job was completed. Some low-quality digital effects devices are extremely dirty or nontransparent. An experienced eye can see the degradation of the picture when such machines are used (see Figure 9-8).

Computer-Generated Graphics

Although there are several types of computer animation devices, all these machines have the same purpose: to create video art. Some have the ability to grab or capture a frame of video so that the animator can design a graphic to go over the picture, while some allow the animator to play or animate multiple frames of video. The more expensive systems can animate the images they create. These devices are often used to create complicated openings. Computer-generated graphics are usually created before the editing session and recorded on videotape.

There are many levels of quality in computer-generated graphics. Simple graphics or animation could be accomplished on an Apple Macintosh or IBM computer system. The major concern when using these systems is getting the computer signal onto videotape with acceptable blanking and video levels. Usually animation of this type has to be transferred one frame at a time to tape. Video paint systems are more sophisticated but more expensive to use. The next level would be two-dimensional and three-dimensional animation. At the three-dimensional level, wire frame models of each object are created in the computer and programmed for motion by an animator/programmer. The computer can then throw light sources, textures, or other effects onto the landscape and/or the wire-framed object. This animation can then be recorded onto film or video. Such high-end computer graphic/animation is extremely expensive, and very impressive.

a

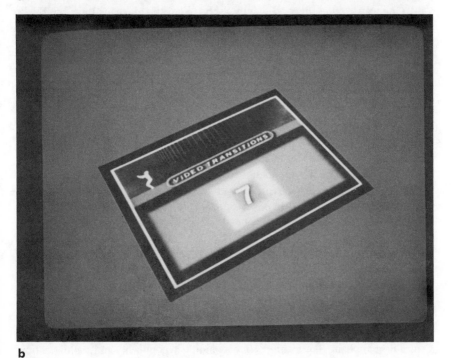

b

Figure 9-8 A full-frame signal reduced in a digital effects generator (a) then reduced and keyed over a background color (b). Photo by Sean Sterling.

SCENE 1	< 45 MINUTES >	SCENE 2

Figure 9-9 The concept behind the B reel. Without cutting the playback tape (which is rarely done), a dissolve from one point to another on the same reel requires a B reel. A tape cannot be at two different places at the same time. D2 editing does not require B reels because the D2 can dissolve from the record machine.

THE B REEL

Videotape effects can be produced by using a *B reel*, which is also called a *B roll* (see Figure 9-9). A B reel is an exact copy of one of the shots used in an effect when the images in the effect come from the same reel.

For example, a dissolve is needed between two shots and both shots are on the same playback reel. Since the record machine can only cut and is recording only the one video signal that the switcher is sending, you must play both shots in the dissolve at the same time, but it is physically impossible for the playback machine to be in two places at the same time.

One way around this problem might be to cut the playback tape, but this is just not done. Instead, an exact copy of one of the shots is recorded on another tape. The effect can then be accomplished by dissolving from the original reel to the B reel. When editing to a D2 record machine, the B reel is not necessary. A D2 machine can play back, then record its own video.

COMPONENT AND COMPOSITE EDITING EFFECTS

Of the two video formats, component and composite, the former is better suited for effects and more expensive. Many effects are easier to perform in a component edit bay. Chroma keying, for example, is much cleaner and more effective in a component bay because the chroma is separate from the luminance information.

Component digital bays are not used for everyday production. However, for creating effects, this type of edit bay is ideal. The separation of chroma from luminance combined with digital quality produces superior effects, and because of digital technology, multiple generations, often an important part of building effects, do not result in significant image degradation. Additionally, digital switchers are usually equipped with frame stores (see the Glossary).

The composite digital effects bay is gaining in popularity and sophistication, although it does not produce the same quality as a component digital video operation. Multiple generations of composite digital video create far less image degradation than do multiple copies of one-inch analog video. However, digital component video (D1) still offers the best quality over multiple generations.

COMPOSITING DIGITAL EFFECTS

As previously noted, digital video technology has made multiple-generation effects commonplace. This improvement has created the potential for more complicated effects, since only one aspect of an effect need be completed in each pass. In comparison, analog video quality deteriorates with subsequent generations; therefore, almost all aspects of an analog video effect must be completed in two or three passes.

Compositing a digital effect essentially uses several record tapes. The following example (see Figure 9-10) uses only two tapes. As one aspect of an effect is completed during a pass, the result is recorded onto the first record tape. This first record tape then becomes a source (playback) tape for the next pass, which is recorded onto the second record tape. The second record tape then becomes a source tape to record back onto the first. The editor continues switching tapes until the effect is complete. Simple in concept, compositing must be meticulously planned. Many parts of an effect will be recorded separately, yet they must fit together precisely.

Compositing a video effect usually requires four elements: the record tape, the playback of the previously created effect, the new video to be added this pass, and a hold out of the new material (see Figure 9-10). The exception to this rule is if you are prereading each effect. Although this puts the effect in jeopardy if you record a pass that is unacceptable (erasing the previous effect), it does eliminate the need for the fourth playback deck. You can protect these effects by recording each successive layer onto another tape. Although time-consuming, this procedure will protect the effect if a mistake is made. A *hold out* is a high-contrast (black and white) image in which the white portion of the signal is the exact shape of the image to be cut out of the background. There will be a matching video image to the hold out, which will be used to fill the hole created by the hold out. Although the human editor keeps track of each playback and record deck, someone or something (the off-line system or client) must carefully manage the new material and its placement, using the hold out.

Sometimes a fifth element is needed to composite an effect: a *reverse hold out*. For example, a cartoon character might be concealed by a cereal box. The reverse hold out would place the character between existing portions of the effect —in this case, in front of the background and behind the box in the foreground.

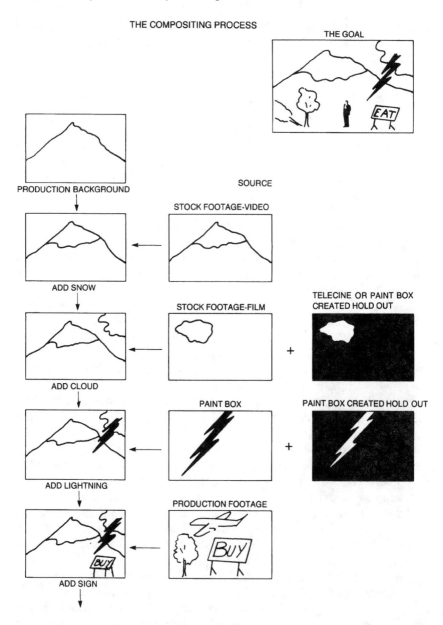

Figure 9-10a The compositing session must be planned. In this example, a nonexistent scene is created piece by piece. A producer, watching the author design this illustration, merely said, "It looks like someone didn't shoot the original footage correctly." In many instances, compositing can enhance a shot, but it is never inexpensive. Another point to note is that in all layers, a DVE device was used to reposition the footage. If the money is available, this effect would be much easier to accomplish using a computer animation system than an edit bay.

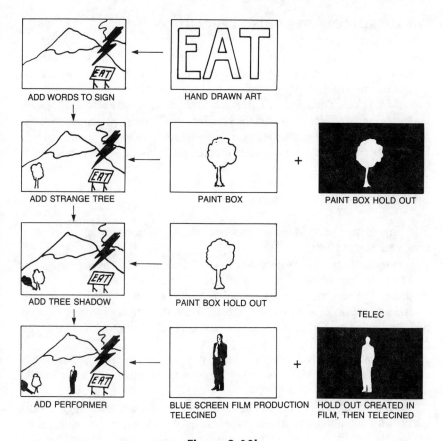

Figure 9-10b

D2 PREREAD

One of the more interesting developments that composite digital video brought to the edit bay was the preread capability. The D2 record machine has a video read head before the record head. This enables the recorder to actually use the existing video as a source before recording over it. This means you can perform a dissolve by using a single playback because the beginning of the dissolve comes from the record machine itself. Preread can also eliminate the need for a B reel. One limitation to this concept is that once the edit is made, the existing video at the point of recording is erased. As in all effects, the dissolve in this case is performed by the switcher, not the record machine.

THE MICROCOMPUTER VIDEO REVOLUTION

Another 1990s growth area in video is the microcomputer and accompanying video accessories. Based on the IBM or compatible computer or Macintosh computer, animation, editing, graphics, and switcher effects are offered at very reasonable prices. There is a virtual explosion of software and hardware. Inexpensive, impressive effects are within the grasp of vitually every computer user. The trick to using microcomputers is to get the images out of the computer onto tape. Several successful shows use effects created on "low-end" effects devices.

SUMMARY

The three types of video effects are switcher effects, external effects, and computer digital effects.

A switcher can create wipes, dissolves, and keys. The purpose of a switcher is to mix the available sources of video and send one video signal to the record machine. The switcher only mixes video sources; it does not create images. Digital switchers come with frame stores and very intricate layering capabilities. The four types of keys are luminance keys, chroma keys, key cuts from external sources, and matte keys.

External effects come from other types of machines connected to the switcher. These machines include character generators and slow-motion devices.

Computer digital effects can be divided into two categories: digital video effects and computer-generated graphics. Digital effects are produced by a digital effects generator, which alters the direction and shape of the picture but cannot create video on its own. Each channel of a digital effects generator can handle only one video signal. Computer-generated graphics are normally created, or built, before the editing session and then recorded on videotape.

Digital video allows for many more video generations without significant signal degradation than analog video does. Composite digital video allows the record machine to preread video before going into record mode. With component video, effects are crisp, and multiple generations do not present any problems.

Another way to create effects is by using a B reel. When the images in the effect come from different locations on the same reel, an exact copy of one of the shots is recorded on the B reel. The two images are then edited together on the record tape.

PART III

Working with the
Image

10

Shooting for Postproduction

This chapter is specifically designed with the editing room in mind. Producing, directing, and shooting a visual program involves many more details than are discussed here, but paying attention to the following suggestions can help improve the overall quality of a show and make the postproduction process much easier and more creative (see Figure 10-1).

PREPRODUCTION

Preproduction planning should be done before any production work is started. Feature films often plan ahead by illustrating every single shot of the planned production. Even on a shoot for the news, the crew and cast need to know where they are going and what equipment they will have available. In producing dramatic shows, scripts must be written, locations chosen, actors cast, and a shooting schedule designed.

The Script

The script is the blueprint of a show. No matter what the format, the script is the plan that the production will follow. It takes less time to rewrite a scene than to shoot a badly planned one. The production team should make sure that what is on paper can be accomplished.

Locations, studio rentals	Legal counsel
Costumes	Script breakdown
Make-up	Props
Additional sound effects	Equipment required for:
Power considerations on location	camera
Weather provisions	sound
Storyboards	lighting
Budget	set construction
Re-shoot days	Actor transportation
Script	Food for crew
Releases	Original production format
Petty cash	On-line format
Transportation	Editing facility
Stock footage	Special effects and their execution
Graphics	Music
Telephone and utilities	Mixing facility
Office location	Off-line editing choices
Insurance	Duplication choices

Figure 10-1 Preproduction considerations.

Script Breakdown

Once the script is ready, a *breakdown* is performed. By critically examining the script, you can determine many factors concerning the location shoot. How many and what kind of sets or locations need to be secured? Where will the shoot take place? Who in the cast and crew needs to be notified and how many days are they needed? How will the effects be created? Will the footage be shot on film or video? Will the effects elements be combined on film or video? At which facility will the effects compositing take place? All these questions and more must be answered before shooting begins. There are several computer programs that help break down scripts, or you can do it by hand. Every nuance of the script, from weather, time of year, type and number of props, cast needed for each scene, types of costumes, to any other aspect of each scene, must be listed and acquired.

The Storyboard

With the possible exception of location news shoots, every production should have some sort of *storyboard* (see Figure 10-2) prepared well in advance of the shoot. This shot-by-shot plan of the show helps avoid possible production and editing problems. It also helps the cast and crew see how the show will be put

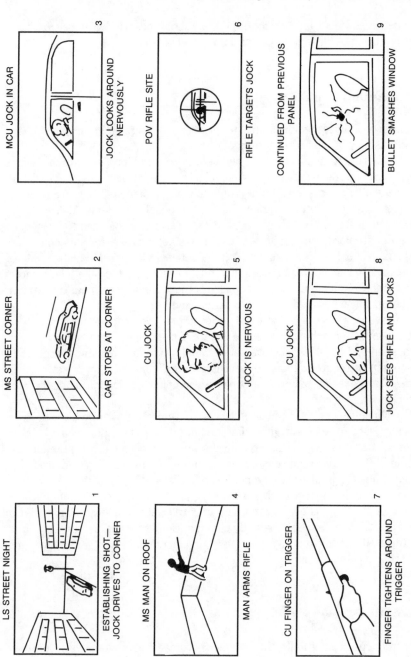

Figure 10-2 A sample storyboard. The storyboard helps identify editorial problems. For example, in this storyboard, panels 1 and 2 will not edit together correctly because the car's direction is reversed.

together. As much information as possible should be included in the storyboard: camera angles, dialogue, type of action, effects, etc.

Production Schedule

The production schedule is a master plan for shooting a program and is the best way to keep all aspects of the shoot organized.

There is no substitute for a detailed and accurate production schedule. As the script is broken down into its individual production demands, the production schedule translates this information into a plan of action. There are relatively inexpensive computer programs, such as Screenplay Systems' Movie Magic®, that automate some of those chores. A *strip board* can be used to keep all the pertinent information organized if money is not available for a computer program. Student productions may rely on detailed outlines. No matter how the production plan is laid out, flexibility must be built into the schedule. Weather, personnel, equipment complications, or other changes can require alterations in originally scheduled production arrangements.

Even if a show is not scripted (for example, a documentary or news show), the production schedule keeps a crew on track and aware of each setup's location and technical requirements. Single-camera productions are usually shot out of sequence to avoid returning to the same location or set. In these cases, it is even more important to have a complete production schedule before the shooting starts.

Obviously, every member of the cast and crew must know where he or she is supposed to be on any given day and hour during the production. *Call sheets* for talent and crew can be organized by using the production schedule as a guide. Equipment requirements can also be determined from the production schedule and circulated to the necessary personnel.

One of the most critical aspects of the production phase is communication. The production schedule, crew and cast call sheets, and all other relevant information need to be constantly communicated to everyone involved in the project. It is ironic that in a communication medium, most mistakes occur due to lack of communication.

Cast and Crew

A production comes to life through the coordinated efforts of the cast and crew. The casting of a show is an important function. Obviously, the most beautiful actress or most handsome actor is not always the best choice for a particular part. Talent and attitude are often more critical factors. Arrogant or lazy actors can cause more problems than they are worth.

Likewise, all crew members should be chosen for their attitude as well as their abilities. An eager individual might be a great assistant to the director but a disaster as a lighting director. Similarly, a performance can be ruined by bad microphone placement or shaky camera operation. Making sure each crew member knows his or her job can make life a lot easier during production.

Equipment/Footage Check

Unless the production equipment has been used the day before or the equipment house has been checked out thoroughly, the equipment should be tested prior to a shoot. If possible, playback equipment should be available during the shoot to check each shot for dropouts, audio problems, tape damage, focus, continuity, and so on.

PRODUCTION

The production phase (see Figure 10-3) is probably the most thrilling aspect of putting a show together, but the cast and crew must not be carried away by emotion. During this phase, extreme caution and attention to detail must prevail. Production may be exciting, but the focus must be on shooting the best footage. Small errors, undetected in the shooting phase, become glaring mistakes in the editing room. A forgotten insert shot or overlooked action in the background can be harmful to the show's overall outcome.

Bars and Tone

Color bars (as discussed in Chapter 4) provide a visual reference signal that indicates how a particular camera is recording pictures. Every production tape should have color bars recorded onto its head for at least 30 seconds, preferably one minute. If a tone generator is available, an audio tone should also be recorded at this time.

Slates

Slates should be recorded visually and on the audio track for every shot and every take. Information containing scene number, date, take, reel, location, and so on, should be at the head of each new recording. It does not matter whether these details are on a film-style slate or on a handwritten piece of paper; what is important is identifying each shot.

Figure 10-3 The Steadicam™ has been commonly used in the motion picture industry. Because small video formats are commonly used, Steadicam adapted its ingenious device for lighter cameras. Photo courtesy of the Steadicam Corporation.

These slates will be used often in the editing process, both in building the master log and in searching for particular takes during the editing session. Not slating a shot during production might save a few minutes during production, but will always cause delays in the editing room. Slate every shot, no matter how trivial or short.

Ambient Sound

Often when editing a picture, the dialogue track is opened, creating an artificial pause. These pauses must be filled with the natural sound of that location. Finding five seconds of perfectly quiet ambience on a production reel is often quite difficult. To solve this problem, 10 to 30 seconds of ambient sound, or room tone, should be recorded at each location. This requires everyone on the set to be quiet, a feat not always easy to accomplish.

Clean Heads and Tails

The head and tail (the beginning and end) of every shot should have a few seconds of nonaction so that the editor can make dissolves, L cuts, or subtle adjustments in pacing. If the cast starts the dialogue immediately after the cue for action, the director should suggest waiting for the count of five after he or she says "action." Likewise, the director should wait a few seconds at the tail end of a shot before calling "cut."

This head and tail rule also applies to pans, tilts, and dollies (see the Glossary). The camera should hold steady for several seconds before beginning a move. Once the move has been completed, the camera should hold again. Even if the camera movement is imperfect, the head or tail of the take may be used by itself.

Reviewing Takes

At the end of each take, it is wise to check that the image was recorded, and that the action, for both the camera and cast, are acceptable. Pay careful attention to the delivery of lines. Were the actors stepping on each other's lines? Were unseen overhead planes or nearby cars creating noise during the dialogue? Is the take perfect? It pays to get it right on tape before continuing to the next camera setup.

If window dubs are being recorded at the same time as the original footage, do not check the window dub for these aspects of the shot. The master footage is what needs to be checked. On more than one occasion, a master record machine has not rolled, meaning that no original footage is produced; then after the take, the window dub is checked instead of the master footage. Because the window dub is available, the mistake is not caught.

Finally, make sure that the master footage is forwarded to the end of the last scene, to ensure that the original footage of the last take is not erased.

Multiple Takes

The recording medium, whether film or video, is relatively inexpensive compared to all the other aspects of the production. Making a second, "insurance" take, if time permits, is a very cost-effective way of providing alternative readings and footage for the editor.

Releases

All performers in a program must sign releases, allowing the producer to use their likenesses in this particular show for all purposes (videocassette, broadcast, commercial use, etc.). Not obtaining a release (or not keeping it on file), can cause incredible headaches later, when a performer decides that he or she can hold up the sale of your program for a lot of money. A signed release must be in hand before the performer steps in front of the camera. There should be no exceptions to this rule. Even student productions must adhere to this rule. When an up-and-coming star performs in a program, the program will be able to be sold if releases are on file. The possible windfall will be lost if a release is not in hand.

Short and Simple

Inexperienced directors and camera operators often plan complicated, difficult shots, such as capturing a reflection in a shiny hubcap, performing a 360-degree pan, or attempting a half-mile dolly for no reason other than to make a big impression. Taking a critical look at a feature film or television show will illustrate the power of simplicity. Camera placement should tell the story, not distract from it. Complicated shots are all too often self-indulgent and pointless.

This simplicity also applies to the physical movement of the cast (blocking). Panning here and tilting there to follow a meandering actor annoys the audience. Unnecessary movement within the frame is a sign that the director is either confused or not in control of the action.

If a camera move is justified, it should be made with ease, smoothness, and—most importantly—purpose. The camera should stop on something that has visual impact and adds to the production. Hand-held shots have the potential of eliciting powerful emotions, but most shots should be made with the camera securely placed on a tripod.

Overlapping Action and Dialogue

Overlapping action and dialogue is an extension of the clean head and tail concept. You should always try to overlap action when changing the camera angle within a scene. The cast should repeat several lines of dialogue or the action that immediately precedes the new dialogue or action. If this overlap is not built into the shot, editing the two angles together will be difficult.

The Close-up

The close-up is an important aspect of any show. Inexperienced film actors tend to embellish emotional moments, and although this might work in a master shot, exactly the opposite approach is needed in a close-up. Since the actor's face fills the screen, even the slightest movement is exaggerated. When shooting a close-up, the director might have to tell the actor to tone down both movement and emotion.

Screen Direction

The screen direction of an action depends on how the action is shot. Action on the screen goes either left to right or right to left. If a woman rides a bike down a street and two shots are recorded—one from one side of the street and the other from the opposite side—when these two shots are edited together, it will appear that the woman has changed direction. She has not, but she has changed *screen direction*.

In sports shows, cameras are placed on one side of the playing field to avoid changing the screen direction of the players (see Figure 10-4). In situation comedies, all the cameras are on one side of the set. In dialogue sequences, the camera setups are on one side of the scene. In every scene, an invisible line dissects the action. If the camera crosses this line, the screen direction will be reversed. If shots are not recorded in the proper order to make the transition from one direction to another, the audience will be very confused.

Consider this example: Two people are talking to each other. The camera is set up in front of the two actors (see Figure 10-5). Now imagine a line drawn straight through the people. If the camera crosses that line, essentially going behind the actors, the screen direction will be reversed. The same problem occurs if a car is filmed going down a street and the camera is placed first on one side of the street and then on the other. In the second shot, the car will appear to be going in the direction opposite to the way it was going in the first shot.

One method of changing the screen direction is to shoot a scene head-on. Placing the camera on the original imaginary line gives the viewer the opportunity to become oriented to a change in screen direction. Crossing the line without a proper transition (see Figure 10-6) results in tremendous editing problems.

Continuity

A program has a certain flow, and this flow, or *continuity*, must be maintained in every shot. For example, if a man picks up a cup with his right hand in the wide shot, audiences expect the cup to stay in his right hand in the medium shot.

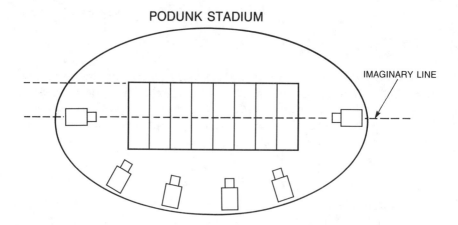

Figure 10-4 Generalized camera placement at a football stadium. In sports shows, cameras are usually positioned on only one side of the stadium to avoid changing the players' screen direction. Recently the "reverse angle" shot has been used, but is clearly identified.

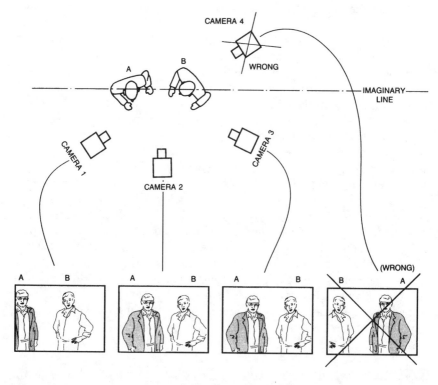

Figure 10-5 Camera placement in a two-person dialogue scene. Placing the camera on the wrong side of the imaginary line reverses screen direction. Note that the camera that has crossed the imaginary line; character B is on the left side of the screen, while the three other cameras have character B on the right.

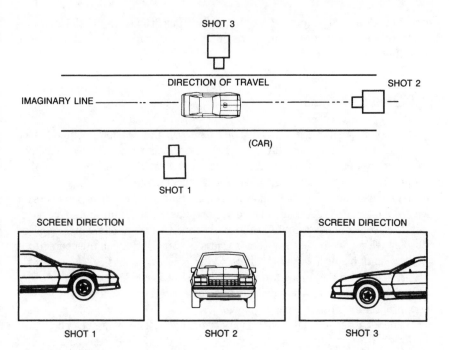

Figure 10-6   Crossing the imaginary line in a motion shot. A head-on shot can help reverse screen direction.

Continuity is not limited to the actions of the characters in a scene. A Boeing 757 parked behind a newscaster should not suddenly change to a twin engine plane. Similarly, anachronisms must be avoided. For instance, a digital watch should not show up in a historical piece.

Most feature films employ at least one person whose main concern is taking notes on every aspect of the show's continuity. Often this person uses a Polaroid camera to help in reconstructing how a scene was played, what type of makeup was used, how background actors were placed, and so on. If continuity is overlooked or ignored, all sorts of editing problems can occur, resulting in a very uneven-looking program.

Cutaways

The *cutaway* is a shot of another location or object that is cut into a scene. For instance, a reporter might be talking about a crack in a local dam. The cutaway might be a close-up of the crack or an aerial shot of the dam, reservoir, and surrounding community. In dramatic shows, the cutaway could be a shot of the murder weapon hidden in a drawer or the clock ticking away precious seconds. The more cutaways that are available, the more freedom the editor has.

A Variety of Angles

Almost every scene starts on a *wide shot*. This sets the location and mood of the scene. The next shot is usually a *medium shot*, which is often framed to include one or more of the main characters of the scene from the waist up. In dialogue scenes, the medium shot is often over the shoulder of one of the characters. The *close-up* is used next. It usually shows the character from the neck or shoulders up.

Most dialogue scenes are played in close-ups and medium shots. Occasionally, the scene might return to a wide-angle shot if a lot of movement is required or to a high-angle shot if the director wants to show how small the character is in relation to his or her surroundings.

A scene can end in a close-up, medium shot, or wide shot. Nearly every soap opera scene closes on a distraught actor's face, but a medium or wide shot is appropriate for other types of shows.

The ideal scene is shot with a variety of angles. The camera can be raised or lowered to create a specific mood or emotion. Raising the camera in a high-angle shot tends to make an actor appear less powerful, while lowering the camera in a low-angle shot tends to make the actor appear powerful and strong. If the director uses a variety of angles and varies the position of the camera, the editor can control the pacing and visual content of a scene to produce a powerful visual experience.

Headroom

In shots where people are present, there should be plenty of headroom at the top of the screen (see Figure 10-7). It looks unnatural if the top of a person's head is cut off. The same holds true for any shot of a building or other object: There must be some space at the top of every frame.

The Lower Third

In a documentary or informational program, the on-camera speakers are usually identified through the use of a key in the lower third of the picture. If there is not enough room in the frame, the speaker's mouth will be covered by the lower-third graphic. It is a good idea to frame individuals in these types of programs so that identifying information can fit in the frame without covering the person's face.

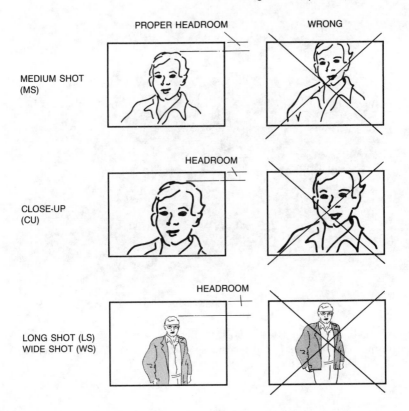

Figure 10-7 Examples of proper and improper headroom composition. Each shot should always have adequate headroom.

Balance

An image's position within the frame has its own balance. For instance, a single shot of a girl running away from a pursuer requires lead room at the head of the picture. Putting the pursuer in the middle of the frame is considered bad framing.

A boat crossing a river has numerous possibilities in terms of balance within the frame. Is the boat participating in a celebration? Is the boat being left behind? Is the boat leading the procession? Each situation requires a different composition, or balance, within the frame.

Safe Action/Safe Title

On a television screen, part of the picture is cut off; therefore, action should be positioned away from the edges of the frame and graphics should be placed in

Figure 10-8 The Sony DVW-700 Digital Betacam. Lightweight digital production cameras provide the power of digital component video at reasonable cost. Photo courtesy of Sony Electronics, Inc.

the center of the frame. If the graphic must appear on one side of the screen, use a crosshatch (Figure 10-9) to determine the point farthest from the center at which the graphic can be placed.

Controlling Background

Locations can provide wonderful and impressive visuals for a program, but unless careful attention is paid to the background, problems can occur. Just as in the earlier example of the 747 turning into a twin-engine plane, the background of an uncontrolled location can be troublesome. It is frustrating to have to redo a perfect reading of an important news story because the camera caught an obscene gesture made by an onlooker or because a microphone crept into the shot. To avoid serious problems, make sure at least one crew member keeps a close watch on the background during every shot. In addition, it is a good idea to check the footage before continuing on to the next camera angle.

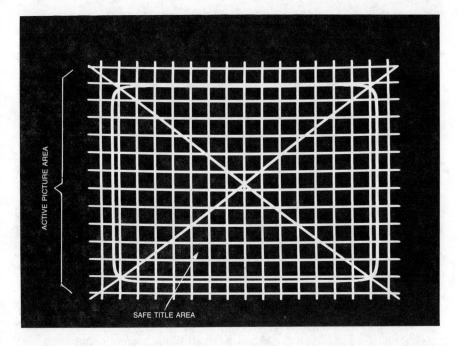

Figure 10-9 A video crosshatch. One way to center a title on a screen is to use a video-generated design. The television-shaped screen is a *safe title area* (that portion of the screen where most televisions will be able to read a title). The center of the X is screen center.

Labeling Original Footage

As soon as a reel is finished, a label must be applied to both the video case and the reel itself. The date, time code, and the names of the locations, production, camera man, scenes, and performers must be written legibly or typed on the reel. Do not wait to get to a typewriter if one is not available. Label the reel before loading another. Memories are short in the heat and confusion of production.

Helpful Suggestions

The actor or sound engineer might have a suggestion about how a shot might be improved or a problem solved. It is always a good idea to listen to suggestions from the cast and crew, as a good production team can often get more out of a shoot than was originally thought possible.

Storing Original Footage

Original videotapes should be stored in a safe, dry place. This might seem obvious, but tapes are often carelessly left on the back seat of a car on a 90-degree day or in a damp garage or basement over the weekend. It makes no sense to spend days on a shoot, then leave the original masters in an unsuitable environment. In addition, you should always note where the originals are stored, as it could be months until they are needed for the on-line edit.

SUMMARY

Preproduction planning is crucial to the production process. The storyboard is a must for any planned production. It is also a good idea to build some extra time into the schedule to accommodate shooting overages. Testing production equipment before the actual shoot and reviewing all shots to make sure the technical and creative aspects are correct are also helpful in avoiding delays.

The production phase of a show requires extreme caution and attention to detail. Identifying slates should precede every shot, both in the picture and on the audio track. In addition, all shots, especially those involving camera moves, should have an ample head and tail. Keep all shots, camera movements, and action within the frame simple and motivated. To facilitate editing, always overlap action and dialogue when changing the angle of a shot.

When a close-up is being shot, the performer should tone down both movement and emotion. To ensure proper screen direction, avoid crossing the center line when moving the camera. If the line is crossed, make sure the proper transition angle(s) are recorded.

In any show, pay careful attention to the details of each shot, including but not limited to the background, the lighting, and the actions and costumes of the extras and principal actors.

You should use a variety of angles in any scene, but always leave plenty of headroom at the top of the frame. Also, you should make sure to leave room for lower thirds, especially in close-up shots of speakers.

Balance is determined by the action within the frame. Action should be positioned away from the edges of the frame so that it is not cut off.

Check all takes for performance, irregularities, and flaws, both picture and audio. Get releases from all performers before they get in front of the camera.

Label all tapes as soon as they are finished with proper information, including date, locations, performers, time code, and scenes. Make sure to store original videotapes in a safe, dry place. Noting their location for future reference will save time later.

11

Editing Pictures

The essence of shooting and editing can be appreciated by watching almost any television commercial. The commercial must tell a story and sell a product in 30 seconds. In addition, commercials are either on the cutting edge of effects and graphics or reflect the current trends.

Only the most necessary shots and audio are included in that half minute. Days, sometimes weeks, will be spent making sure all 900 video frames are exactly the ones that should be shown.

A visual program is created by selecting a series of images and sounds. The editor, along with the director, chooses the specific images and audio that will be included (or discarded) in the show. This selection process makes an immense difference in how an audience reacts to a particular production.

In feature films, TV programs, and videos, the editor gets single-card credit, just as the writer and director do. Knowing the power of the editing process, the feature film director negotiates for control of the final cut, although he or she rarely gets it. In a television program the producer often has the ultimate creative control. Once production is completed, whoever controls the editing process controls the program.

ORGANIZATION

The novice editor might think that the professional glances at the program script, then whips out a first cut that is brilliant, approved, and sent to on-line. Nothing could be further from the truth (see Figure 11-1). A high-caliber editor takes the time to log the available footage. Then, after consulting with the director, he or she begins the methodical process of cutting a program together.

This is neither a quick nor an easy job. Knowing the existing footage, understanding the show's purpose, and being familiar with the script are just the beginning of the task.

THE EDITING FLOWCHART

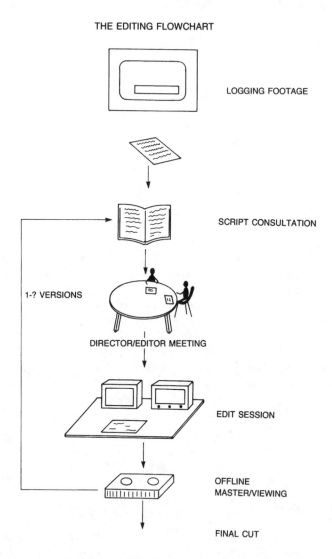

Figure 11-1 An overview of the editing process. The postproduction process is carefully planned and executed. Rarely does a show go through one simple, off-line edit. Changes often occur during the refining of a program, whether it is a 30-second commercial or a six-hour mini-series.

Creating a show from the beginning cannot be a haphazard affair, or the result will be equally haphazard. The master log, and the thought process that includes planning an editing approach, are as important as learning which button to push.

THE SHOW'S PURPOSE

Every show has a purpose. This might be to sell a product, to train or inform, to amuse, to frighten, or to excite. The show's purpose should be decided long before any footage is shot.

The editor places the images and audio in an order that supports the show's purpose. This is true in feature films as well as propaganda pieces, news, comedies, dramas, and documentaries. If the editor is confused about the show's purpose, this will be evident in the final product.

THE INTENDED AUDIENCE

Each program has an intended audience, which may be broad or very limited. A training tape about the installation of car stereos is geared toward the technicians who will use the tape for instruction. Such a tape is edited differently than a documentary on the life of a car stereo installer because the intended audience is different. The editor must know the intended audience of a program to satisfy that audience's expectations through the pacing and presentation of information.

CHOOSE, EDIT, AND TRIM

The editing process is one of elimination. Shot by shot, a show evolves out of the images and dialogue chosen. In the first step, the editor views the footage and chooses the best images for the show's purpose and intended audience.

Viewing the footage involves building a master log, as discussed in Chapters 5 and 6. The master log indicates which shots are technically correct and which have the proper delivery or performance. Perhaps only a portion of a shot is usable, but if it contains the proper balance of composition, performance level, and background action, this is noted in the master log. As the editor views the footage, he or she notes that one shot might connect well with another or that a particular length of footage might be appropriate for the opening titles, graphics background, or other purpose.

The editor then begins to piece the shots together during an editing session, using the master log as a guide. If the tape is for news, the results of the first edit might end up on the air. In dramatic or documentary programs, however, the first cut is usually done in an off-line editing session, then refined.

Edits are often trimmed (lengthened, but usually shortened) even as a show is being cut for the first time. Most editors, once they have determined the IN points on the record and playback tapes, will let the edit run long on the OUT end. The extra footage at the end of the edit can be used to make sure the next edit comes in at exactly the right moment. This method takes a little more time than just slamming a rough cut together. Many editors come close to a fine cut if they examine each edit thoroughly. In larger budget shows that have the luxury of going through the off-line process, trimming takes more time. Edits are often cut in different sequences until the scene plays to everyone's satisfaction.

When editing on a random-access editor, this trimming process can happen as soon as the following edit is placed, because the linearity of videotape is not a concern in random-access editing.

PACING

Each shot has its own pacing, and the connection of several shots creates the pacing or rhythm of one scene. The relationship of one scene to another creates the pacing of the entire show. Through the careful use of pacing within a shot, a scene, and the entire show, an editor can create tension, laughter, relaxation, arousal, or anger in the audience. The entire spectrum of human emotions is available to a sensitive editor with the proper footage.

One of the most powerful tools an editor has is the ability to compress or expand time. With the proper editorial choices, a scene can affect the audience's perception of time.

For example, a training tape about installing car stereos is intended to impart information about a technical process. The shots will be more than long enough to demonstrate the specific facts concerning the installation process. Some footage may be repeated. The pacing of the program will be slow and methodical. This does not mean boring, but it will be paced for maximum content absorption.

On the other hand, an action-adventure program will be quickly cut. The pacing will come from the action and movement within the frame as well as from rapidly occurring edits that accent that action. There will also be scenes within the program in which the pacing will slow to keep the audience members from being too shocked, to let them catch their breath.

Controlling the Pacing

A program's pacing can be controlled in several ways. The first and most obvious is the length of each cut. An edit can have extra time on the in and out portions. This added time affects how the edit "plays." For instance, you may edit a close shot of a gun being raised, then fired, as in the sequence of Figures 11-2 through 11-8. An edit that uses the whole raising action and firing, including the moments after the firing, will be paced more slowly than the edit that starts just as the gun stops its upward motion and ends as soon as the shot is fired. The slower edit would be at least one second longer than the quick-paced edit.

Another method of controlling the show's pace is with the number of cuts. Again, referring to the raising of a loaded gun, the same real-time shot could be used to show the raising of the gun, but intercut with the intended victim's face and the assailant's expression. The raising of the gun would take just as long, but the added footage would alter the scenes timing.

A scene may not have the same pacing throughout. The beginning might have quick cuts, with great tension, then the pace might slow down, only to speed up again as another threat or character is introduced. A show with no rhythmic change is boring. This is another reason to shoot several angles of a particular scene. The multiple angles allow for a flexible adjustment of pacing.

WHEN TO CUT

Cutting from one camera angle to another should be invisible to the audience. One of the best places to cut is during action. The eye is usually drawn to motion, so when a change in camera angle occurs during the motion, the mind automatically connects the action.

Another ideal time to cut is when the audience expects it. If two on-screen characters are having a discussion and another off-screen person is secretly listening at the door, a perfect time is when the on-screen characters discuss the eavesdropping friend. Similarly, if a narrator is describing Niagara Falls, this is a good time to cut to a shot of the falls.

In all cases, an edit must be motivated. Without motivation, either by concept, such as a narrator's line, or a physical action by an object or character, the edit will be jarring and obtrusive. When an edit occurs with motivation and on-screen action, the audience will be unaware of the shot change. Part of the editor's purpose is to mask the fact that an edit has taken place.

The eye naturally jumps to objects or subjects that relate to what is happening or that appear interesting. If the viewer feels a need to see something, the editor, unless he or she is trying to elicit a specific emotion (terror, laughter, suspense, etc.), should let the viewer see it.

Figures 11-2 through 11-8 Time can be compressed or expanded, depending on how images are edited together. Using all of the images, the picture sequence elongates elapsed time by keeping all of the gun being raised and cutting to different angles. Using only the fourth, fifth, and sixth images collapses the time in which the action takes place, providing a different pacing, yet still expressing the full action. Photos courtesy of Sterling Productions.

FOUR TYPES OF EDITS

A show that has been properly edited should appear not to have been edited at all. Viewing a program should be an uninterrupted visual experience. Edits appear to be natural or invisible when the cut follows one of four basic editorial concepts: *action, screen position, form*, and *idea*. One exception to this rule is an edit specifically made to jar the audience, a *shock cut*; another is in a music montage sequence, where edits are often made on the beat, making the cuts or effects obvious.

Action

Even a simple gesture, such as raising one's hand, allows an editor to cut at numerous points during that action. An editor might cut at the start of the move, in the middle, or toward the end, but cutting during the action is one of the best ways to change the camera angle within a scene.

Screen Position

If the eye is led to one side of the screen, the action or character in the next shot might be located on that side also. Again, the purpose of the cut is to allow the eye to follow the movement of the shot. In commercials, an image is often flipped to help an edit flow. Reversing screen position just to make an edit work better is a common practice. Of course attention must be paid to any signs or other lettering in the shot, because they will be backwards.

Form

A cut from a porthole to a full moon is an example of an edit using form. Cutting from a Frisbee™ to the sun or dissolving from a burning match to a roaring fire are other examples. This type of edit often uses screen position to be most effective.

Ideas

Ideas are used to smooth the visual transition in edits. A dissolve from a crying woman to a rain-streaked window is an example of an idea edit.

The most powerful edits are those that combine two or more of these concepts. An example of a combination would be cutting from a high-angle shot of a diver leaping off a diving board to a side-angle shot of an ice cube landing in a glass. In this case, action, screen position, and idea are combined to create a transition.

L CUTS

The *L cut*, or *split edit*, is an edit in which the audio or picture leads a *both cut* (see Figure 11-9). This type of edit is extremely powerful, offering many possibilities for controlling dialogue and making shot transition smoother.

The L cut can be used in any type of editing situation. An audio cut that precedes the picture can be used to prepare the audience for the next scene. For instance, the sound of waves might precede a picture of the stormy ocean. Alternatively, a picture leading into an audio split might be a close-up of a woman's lover as she finishes talking about him.

The L cut is most often used in static dialogue scenes (in soap operas or television dramas) where there is little variation in angles. For instance, one character's lines might be edited over the other person's picture.

AUDIO TRANSITIONS

Audio is often ignored as a primary source of transition from one shot to the next. Although the most popular type of audio transition is the L cut, in which

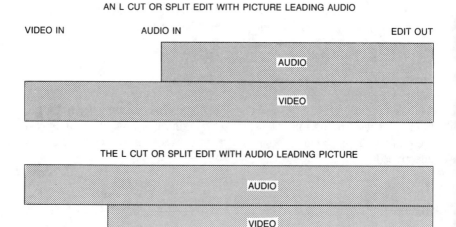

Figure 11-9   The L cut, or split edit.

the incoming audio is edited into the outgoing scene, audio can also be used for shock cuts: A sudden scream occurs frames before the visual is introduced. Another use of audio is in a street scene that is enhanced by the sound of a police siren in the background, even though no squad car is ever shown.

Each edit should be examined in terms of its audio as well as its visual potential. Sounds that are not recorded during production can be taken from effects records or created later at a makeshift sound session. A door slam or a baby's cry can be enhanced, adding to the overall production value of a program. Many production companies purchase tape or CD sound libraries that contain hundreds of sound effects. These effects are edited into the sound track of the program to make it that much more interesting.

AUDIO INCREASES PRODUCTION VALUE

The motion picture industry recognizes the value of a carefully executed sound track. An excellent audio track undoubtedly enhances the viewer's perception of a program. The final audio mix of a film contains hundreds of dialogue lines, special effects, music tracks, Foley effects, and ADR lines. Foley audio effects are created on a sound stage by individuals as they watch a copy of the production footage. ADR (automatic dialogue replacement) tracks are created by performers as they listen to a loop of their own voices while watching the footage of themselves. Hearing themselves repeatedly helps the performers recreate the same inflections used during production.

When the editor is performing off-line editing, edits should be included for audio work. Beyond the obvious sync sound edits, other aspects such as ambient sound, effects, and music should be continuously considered while building the EDL. If the budget does not allow for professional sweetening (Chapter 18), and if the mixing will take place during the on-line edit, building A/B audio tracks on the off-line system can speed the mixing process and keep costs for audio work low. With complicated audio mixing, it may be worthwhile to go to an audio facility, because mixing a great deal of audio in a video bay is usually expensive and often ineffective.

FAST CUTTING EQUALS PERCEIVED ACTION

Editors of adventure films heighten the feeling of action by cutting often. Most shots last less than five seconds. In action sequences, an edit occurs at least every two seconds, if not quicker.

Even when cutting a lecture, the editor should use as many visuals as possible. The number of (motivated) edits will determine whether the production seems long or short to the audience. In the limited settings of television sitcoms, for example, camera angles and shots are constantly changing to give the show its quick pacing.

Occupying the eye with new and different images that are consistent with the intent of the show will prevent the audience from becoming bored. Of course, a quick cut during a drawn-out funeral scene might be totally wrong, considering the content of the scene.

USING SPECIAL EFFECTS

There is a time and place for special effects. In the early days of live television, every transition seemed to be a wipe or other effect. In the 1980s, the digital video effect, usually flying boxes or flips, was seen numerous times per hour. Digital effects are used to enhance programs as a compositing tool, to correct production errors, or to create subtle yet powerful frames. The feature film uses cuts for transitions, yet a film director will spend tens of thousands of dollars to create an illusion. The effect within the shot is transparent, but the transition between shots is almost always a cut. Movies use effects within the shot, not for transitions. You should use effects sparingly and with taste. Gratuitously flying images in and out, flipping graphics, or making every transition a new viewing experience does nothing to enhance the show's purpose. As each shot is selected for its contribution to the program, so should any effect be chosen to increase the overall impact of a program rather than to draw attention to the effect itself.

Opens, Closes, and Bumpers

Some of the most important areas for effects are the show's open, close, and bumpers. *Bumpers* are three-to-five-second shots that identify a television program, usually placed before, after, and inside commercial breaks. Bumpers can be a single card with a voice-over announcer or complicated multithousand effects created in a digital computer graphics station. These expensive bumpers can be seen on broadcast and cable networks. They are often bright, incredible effects ending in a logo of the network. A carefully crafted open and close will make the viewer think the content of the show is important. Since these elements are crucial to the way in which the show is perceived, special care should be taken to make them unique and impressive.

SHOTS AND ANGLES

As discussed in the previous chapter, a scene usually starts with a wide or long shot, moves to a medium shot, then alternates between close-ups and medium shots. Most scenes are shot and edited in this manner for good reason: It works, as shown in Figures 11-10a and 11-10b.

Occasionally, this rule can be broken. A new scene that cuts to a close-up of a knife can quickly build suspense. Cutting to a wide-eyed victim is also a powerful transition when coupled with the correct audio. As a rule, however, the audience wants to know where the action is taking place and what is happening at that location. Being obvious is better than being confusing.

A variety of angles increases audience interest. Cutting back and forth to the same shots quickly becomes boring. Ideally, the director will provide the editor with enough editorial choices to allow him or her to incorporate a variety of different shots in the program.

DISSOLVES, WIPES, AND DIGITAL EFFECTS

The most important and powerful tool at the editor's disposal is the cut, but other effects are useful when editing a program.

a

Figure 11-10a   A variety of angles keeps the pace flowing and the audience interested. The change in camera angle can also mask small continuity problems, such as hand placement. (See Figure 11-10b.) Photo courtesy of Sterling Productions.

b

Figure 11-10b Photo courtesy of Sterling Productions.

In the early days of filmmaking, dissolves were used to indicate that time had passed. Today, audiences are more sophisticated, and with the proper clues, they understand a cut to another time or location without the aid of a dissolve. However, the dissolve is still occasionally used as a time-passage device.

As discussed in Chapter 9, digital effects are often used to give motion to still pictures or to move from one image to the next. Other uses of the digital video effects device (abbreviated DVE—see the Glossary) are to move graphics, or alter words and images from videotape sources or character generators. The DVE can stretch, expand, rotate, or reposition these elements to other areas of the frame. DVE repositioning is commonly used when combining elements in effects. Creating a mirror image is also a function of the DVE.

No matter what the effect, it should fit with the concept and feel of the program. It is also important to remember that any visual effect occupies the mind and, during the effect, the viewer usually does not recognize anything else. For instance, if audio information is given during an effect, the audience members might be distracted by what is happening on the screen. This "effect" time should not, therefore, be used to convey important information. Also, the editor must be sure that the images involved in the effect are on the screen long enough for the audience to really see them. (Exceptions to the rule are the flash cuts like the ones used in music videos and some commercials.)

Planning Effects

When editing a complicated effect off-line, it is important to keep the various sources involved in that effect labeled and organized. When contemplating more than a wipe or dissolve, you should be very sure how to execute the effect. Once the process is firmly established, the elements (playback sources) need to be marked in the EDL. If there are more than a few effects to be accomplished, perhaps an effects-editing session should be scheduled to complete the required effects without impeding the show's on-line session.

MORE INFORMATION EQUALS MORE INTEREST

The editor's purpose is to create a show in a cohesive, understandable, and orderly fashion. The more visual and aural experiences you can present (in context with the purpose and story), the better the show will be.

Often a production contains more than one story line. There are two methods of editing multiple story lines. The first is to tell one story, then go on to the next. This type of storytelling is called *continuity editing*. The second method is to tell the stories side by side, as they happen. This is called *parallel editing*.

For instance, if two brothers went to war and the editor wanted to show what happened during those years, she could tell the story of one brother, then focus on the other. That would be continuity editing. If she took both brothers' experiences and intercut them, that would be parallel editing.

Both methods of storytelling are effective, but in parallel editing, special care must be taken to make sure the audience knows which story is being told.

EDITORIAL PITFALLS

Shot Selection

A shot must have some specific purpose if it is to be included in a show. Ideally, each shot should have more than one purpose. For instance, a multipurpose shot might establish location, a character's mood, and climate all in one brief image. The audience will pick up on shots that do not belong.

Another point to remember is that each shot should be as short as possible. Once the shot's purpose has been fulfilled, the editor should make the next edit. The more visual information an editor can include in a production, the more interesting it will be to the audience.

Finishing the Action

One of the most annoying editorial flaws is not allowing a character or object to complete an action within a scene. If an action takes too long, time can be compressed through editing, but the action should be concluded. Cutting away from something in motion before the action is completed is as bad as lingering on a stagnant or slow-moving shot. An exception to this rule is in the editing of commercials or music videos. In these programs, the intent is to catch the audience's attention, not impart plot or pass along complicated information. The rapid edits and unfinished action are consistent with the program's purpose.

Similarly, it is important to remember that it takes a few seconds for a particular shot to register in a viewer's mind. The editor, having seen a shot over and over again, might cut away from a shot before it has time to register with the viewer. The editor should let the viewer see what he is meant to see before cutting away. An editor must not let familiarity with a shot fool her into cutting too soon.

Continuity

As mentioned in the previous chapter, continuity is a major concern during production and is just as important during the editing process. A show should appear seamless. In some cases, the editor might have to change the sequence of shots or even scenes to maintain the show's continuity. Having a character running in one direction in one shot and then suddenly going in the other direction in the next can ruin the best-edited scene and confuse the audience.

Jump Cuts and Cutaways

A *jump cut* occurs when two extremely similar shots are edited together. When a jump cut is viewed, everything in the frame seems to jump. This effect can be used to pop people or objects in or out of a frame, but in most instances, the jump cut is annoying.

In news editing, jump cuts are purposely made to piece together a reporter's story. Once the narration has been built, the jump cuts are covered by cutaways. Some commercials and documentaries use wipes or dissolves to mask jump cuts. Often an editor can avoid jump cuts by cutting to a different angle or frame of an object. Music videos and some commercials now purposely use the jump cut.

One of the easiest ways around mismatched action or dialogue mistakes is through the use of a cutaway. Although the cutaway is a powerful tool, it can be very disruptive if used improperly (without audience expectation). An editor must choose cutaways carefully and with purpose. As with every edit, the cutaway should be motivated.

Cutting from one location to another or from one point in time to another is a perfectly acceptable transition. Television has trained the audience to accept these abrupt changes. To avoid confusion, however, an editor should try not to have the character in an outgoing shot appear immediately in the incoming shot when changing location or time frame. This rule might be broken for effect—for example, if the director wants a man to jump from a train and land in a bed.

Respect for the Character

The audience is keenly aware of any character's expressions. Editors can forget that the images in front of them will always be recognized by the audience as human. Editors should treat screen characters as respectfully as possible. There are several specific rules about editing facial expressions and dialogue that are to be broken only for a specific effect.

Lip Flap

When using a close-up for a cutaway, the subject should not appear to be talking. This rule also applies to a character about to speak. If the edit requires cutting away from the person about to speak, the cut should happen before the speech, not as the talking begins.

No Closed Eyes or Open Mouths

An expansion of the previous concept: You should not cut to a character with his or her eyes closed or mouth open unless the shot is specifically designed to do so.

Careful Background Choices

Cuts to background characters should be made just as selectively as to those of the principals. Just throwing in a shot of people milling around can destroy the illusion of the program. When the editor is including shots that contain extras, the background actors should be dressed correctly and acting in character.

CONCLUSION

It really does make a difference how pictures are edited together. Through a combination of technical and creative skills, the editor can save a poorly shot program and make a good one even better. He or she can also change the focus or tone of a show, a fact that makes the editor's position very powerful.

SUMMARY

Editing determines the pacing of a show, the timing between dialogue lines, the expansion or compression of time, and the specific images that are placed against each other.

The concept of a show should be decided on before any editing begins. It is a good idea to know the intended audience and to be aware of that audience's expectations and limitations.

The process of editing is to choose, edit, and trim each shot to its minimum length while keeping its proper pacing and impact within the scene. Each shot has its own pacing. How these shots are connected creates the rhythm within a scene. How these scenes are connected determines the overall feel of the program.

There are four types of edits: action, screen position, form, and idea. The most effective edits are those that combine two or more of these concepts. The number of edits in a show will often determine whether the production seems long or short to the audience.

One of the most powerful tools in editing is the L cut. Each edit must be examined in terms of its audio potential as well as its visual impact. It is important to remember that audio can come from sources other than the production.

As a general rule, you should begin a scene using a wide shot, cut to a medium shot, and then edit the scene, alternating between medium and close shots. If it is possible and is within the context of the show's intent, a variety of angles should be used to increase the interest of the audience.

In almost every type of program, the cut is the most powerful and often the best method to change from one visual to another. Dissolves, wipes, and digital effects are other useful editing devices. It is important to remember, however, that effect time should not be considered content time. In addition, any edit, including transitional effects, should fit in with the concept and feel of the program. There are two ways to edit multiple story lines: continuity editing and parallel editing.

Several editorial pitfalls exist. A shot must have a specific purpose to be included in any show, and each shot should be kept as short as possible. One of the most annoying editorial flaws is preventing a character or object from completing a motion within the scene. Cutting away from a scene too soon also can confuse the audience. Editing should create a seamless flow of information to the audience. An editor should avoid breaks in continuity, such as jump cuts and improperly used cutaways. The editor should also avoid having the character in an outgoing shot appear immediately in the incoming shot when changing locations.

Editing is one of the most important tools of the visual media.

PART IV

Working at the Keyboard

12

Operating Control Track Editors

Control track and cuts-only time code editors perform many postproduction chores despite the onslaught of computer editing systems. Learning how to operate a control track editor can be easy, which can fool a novice into thinking that the process of editing pictures is as easy as learning the keyboard. The editor must realize, however, that each edit affects the audience and the outcome of the program. Each picture and sound element requires all the detail discussed in Chapter 11 (continuity, pacing, purpose, and other considerations). Just because a person can get a machine to perform a cut does not mean that the person is an editor. Practicing, studying how other editors work on their shows, and then more practicing are the only ways to become a competent editor.

Control track editors can be upgraded to read time code, but there is a big difference between a control track editor that reads time code and a computer editor. A computer editor has a completely different set of commands than a random-access editor does. Besides being able to perform the all-powerful cut, the computer editor allows you to store, recall, and change the EDL. Some more advanced editors can communicate with peripheral equipment, such as switchers and DVEs. Because the control track editor does not have an edit memory, careful note-taking is suggested during an on-line editing session and required during an off-line session. These notes might include where certain shots are located, comments about audio fixes, shots that should be changed, and so on. The pressures of editing should not overshadow the importance of taking notes. An editor must take the time to write down the details that might otherwise be forgotten.

EDITOR OPERATION

Most control track editors are similar in operation. To make a recording, both the record deck and the playback deck must be given IN points. This is usually accomplished by pausing the decks. Some controllers also require an additional keystroke (Enter or Return) to input the edit IN point. Once the IN points are programmed, an OUT point can be determined. An edit without an OUT point is called an open-ended edit.

A preview is the next step in performing an edit. This is the stage at which an edit is rehearsed but not actually recorded. Once the edit has been previewed, the INs or OUTs might have to be adjusted. The edit can be modified by pressing " + " or " − " and then entering the number of frames by which the IN point needs to be adjusted. Finally, the In or Out button is pressed. Some control track editors do not return to their original IN positions after a preview, so trimming the edit might be required even if the edit preview was exactly right. When the edit has been perfected, it is recorded.

THE SONY RM 450

The Sony RM 450 (see Figure 12-2) is another popular control track editor. It has separate bi-directional shuttle control of the source and record machines.

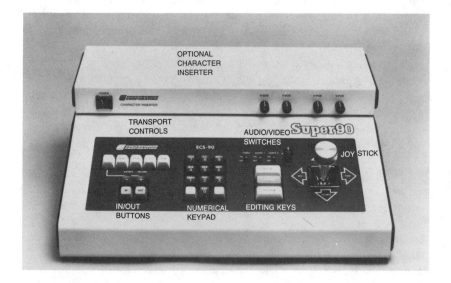

Figure 12-1 The Convergence Corporation's℗ Super 90. Photo Courtesy of Convergence Corporation.

Figure 12-2   The Sony RM 450 editor. Courtesy of Sony Electronics, Inc.

Setting up an insert edit on the RM 450 is easy, as it is on the built-in editors in the Sony 500, 800, and 900 series of three-quarter-inch U-Matic® video tape machines. You choose an IN point on the record machine, then an IN point on the playback deck. With the RM 450, you can either perform open-ended edits or determine the OUT point before the edit is made. You can trim edit points once they have been loaded into the machine by using the trim function keys, located below the center blue mode keys.

The audio and video modes are selected using the blue upper center keys. Assemble edits as well as any combination of video and two tracks of audio can be made. The Auto Edit button, which is used for most edits on the machine, is located at the center bottom. Split edits are also available, using the brown key just to the left of the white trim keys.

MACHINE-TO-MACHINE EDITING

In many postproduction situations, there is no edit controller between the record and playback decks. In some cases, recent editing advances have been built into the machines themselves. Although a controller simplifies the editing process, many producers do not have the income to justify purchasing a controller, thus leaving the editing as a machine-to-machine configuration.

There is little difference between a machine-to-machine editing situation and using a control track editor. There are edit In and edit Out indicators on the record deck. In most cases, the record deck will control the playback source deck. Trims are also available with machine-to-machine editing. The edit type (Audio 1, 2, both tracks, and/or video) is selected on the front panel. Again, this type of editing does not result in an EDL of any sort, but certainly makes edits quickly, efficiently and, in a pressure-filled environment, can be the difference between making the air in time or missing the deadline.

Figure 12-3 shows a Sony Betacam SP videotape recorder front panel that can be used as an edit controller. Attaching this deck to another compatible machine (a Betacam or one-inch, for example) can offer excellent cuts-only capabilities without adding the cost of a controller between the two decks. Engaging the specific insert button(s) (center right) or the assemble buttons starts an edit.

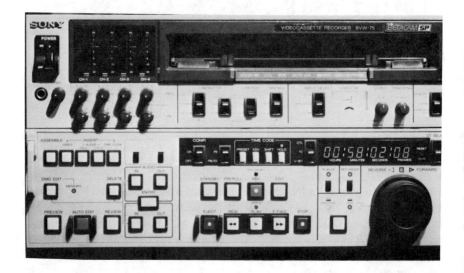

Figure 12-3 The front panel of a Sony Betacam SP. This sophisticated machine has a built-in editor; it can also sense the difference between SP tape and regular videotape. Note the four channels of audio displayed at the top left of the deck. Courtesy of Sony Corporation.

When you press the buttons to the left of the shuttle knob (right side of the machine), the player or recorder is engaged. Record and playback INs and OUTs are selected through the entry buttons to the left of the center shuttle controls. Pressing the entry key along with the In or Out button will program the edit.

The machine is also capable of making split edits by programming audio separately from video INs. There are input levels for the four audio channels as well as an inboard VITC generator (see Chapter 2). The internal generator should be on when you are using VITC time code.

In addition, there is a dynamic motion control memory for the playback deck located on the left side of the control panel. This allows limited slow-motion programming of the playback deck. Like most simple editors, there is no memory on the deck, but it will lock to time code or control track.

Setting the edit INs and OUTs remains a constant in any editor. The record and playback INs are selected, and the duration is determined by the OUT point, whether it's the playback OUT or the record OUT. Preview and record (auto edit) are found at the bottom left of the deck. Many television stations use two Beta decks to accomplish their news editing chores.

SPLIT EDITS

Some control track editors cannot make split edits (also called L cuts) automatically. The method for making a split using a control track editor varies depending on the type of split required. With an audio-leading-video split, the leading audio is recorded in a separate edit. When the edit becomes a both cut, it is made as an audio-video edit. In the case of video leading the both cut, the audio portion is recorded first; then the video portion is recorded in a one-video-only edit. (The video portion includes both the leading section and the section that is in sync with the audio.)

PAUSE AND RECORD

Some editors use the pause and record method of editing, which prevents the control track editor from slipping a frame or two during a preview. It also eliminates the luxury of previewing an edit. This method requires that the operator be experienced enough to know whether the edit will work without the use of a preview.

In this method, the editor finds the record and playback IN points and checks both images visually, conceptualizing the edit. Now, rather than previewing, the editor records an open-ended edit, stopping the recording when

"Courtesy of Sony Electronics Inc."

Figure 12-4 The Sony BVU-950 U-Matic® editing deck. This three-quarter-inch machine has a built-in editor similar to other decks. Note that this built-in editor does not have split capabilities, and has only two tracks of audio available.

more than enough of the edit has been recorded. The next edit will erase this extra video and/or audio (the tail of the previous edit) and will also be recorded long.

In some cases, this use of a control track editor is perfectly acceptable. For example, demo reels that consist only of commercials do not require that edits be previewed. Likewise, in fast-paced news situations, this method can get the job done quickly and well.

AN EDITING EXAMPLE

A news reporter rushes into the editing bay. He has the story. It's only 20 minutes to airtime. The editor grabs a fresh, preblacked 10-minute cassette off the shelf for the edit master and puts it into the record machine. Luckily, she has just finished recording color bars and tone on the head of the tape.

"We've got two versions of the introduction and one close, a great interview that's too long, and some cutaways," the reporter says breathlessly.

The editor puts the playback reel into the playback machine. She uses the playback controls to shuttle the tape at high speed until it reaches the beginning of the introduction. She presses Play and watches the two takes of the introduction. Both editor and reporter agree that the first take is better. The tape is then shuttled back to the head of the interview.

Now the editor works with the record machine. Thirty seconds past the end of the bars and tone, she puts the machine in pause. This will mark the IN point on the record machine. The source tape is paused three seconds before the reporter starts talking, marking the IN point on the source tape. Since this is the first edit, there is no need to worry about erasing any previous edit, and it is immediately recorded.

When the introduction has been completely recorded, the editor backs up the record tape to the end of the reporter's speech. The playback reel is shuttled to the interview, which the editor and reporter view in its entirety. They take notes during the viewing and discuss the selected segments when the viewing is over.

After they devise a plan, the editor shortens the interview by making a series of audio and video edits, thus eliminating unnecessary or unwanted sections of dialogue. This process results in a series of jump cuts. When the interview is finished, the reporter and editor play it back, listening with their eyes closed so that they are not distracted by the jump cuts and can concentrate on the audio, making sure the interview sounds natural. Once the sound has been finalized, the jump cuts are covered by using the appropriate cutaways. These edits will be recorded in the video-only mode.

The playback tape is shuttled to the reporter's close and put in pause. The record tape is paused at the end of the interview, and the close is edited onto that point. The editor rewinds the record tape, and she and the reporter view the story one more time to check for any mistakes or flaws that might have been overlooked.

"It's fine," the reporter says. "Let me have it."

The editor rewinds the record tape to the head, ejects it from the machine, and writes the name of the story, the date, and the reporter's and editor's names on the cassette.

"Thanks," the reporter says. "See you tomorrow."

"Sure," the editor replies. "About 20 minutes before airtime, right?"

There is no answer: The reporter and the tape are gone.

13

Reading the Computer Edit

Until computer editing arrived in video postproduction, editors had little control over the accuracy or remaking of a specific edit. Although computer editors offer greater control, using a highly accurate computer does not mean that all edits will be brilliant or easy to reconstruct. A person must still decide which edit is to be recorded. What the computer editor offers is extreme accuracy and a set of standardized codes to note how an edit was accomplished.

AN EDITING EXAMPLE

The first edit on the record tape should begin at the most convenient time code number. To make the show's duration easy to calculate, we will start the program material at 01:00:00:00. But several recordings must be made before the program itself begins. We must record one minute of bars and tone, 10 seconds of black, 10 seconds of slate information, and a 10-second countdown. This adds up to one minute and 30 seconds. To have the first edit of program material at 01:00:00:00, we must begin this series of preliminary edits at 00:58:30:00—one minute and 30 seconds before 01:00:00:00.

Preliminary Edits

Our first edit will be of color bars and audio tone. The color bars are a reference for calibrating the various video components. The tone is a reference for the audio record level. (See Chapter 4.)

For this example, let's assume that we have two tracks of audio available (many formats have four channels available; D1, D2, and Betacam are three of them) on our record machine. We will record the tone on both channels. Once the recording is completed, the computer will store the edit in memory in a standard SMPTE format (see Chapter 1). The computer listing of this format looks like Figure 13-1.

The first number we see, reading left to right, is our edit number, 1. The next piece of information is the source or reel from which the edit came. In this case, it is color bars (shortened to CBR). Then comes the mode description. Edit 1 was recorded on both tracks of the audio and video (B), and the edit was a cut (C). Since there was no effect, no effect duration is listed. Four sets of eight-digit numbers follow. These numbers represent the playback IN point, the playback OUT point, the record IN point, and the record OUT point. Since color bars are not a moving source, as is a videotape machine, the playback IN time will be 00:00:00:00 and the OUT time will be the edit duration. The record IN number is the first frame in which the source will be copied to the record machine. The last number in the computer listing is the record OUT location.

The second edit is both an audio and a video edit to video black for 10 seconds and is listed like this:

2 BLK B   C   00:00:00:00   00:00:10:00   00:59:30:00   00:59:40:00

The third edit is a both cut recording the video slate. The purpose of a video slate is to explain exactly what is on the tape, including the date it was edited, the show name, the running time, the audio configuration, the production

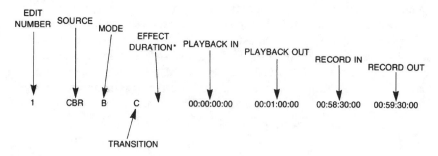

*Because a cut is an immediate transition, the cut has no effect duration.

Figure 13-1   Diagram of edit 1.

company, the director's credit, and any other important information about the show. Usually, the source of this information is an auxiliary input (AUX) on the switcher, often a character generator or video camera. It is listed like this:

3   AUX B   C   00:00:00:00   00:00:10:00   00:59:40:00   0:59:50:00

The fourth edit starts where edit 3 left off. This edit is a countdown with a duration of 10 seconds. The countdown's source is reel 50:

4   50   B   C   00:10:00:00   00:10:10:00   00:59:00:00   01:00:00:00

Program Edits

The fifth edit of the computer list, and the first edit of program material, is from reel 7 and is a shot of a tree. The director checks his master log and finds that the tree shot is located at about "seven-o-one-even," or 07:01:00:00. Reel 7 is put into a playback machine and scanned at high speed. "It's the shot of the big tree," the director says. "You can't miss it." We do and have to back up the tape until we locate the shot. The exact time code of the shot is 07:01:15:03 ("seven-o-one, fifteen-o-three").

The editor decides that a 30-frame fade-up from black should start the show. The computer listing for a fade is different from that for a cut. The dissolve or wipe has two lines of information. The first line identifies for the computer the point in the previous edit at which the new effect will take place. The second line represents the incoming material that will be subjected to a dissolve or wipe:

5 BLK B1   C   00:00:00:00   00:00:00:00   01:00:00:00   01:00:00:00

5   7   B1   D   30   07:01:15:03   07:01:27:03   01:00:00:00   01:00:12:00

In edit 5, we made a cut (C) to black at 01:00:00:00 on the record tape and then immediately dissolved to reel 7. (An effect occurs immediately if the record IN points of a two-line event are the same.) The edit was both audio and video, but the audio was recorded only on channel 1 of the record tape. The second line of the edit indicates that the effect was a dissolve (D) that had a duration of 30 frames. The edit ended at 01:00:12:00 on the record tape (see Figure 13-2).

The director informs us that the second edit of the show (the sixth edit on the record tape) will be a video-only edit from reel 10. It will begin at the end of a zoom-out from a closeup of a flower and will stop when the flower is out of focus. Reel 10 is loaded into a playback machine. With some searching, we find that the zoom stops at 03:41:15:02. This is the playback IN. The flower is out of

RECORD TIME CODE

	00:58:30:00	00:59:30:00	00:59:40:00	00:59:50:00	1:00:00:00
AUDIO TRACK 1	TONE	SILENCE	SILENCE	SILENCE	30 FRAME FADE UP ON AUDIO
AUDIO TRACK 2	TONE	SILENCE	SILENCE	SILENCE	SILENCE
	COLOR BARS	VIDEO BLACK	VIDEO SLATE	VIDEO BLACK	FADE UP ON FIRST PICTURE

(PLAYBACK TIME CODE) 07:01:15:03   07:01:27:03

EDIT	REEL	MODE	TYPE	DURATION	PLAYBACK IN	PLAYBACK OUT	RECORD IN	RECORD OUT
1	CBR	B/12	C		00:00:00:00	00:01:00:00	00:58:30:00	00:59:30:00
2	BLK	V/12	C		00:00:00:00	00:00:10:00	00:59:30:00	00:59:40:00
3	AUX	B/12	C		00:00:00:00	00:00:10:00	00:59:40:00	00:59:50:00
4	BLK	A/12	C		00:00:00:00	00:00:10:00	00:59:50:00	01:00:00:00
5	BLK	BV/1	C		00:00:00:00	00:00:00:00	01:00:00:00	01:00:12:00
5	7	BV/1	D	30	07:01:15:03	07:01:27:03	01:00:00:00	01:00:12:00

Figure 13-2   Diagram of edits 1 through 5.

focus at 03:41:25:12. This is the playback OUT. If we subtract the IN from the OUT, we find that the duration of this edit is 10 seconds and 10 frames.

Suddenly, the director changes his mind and wants to end the shot half a second before the flower is out of focus. If the flower is out of focus at 03:41:25:12, we must subtract 15 frames (half a second) from the OUT point so that the edit will end half a second earlier. We now have a new playback OUT point of 03:41:24:27. As a result, the edit duration is changed to nine seconds and 25 frames.

Now that the edit is defined, we can go to the record tape. The director indicates where he wants the flower shot to cut into the image of the tree. We discover by pressing a key on the computer editor (see Chapter 15) that the time code at this point on the record machine is 01:00:06:00. If we record the edit at this point, we will erase the last six seconds of the tree shot, since the tree edit lasted until 01:00:12:00. The edit listing from the computer after the recording looks like this:

6   10   V   C   03:41:15:02   03:41:24:27   01:00:06:00   01:00:15:25

This edit listing indicates that edit 6 came from reel 10; the edit was a video-only cut; playback IN was 3 hours, 41 minutes, 15 seconds, 2 frames; playback OUT was 3 hours, 41 minutes, 24 seconds, 27 frames; record IN was 1 hour, 0 minutes, 6 seconds, 0 frames; and record OUT was 1 hour, 0 minutes, 15 seconds, and 25 frames.

There are several ways to communicate time code verbally. One way is to list the numbers followed by *hours, minutes, seconds,* and *frames,* as above.

Another is to list just the numbers with no designations. In a case where there are no leading hours, such as with our video slate at 00:59:40:00, this time code number would be said without the leading zeros: 59, 40, 00, or 59 minutes and 40 seconds.

The third edit of our show, and the seventh to be recorded, is an audio-only edit—the sound of a bee buzzing—found near the end of reel 13. Reel 13 is loaded into a playback machine, and we find the buzzing at 13:55:05:10. On the record machine, we have decided to start the audio of the bee just before the beginning of the flower shot. The video edit of the flower starts at 01:00:06:00 on the record tape, so we start this audio a third of a second (10 frames) earlier than the picture. That puts the record IN at time code 01:00:05:20. The director instructs us that the bee noise should end where the flower shot ends and that the bee noise will be on the other audio track, track 2 (the background audio from the tree shot was recorded on track 1 in edit 5).

After we record the edit, the computer listing looks like this:

7   13   A2   C   13:55:05:10   13:58:15:15   01:00:05:20   01:00:15:25

Edit 7 is from playback reel 13; it is an audio-only edit onto track 2; record IN is 1, 00, 05, 20, and record OUT is 1, 00, 15, 25 (see Figure 13-3).

Until one-inch videotape came along, computer editors could access only one audio track because quad had only one track available.

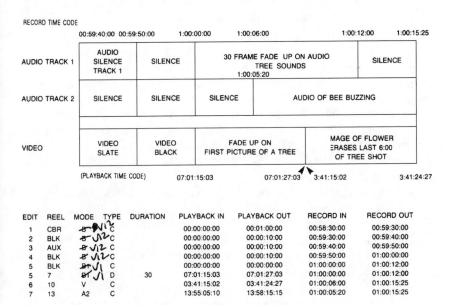

Figure 13-3 Diagram of edits 1 through 7.

There are currently two generally accepted industry standards for two-track audio EDL listings: the CMX format and the SMPTE format.

Now that we have looked at several edits, let's examine the dissolve and wipe listings a little more closely and see exactly what happens during a dissolve or wipe.

The director decides that he wants to dissolve from the flower to a shot of the sky. The sky is found on reel 25 at 11:11:12:00. We keep reel 10 in a playback machine because we will be dissolving from it, then load reel 25 into another playback machine and find the shot. The edit duration is to be 15 seconds and the dissolve rate three seconds.

Fortunately, the computer editor is able to make edits on the exact frame. This is called a *match cut* or *in-frame edit*. We make a match cut edit where we left off on the flower shot and dissolve to the sky shot. The edit listing looks like this:

8	10	V	C		03:41:24:27	03:41:24:27	01:00:15:25	01:00:15:25
8	25	V	D	90	11:11:12:00	11:11:27:00	01:00:15:25	01:00:30:25

The first line of the listing is the continuation of the video that will be dissolved out (the flower shot). The second line is a continuation of edit 8, the sky shot. (The second line of a two-line event always indicates the beginning of the effect.) Note that in this example, the duration of the top line is zero frames. This indicates that the effect will start immediately. The new incoming video, from reel 25, starts at the same record IN time, 01:00:15:25. The edit is a video-only, and the dissolve rate is 90 frames.

The dissolve starts at 01:00:15:25 on the record machine and ends 90 frames, or three seconds, later. From 01:00:15:25 to 01:00:18:25, video from reels 10 and 25 is involved in the transition. The video from reel 25 at 11:11:12:00 will not be seen, however, because it is the beginning of the dissolve. Ninety frames later (the duration of the effect), the video from reel 25 will be full, and there will be no trace of reel 10 (the outgoing video). Nevertheless, there must be usable video on reel 10 up until 03:41:27:27. Even though the list does not show it, those additional 90 frames are used in the dissolve. That is why the heads and tails of all planned effects must be checked during an off-line edit if you are using a cuts-only system.

For a match cut to work properly, all the video components of the outgoing scene must be matched exactly to where they were when the first part of the edit was made. If the match is not exact, the picture will shift in color, video level, or position on the screen.

One way to help ensure the match cut's success is to keep the playback reel on the same machine and make no adjustments until you are sure that it is not needed for an effect. In this way, all the aspects of the video (video, setup, chroma, luminance, and vertical and horizontal alignment) will be the same. Sometimes, depending on the machines involved, it is impossible to make an in-frame edit at a later date. In this case, you must rerecord the video prior to the effect. This might not be a problem in a single dissolve sequence, but if 15 dissolves occur in a row, changing one could be very time-consuming.

In our case, since edit 6 is a cut and the OUT point of the second part of the dissolve is also a cut, the edit could be listed and performed in the following way:

8   10   V   C   03:41:15:02   03:41:24:27   01:00:06:00   01:00:15:25

8   25   V   D   90   11:11:12:00   11:11:27:00   01:00:15:25   01:00:30:25

The top line of the new edit is identical to edit 6. The computer editing system will perform the dissolve as one continuous edit, eliminating the match cut.

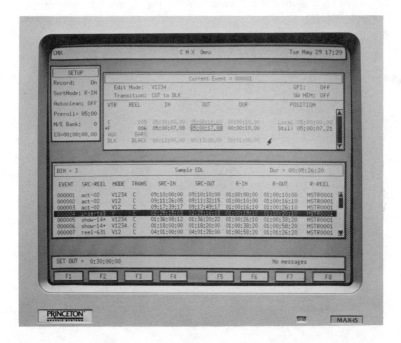

Figure 13-4   This display of a CMX Omni edit controller shows an actual EDL. Note that the edits displayed in the large center rectangle are accessing either channel 1 and 2 or all four channels of the record deck. Other available information includes the status of the machines in the top rectangle. The setup function on the top left indicates other parameters, such as whether the record function is active, or whether the automatic list cleaning function is on, and the length of preroll. Photo courtesy of CMX.

If the director decided to change the dissolve to a circle wipe, the listing would look like this:

```
8   10   V   C         03:41:15:02   03:41:24:27   01:00:06:00   01:00:15:25
8   25   V   W19   90   11:11:12:00   11:11:27:00   01:00:15:25   01:00:30:25
```

The W stands for a wipe, and the 19 refers to a computer code for a circle wipe. The computer wipe code indicates certain wipe patterns (see Figure 13-5) and does not have any way to note the softness of the wipe border, the color of the border, the position of the wipe, or the pattern modulation.

SUMMARY

The listing that results from a computer edit represents most of the information required to re-create the edit. One of the most important tasks for the new-comer to time code editing is to become accustomed to reading and interpreting the computer listing.

CODE 1	SKETCH 2	CODE 1	SKETCH 2
00	NONE	12	
01		13	
02		14	
03		15	
04		16	
05		17	
06		18	
07		19	
08		20	
09		21	
10		22	
11		23	

WIPE PATTERNS

NOTES:　1　WIPE CODE IS FOR NORMAL-DIRECTION WIPE. ADD 100 FOR REVERSE-DIRECTION WIPE.

2　SKETCH SHOWS EFFECT. NORMAL DIRECTION OF CHANGE IS TOWARD INCREASING WHITE AREA.

WIPE CODES FROM 24 TO 85 HAVE NOT YET BEEN STANDARDIZED SINCE EXPANDED WIPES ARE ONLY AVAILABLE ON NEWER MODEL SWITCHERS.

Figure 13-5　Common wipe pattern designations. The numbers under the code are generally accepted wipe patterns, although some switchers use other numbers for the same patterns.

14

Creating the Off-Line EDL

This chapter gives specific information about logging off-line edits made with a control track or time code editor and window dubs (not computer or random-access editors). This type of editing is commonly used for industrial programs, segments for magazine format shows, feature news stories, and prime-time programs.

Keeping track of all the edits made in an off-line session is not always easy. On many occasions, the video portion of an edit is erased, but the audio portion remains. Shots can come from many different sources. Reels might be borrowed from other shows or companies. Locating the original source of a stray audio or video edit can be a very discouraging task if proper notes are not taken during the editing session.

Three things must be done to ensure a successful off-line edit using a control track editor. The first, as mentioned in Chapter 5, is to build a master log of all the playback material. The second is to write down every edit that contains audio as it is performed. When creating the EDL, you may find that the time code window of the playback source might not represent the source of the audio on the off-line master. The third important task in off-line control track editing is to make notes about the edits that have been recorded (audio, effects, source reels, titles that must be added during the on-line edit, etc.). If the editor is pressured and does not have time to make these notes clearly and precisely, important edits, changes, effects, and reel identifications might be lost or forgotten. It is vital that everything be written down, not just kept in someone's head. By the time the workprint has changed 15 times and the edit sessions have turned into marathons, nothing will be clear in anyone's mind. See Figures 14-1 and 14-2 for examples of master logs.

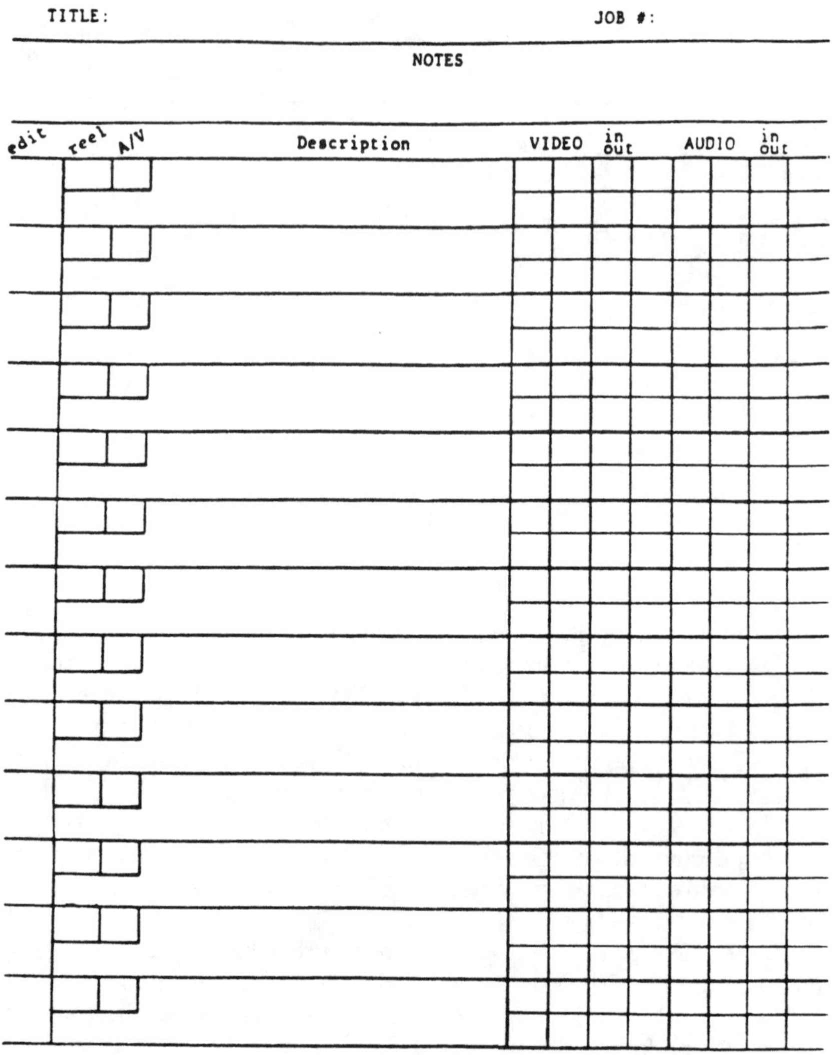

TITLE :   JOB # :

NOTES

edit	reel	A/V	Description	VIDEO in out	AUDIO in out

Figure 14-1   An example of an edit log sheet used for writing EDLs. The sheet has spaces for each edit in which to log the edit number, source reel, edit mode, source IN and OUT, and other important information.

Since the on-line editing session will be based on the EDL, it stands to reason that this list must be accurate in every respect. A sloppy EDL defeats the purpose of the off-line edit.

Control track EDLs are not usually based on the record tape time code but rather on the source reel time code. A complete edit entry consists of the source

EDIT #	INSERT SYNC POINT	REEL #	PLAYBACK NUMBERS	V A1, A2	TECHNICAL PROBLEMS	CONTENT	NOTES

Figure 14-2 An example of an edit log sheet. This sheet has a space for insert sync points, discussed later in this chapter.

reel number, the mode (audio, video, or both), the source IN and OUT points, and any effect that might be required. All this information can fit easily on one line of a sheet of paper.

LOG SHEET FORMATS

The world of professional video has never settled on any particular format for handwritten log sheets. Many editors create forms to match their style of note-taking. The form itself is not important, nor is the manner of notation. The crucial part is that the IN and OUT points of every edit are logged, along with the source reel number, any sync points and offsets, and any special notes about the edit that might be required.

SYNC POINTS AND OFFSETS

Sync points and offsets indicate where, in the middle of an edit, another edit is to take place. A *sync point* is the time code number in the earlier edit where the new edit is to occur. An *offset* is the duration from the head or tail of the edit that

TWO EXAMPLES OF LOGGING SYNC POINTS AND OFFSETS
(Working with playback numbers only)

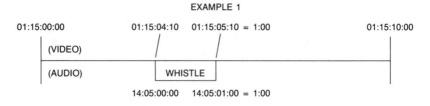

EXAMPLE 1

EDIT #	OFFSET AND SYNC POINT	REEL #	PLAYBACK # IN & OUT	DUR	V A1, A2	TECH
47		52	01:15:00:00 TO 01:15:10:00	10:00	V, A1	
48	01:15:04:10	14	14:05:00:00 TO 14:05:01:00	1:00	A1	

EXAMPLE 2

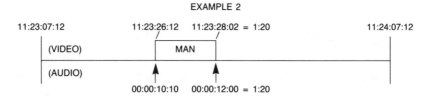

EDIT	REEL	A/V	DESCRIPTION	VIDEO IN/OUT	AUDIO IN/OUT
17	12	B1	STREET SCENE	11:23:07:12	11:23:07:12
				11:24:07:12	11:24:07:12
18	5	V	MAN STARING << 11:23:26:12 >> < +19 FROM EDIT 17 >	00:00:10:10	: : :
				00:00:12:00	: : :

Figure 14-3 An example of logging an insert edit.

immediately precedes the spot where this edit is to take place. See Figure 14-3 for an example of a log sheet used for an insert edit.

Let's say that a both (audio and video) cut starts at 01:15:00:00 on a playback source and ends at 01:15:10:00, making a 10-second edit. Four seconds and 10 frames into the cut, a train whistle (from another playback source) is to be cut onto the audio track. The sync point for that whistle would be 01:15:04:10 and the offset would be 04:10 from the head of the edit.

Here is another example: A both cut is made starting at 11:23:07:12 and ending at 11:24:07:12—a one-minute edit. A video edit is slated to occur when a dog crossing the street reaches the yellow line. The playback time code at that point is 11:23:26:12, or 19 seconds into the cut. At this point, a video-only shot of a man looking at the dog is to be inserted into the street-crossing scene. The both cut will be logged on the EDL followed by the video insert, the offset, and/or the sync point. The sync point is found by looking at the time code in the window of the off-line master. The offset is calculated by subtracting the time code IN point of the video edit from the time code at the sync point. Again, the idea is to note these numbers accurately, as each cut is performed.

L CUTS

Another use for the sync point or offset is in logging L cuts, or split edits. An L cut is made to delay either the video or audio for a portion of the edit. Looking at a diagram of an L cut shows where this type of edit gets its name: It looks like a sideways L. The term *split edit* comes from the idea that the IN point of the audio has been split from the IN point of the video. Split edits are extremely common in dialogue scenes. The split is used to show the audience how characters react to another performer's dialogue. It also speeds the pacing of a scene because the audience is occupied by both the dialogue and the reaction.

Most edits are L-cut at the head of the edit (a *split in*) rather than at the end (a *split out*). It is easier to make a split in than a split out because you do not have to wait until the end of the edit to find out whether the split will work.

In logging the L cut, you may choose to log the edit using the time code for the IN point of the leading portion of the split, the point where the edit becomes a both cut, and the OUT point of the edit. Offsets can also be used to determine where the split becomes a both cut. The offset is the time from the head of the edit to where the both cut begins.

LOGGING AN L CUT

A well-built man is bowling. Two women are sitting at the scoring table talking to each other in a two shot. In the first edit, the man gets up to bowl; his back is toward the camera. As he gets ready to release the ball, a split IN is performed. In the audio leading the picture, we hear the two women say, "That's a sight to behold." The picture now joins the audio as the two women look at each other and smile. Their dialogue starts on reel 5 at 05:55:10:00 and ends at 05:55:15:00. The entire edit ends at 05:55:25:00.

Let's look at the same edit using two tracks of audio. We continue the bowler's ambient bowling lane sounds on track 1 and start the split edit within the first edit, using sync points. The bowler's reel is 17, the IN time is 01:00:00:00, and the OUT time of the ambient audio is 01:00:20:00. The sync point used for the audio edit of the two women talking will be 01:00:05:00, which happens to be five seconds into the bowler's shot. This example is about as complicated as a cuts-only log entry can get for two edits (see Figures 14-4a and 14-4b).

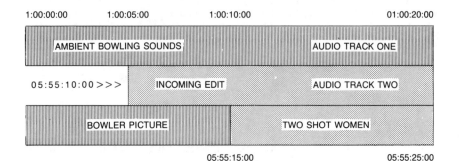

LOG SHEET 1

EDIT #	OFFSET AND SYNC POINT	REEL #	PLAYBACK # IN & OUT	DUR	V A1, A2	TECH
22		17	01:00:00:00 TO 01:00:20:00	20:00	V, A1	
23	SPLIT: DELAY VIDEO 5:00 01:00:05:00	5	5:55:10:00 TO 5:55:25:00	15:00	A2, V	

LOG SHEET 2

EDIT	REEL	A/V	DESCRIPTION	VIDEO IN/OUT	AUDIO IN/OUT
22	17	B1		1:00:00:00	1:00:00:00
		MAN BOWLING		1:00:20:00	1:00:20:00
23	5	B2	5:00 V DELAY GIRLS TALKING << 1:00:05:00 >> < +5:00 FROM EDIT 22 >	5:55:15:00	5:55:10:00
				5:55:25:00	5:55:25:00

Note: As you can see, the second log sheet allows for much more information than the first, even explaining the in and out times for the video as well as the audio.

a

Figure 14-4a   An example of logging an L cut with one audio track.

LOGGING THE "L" CUT. . . . A SPLIT "IN" EDIT
(WITH AUDIO LEADING PICTURE — ONE TRACK OF AUDIO)

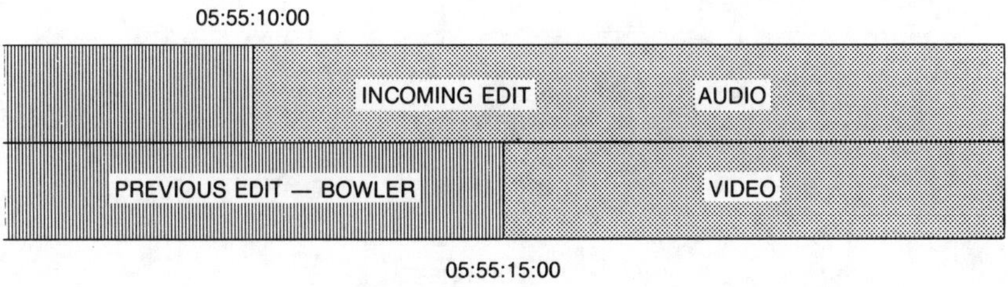

05:55:10:00

	INCOMING EDIT	AUDIO
PREVIOUS EDIT — BOWLER		VIDEO

05:55:15:00

LOG SHEET 1

EDIT #	OFFSET AND SYNC POINT	REEL #	PLAYBACK # IN & OUT	DUR	V A1, A2	TECH
23	AUDIO LEADS FOR 5:00	5	05:55:10:00 TO 05:55:25:00	15:00	A1, V	

LOG SHEET 2

EDIT	REEL	A/V	DESCRIPTION	VIDEO IN/OUT	AUDIO IN/OUT
23	5	B1	SPLIT EDIT	05:55:15:00	05:55:10:00
			DELAY V 5:00 BOWLER AND AMBIENT SOUND	05:55:25:00	05:55:25:00

b

Figure 14-4b   An example of logging an L cut with two audio tracks.

To recap, there are three points to log for split edits: (1) the time code for the leading portion of the edit, (2) the sync point or offset where the edit becomes a both cut, and (3) the time code of the OUT point of the edit.

LOGGING DISSOLVES AND WIPES

Logging simple effects such as dissolves and wipes is almost identical to noting a cut. The only additional information needed is the type of effect (wipe or dissolve) and its duration. In some cases, sync points and offsets might be needed if the dissolve is to be a video-only edit that allows the audio from the original edit to continue.

You must be aware of several items when logging simple effects. First, most off-line editors use the cut point of an edit as the head or beginning of the effect. Some editors, usually film editors, use the cut point as the mid-point of

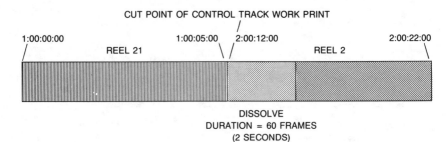

CUT POINT OF CONTROL TRACK WORK PRINT

DISSOLVE
DURATION = 60 FRAMES
(2 SECONDS)

LOG SHEET 1

EDIT #	OFFSET AND SYNC POINT	REEL #	PLAYBACK # IN & OUT	DUR	V A1, A2	TECH
52		21	01:00:00:00 TO 01:00:05:00	5:00	V	
53	DISSOLVE FROM 52 60 FRAMES	2	2:00:12:00 TO 2:00:22:00	10:00	V	

LOG SHEET 2

EDIT	REEL	A/V	DESCRIPTION	VIDEO IN/OUT	AUDIO IN/OUT
52	21	V		1:00:00:00	: : :
			FIRST SCENE	1:00:05:00	: : :
53	2	V	60 FRAME DISSOLVE FROM	2:00:12:00	: : :
			EDIT 52 SECOND SCENE	2:00:22:00	: : :

Figure 14-5 An example of logging a simple dissolve.

an effect. If you are using the latter procedure, it is important to tell the on-line computer editor, to avoid confusion. The on-line editor can then manually adjust each edit by backing up the cut point to half the duration of the effect.

Second, if a dissolve or wipe is being planned during a cuts-only off-line session, you must make sure that the head of the incoming shot and the tail of the outgoing shot have enough picture to complete the effect. If an effect is going to last three seconds, one and a half seconds of the incoming video and one and a half seconds of the outgoing video will not be seen on the off-line workprint (assuming that the cut is the mid-point of the effect). A full three seconds would be needed at the tail of the footage if the effect was logged using the head of the shot. Figure 14-5 shows how a simple dissolve from reel 1 to reel 11 would be logged.

LOGGING MULTIPLE EFFECTS

Logging complicated effects such as quad splits or multiple-source effects is not difficult if you use sync points and offsets. Let's say there is an animated background for a network promotion of *Saturday Night at the Movies*. This background is to run for 10 seconds, after which four digital effects boxes are to appear, one every two seconds. The EDL would look like Figure 14-6.

FIELD DOMINANCE

A frame in video comprises two fields. An edit can occur at the beginning of field 1 (between the frames) or at the beginning of field 2 (in the middle of the frame). The standard is for edits to occur at the beginning of field 1; this is called *field 1 dominance*. When you are editing to three-quarter-inch, especially when using the Sony 500 or 800 U-Matic series, edits will occur between the frames (field 1 dominance). So, when you edit off-line on three-quarter-inch and then conform on a system using field 2 dominance, the edits will begin and end a field late (in relation to the off-line master).

THE LAST FRAME

Computer systems do not record the last frame of an edit time code number because of the way durations are calculated. For example, let's say we want to record one frame of video starting at time code 01:00:00:00. To do this, the computer system calculates the duration of the edit by subtracting the IN point from the OUT point. To get a one-frame edit, the edit must start at 01:00:00:00 and end at 01:00:00:01, but the only frame that the computer will record is 01:00:00:00.

If you are using a computer system for off-line and on-line editing, this frame difference will be consistent, and you need not be concerned about it. If you are translating a handwritten log to a computer system, however, the last frame will be dropped. If it is important to have the last frame of an edit recorded, add one frame to the OUT number. You would not add the frame only if the off-line editor were editing on the second field or if the window dub were delayed by one field. To check for this, you must carefully examine the first frame of an edit on the record tape. There should be two frame bars before the time code frame number changes. If there is only one frame bar, and the number changes, then only field 2 of the time code window is being recorded. In this case you should not add a frame. The editing system may be editing on frame 2, or the window dub may be one field off from the original footage, which occasionally happens in video processing.

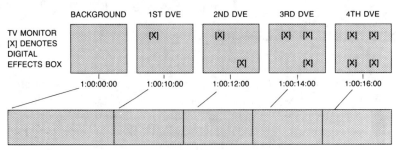

LOGGING COMPLICATED EFFECTS

RECORD TAPE

LOG SHEET 1

EDIT #	OFFSET AND SYNC POINT	REEL #	PLAYBACK # IN & OUT	DUR	V A1, A2	TECH
1		100	01:00:00:00 TO 01:00:20:00	20:00	V	
2	1:00:10:00 BOX 1 DVE OVER BACKGROUND	1	1:00:40:00 TO 1:00:50:00	10:00	V	
3	1:00:12:00 BOX 2 DVE OVER BACKGROUND	2	2:00:10:00 TO 2:00:18:00	8:00	V	
4	1:00:14:00 BOX 3 DVE OVER BACKGROUND	16	16:00:30:00 TO 16:00:36:00	6:00	V	
5	1:00:16:00 BOX 4 DVE OVER BACKGROUND	8	22:44:12:15 TO 22:44:16:15	4:00	V	

LOG SHEET 2

EDIT	REEL	A/V	DESCRIPTION	VIDEO IN/OUT	AUDIO IN/OUT
1	100	V		1:00:00:00	: : :
			BACKGROUND FOR DVE EFFECT	1:00:20:00	: : :
2	1	V	DVE BOX 1	1:00:40:00	: : :
			<< 1:00:10:00 >>	1:00:50:00	: : :
3	2	V	DVE BOX 2	2:00:10:00	: : :
			<< 1:00:12:00 >>	2:00:18:00	: : :
4	16	V	DVE BOX 3	16:00:30:00	: : :
			<< 1:00:14:00 >>	16:00:36:00	: : :
5	8	V	DVE BOX 4	22:44:12:15	: : :
			<< 1:00:16:00 >>	22:44:16:15	: : :

Note: This edit would require a four-channel digital effects generator or going down four generations of video.

Figure 14-6 An example of logging a complicated digital effects sequence.

LIST CLEANING AND MANAGEMENT

List cleaning is the elimination of all unnecessary edits in an EDL. Before any on-line assembly can be performed from an off-line list, the EDL must be cleaned (unless this is a random-access editor list; these EDLs are always "clean"). When an off-line video edit is made, it most often erases a portion of the previous edit. It does not make sense to go through this same recording/erasing procedure during the on-line edit, so any unnecessary edits should be eliminated from the EDL.

A computer EDL can be cleaned in two ways. The first is to have a person sit at a computer editor and manually change the list. The second is to run the EDL through a computer program that automatically cleans it. Dave Bargen, an ingenious computer programmer, created the first cleaning program, called 409®.

Cleaning a list by hand can be very tedious, but doing so can save a great deal of time and money during the on-line edit. When cleaning a list by hand, you must keep a copy of the original EDL for reference.

Another type of computer program, created for list management, is the Trace® program. Let's assume an off-line edited master has been created. To make changes, the editor uses the off-line edited master as a playback rather than recreating every edit. In the EDL, however, one edit from the playback of the off-line master might represent many edits made from other reels during the original creation of the workprint. The Trace program searches through the EDLs to find where the original edits came from.

A, B, C, D MODE ASSEMBLIES

Once the EDL has been loaded into a computer editing system, there are several methods by which the video specified by the EDL is recorded from source tapes to a record tape. The first method, called A mode, is a linear editing process. Edit 1 is followed by edit 2, edit 3, and so on until the show is completed. A second method, called B mode, or *checkerboard*, assembly, records all of the edits from one group of playback reels, then moves to a new group of playbacks. A third method of organizing an EDL is an enhancement of B mode called *C mode*. C mode is also a checkerboard arrangement of the EDL, except that the edits are executed in the sequential order in which material is located on each playback tape. Thus, the record tape shuttles back and forth to edit destination points while the playback tape simply rolls forward, stopping to copy designated material.

D Mode is an A mode list with all the edits other than cuts listed at the bottom of the EDL. *F mode* is a C mode list with all edits other than cuts listed at the bottom of the EDL.

The copyrighted computer program Prereader® offers an even more advanced feature. This program, designed to take advantage of D2's prereading function, can arrange an EDL so that only one machine is needed to perform dissolves, and organizes the list for the least amount of shuttle time. For an hour program, it would be silly to shuttle the record tape from one end to the next in order to shuttle the playback five seconds if the following edit would cause the record tape to travel all the way back to the beginning of the program. The program figures out the most efficient method of assembling the edits.

The advantage of these approaches in EDL preparation is that each reel is put on the playback machine the minimum amount of times. The disadvantage is that the EDL must be totally accurate and clean, with no edits erasing other edits. In these checkerboard assemblies, the final edited show cannot be viewed until the editing session is completed. However, these preparations can save up to 50% of on-line time (and expenses), depending on the length of the show and the number of reel changes required.

SUMMARY

As this chapter shows, a control track editor can be an effective off-line tool. However, the editor must take detailed notes during the off-line session and use these notes to produce a legible and accurate EDL.

15

The Computer Keyboard

Numerous types of computerized time code editing systems are available, each with different keyboard layouts and functions (see Figure 15-1). Despite these differences, there are many similarities between brands. This chapter briefly explains some of the more common computer editing keys and typical keyboard layouts.

When CMX introduced its first video editing systems, their keyboard became an industry standard. Since then, many editing keyboards have followed the same general pattern of key placement. Keyboards that differ radically still have similar function keys. Other editing systems have additional keys that enhance the system's edit and list management capabilities. (*List management* refers to the ability to alter edits once they have been recorded.) See Figure 15-2 for an example of a computer editing keyboard.

SOURCE KEYS

Source keys access particular machines and other switcher inputs, such as color bars, matte cameras, color cameras, character generators, and digital effects generators. Once the machine has been selected by pressing a source key, other functions can be applied to that machine.

Figure 15-1 An on-line editing console. Photo by Sean Sterling.

TRANSPORT KEYS

Transport keys move or stop a selected machine. Normal keyboard functions are Rewind, Fast Forward (FFWD), Slow (usually 25% of normal play), Stop (or Still), and Play. Most keyboards also have a Cue, or "go to" key, which sends a

Figure 15-2 A computer editing keyboard. Photo courtesy of Editing Technologies Corporation.

tape to a specific time code number. Some computer editors have joysticks, others have circular knobs; both the joystick and knob are used to shuttle the selected tape machine at various speeds.

TIME CODE KEYS

Time code keys are used to enter time code from a selected machine into the computer.

SET IN/OUT KEYS

Set In and Set Out are used to enter known time code numbers into the computer. These numbers are known because someone has already noted them during an off-line edit or viewing session.

MARK KEYS

Mark In and Mark Out enter time code while playing a selected machine. When either the Mark In or the Mark Out key is pressed, the machine's time code is marked and loaded into the computer. Mark In enters the time code into an IN position on the CRT; Mark Out enters the time code into an OUT position on the CRT. In some editing systems, the mark keys must have the VTR in motion to access the correct time code number. The exception occurs when vertical interval time code is being used, because VITC is accurate whether or not the tape is moving.

TRIM KEYS

Trim In and Trim Out alter time code numbers already entered into the computer. The time code numbers in the IN or OUT positions, and the duration of the edit can be altered by either a plus or a minus. If an IN point was marked ten frames too late, it can be changed by trimming it − 10 frames.

EFFECTS KEYS

Effects keys instruct the computer to cut, dissolve, wipe, or key. The following paragraphs explain how these effects are programmed on each keyboard.

Cut

Pressing the Cut key will change a dissolve, wipe, or key to a cut.

Dissolve

Pressing the DIS (dissolve) key initiates a dialogue between the operator and the computer. Usually the computer asks, "Dissolve from?" The operator then presses the source select key of the deck from which the dissolve originates. The computer then asks, "To?" The operator again presses the source select key of the machine from which the incoming picture or audio originates. Finally, the computer asks, "Duration?" The operator types in the number of frames the dissolve entails, then presses the Enter or Return key.

Wipe

Wipes are programmed almost exactly the same way as dissolves. When the operator presses the Wipe key, the computer starts a dialogue. Usually the computer asks, "Wipe from?" The operator presses the source select key of the deck from which the wipe originates and the computer asks, "To?" Again, the operator presses the source select key of the machine from which the picture or audio originates. Then the computer asks, "Duration?" The operator types in the number of frames the wipe entails, then presses the Enter or Return key. Finally, the computer asks, "Wipe number?" As discussed in Chapter 13, wipes are programmed by number. Most switchers have various patterns available.

Multiple-Source Effects

Effects requiring multiple-source machines to be rolling at the same time can be accomplished in different ways depending on the edit system. One of the most common commands is "Master/Slave." When this key is pressed, the computer asks which machines will be linked together; multiple machines can be put into play during the edit. For simple two-machine effects, a dissolve with a duration rate of 0 can be used to roll two playback sources. The Master/Slave key can also be used to enable editing to multiple record machines.

AUDIO/VIDEO KEYS

Audio/video keys are used to tell the computer whether the edit is to be an audio-only edit, a video-only edit, or both an audio and a video edit. Some systems also have keys that determine on which track the audio is to be recorded. Various keyboards have different key names for these functions. For instance, an audio-only key might be labeled A, AUD, or A Only. A video-only key might be labeled VID, VID Only, or V Only. A key for both an audio and video edit might be labeled B, Both, AUD/VID, or Audio/Video. In advanced editors, there are five selections to be made, which turn each choice on and off: V, A1, A2, A3, and A4.

PREVIEW KEYS

Preview keys are used to rehearse edits without actually recording them. Each video edit comprises three sections: (1) the picture and audio on the record tape located just before the edit, (2) the edit material that has been chosen for the preview, and (3) the material located just after the edit.

Three types of preview are described in the following paragraphs and illustrated in Figures 15-3, 15-4, and 15-5. Figure 15-6 compares the three types.

Video-Video-Video

The video-video-video (VVV) preview (see Figure 15-3) is the most common preview. It shows a portion of the outgoing edit, the incoming edit, and a portion of the next edit.

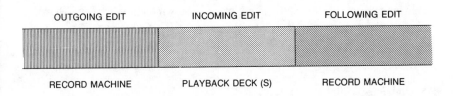

Figure 15-3   Diagram of the VVV preview.

Figure 15-4   Diagram of the VBV preview.

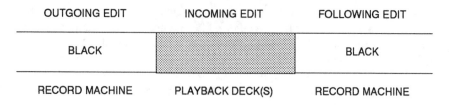

OUTGOING EDIT	INCOMING EDIT	FOLLOWING EDIT
BLACK		BLACK
RECORD MACHINE	PLAYBACK DECK(S)	RECORD MACHINE

Figure 15-5 Diagram of the BVB preview.

EDIT IN POINT   EDIT OUT POINT

RECORD MACHINE

VIDEO	VIDEO	VIDEO	VVV SHOWS ALL OF THE REHEARSED EDIT.
BLACK	VIDEO	BLACK	BVB SHOWS ONLY PLAYBACK SECTION OF THE EDIT.
VIDEO	BLACK	VIDEO	VBV SHOWS ONLY THE RECORD OF THE EDIT.

Figure 15-6 Diagram of the three types of preview.

Video-Black-Video

The video-black-video (VBV) preview (see Figure 15-4) shows only the record machine material. At the edit IN point, black is shown on the monitor. When the edit ends, the picture returns to the record master. This preview is often used to examine exactly what is on the record machine at the beginning and end of the edit.

Black-Video-Black

The black-video-black (BVB) preview (see Figure 15-5) shows only the play-back portion of the edit.

REPLAY KEY

The Replay key rewinds the record machine and shows the last edit that was recorded. Most editors do not bother with this key and instead manually rewind the tape to review the edit.

RECORD KEY

The Record key instructs the computer to record the video and/or audio information indicated on the CRT onto the record tape. CMX-type editors often require the operator to press the CTRL (control) key and the Record key simultaneously to perform the record function.

EXIT KEY

All computer editors have some sort of exit key. Pressing this key aborts any dialogue between the operator and the computer and returns the menu to a noninteractive status. This is the key to use to cancel whatever is currently on the screen.

MASTER/SLAVE KEY

Depending on the controller used, there is a function on computer editors that will tie multiple playbacks and/or record decks together. Once the relationship is established, a trim on one of the decks will change the others equally. In addition, all decks involved in the master/slave setup will roll when the edit is performed.

The master/slave option is used to create multiple playback effects. The basic dissolve function can drive only three decks (the record machine and two playbacks), but the master/slave function can roll as many sources as are available.

PERIPHERAL CONTROL

Again, specific to individual controllers, a series of keystrokes can trigger peripheral devices. Usually these triggers are grouped into three basic categories.

Switcher Operation

Advanced switchers can often have their complicated effects setups stored in memory or even within the EDL. The Grass Valley Group, a major manufacturer of switchers, calls its remote-controlled triggers *PEGs* (Program Motion, E, Mem, GPI, Strings). Effects can be loaded into the switcher or merely triggered.

General-Purpose Interface (GPI)

The GPI is a single pulse sent to an external device, such as a DVE (see Chapter 11). This pulse indicates that the device is to perform a prearranged event (run forward, stop, freeze, run backward, etc.).

Playback Speed Control

The third type of external triggering apparatus controls the playback speed of one or more decks. Each controller creates this command differently, but all controllers require two vital pieces of information: what speed the deck is to travel and when it is to begin its variable-speed function. Some computer controllers cannot preroll at variable speeds, preventing a slow-motion effect from entering an edit at its exact, predetermined frame. Other controllers, CMX and Sony controllers, for instance, can preroll at the variable speed and enter an edit at the exact frame desired.

ALL STOP KEY

The all stop key on most computer systems is the space bar at the bottom of the keyboard. Pressing this key aborts any action that is being performed by the system, including recording.

You must be careful when aborting a recording in progress. If the all stop key is pressed while you are recording an edit, there will be no evidence of that edit in the EDL, even though there will be video and/or audio placed on the record tape. There is always a different key that cancels the recording process, but maintains an accurate edit record. In most computer editors, you simply press the Record key again; however, you should check the editor's operating manual first.

EDL KEYS

The computer editor creates an EDL as it edits. The EDL keys enable the computer to store and make copies of the EDL in different formats. The operator can also load an EDL into the computer by using these keys. The two computer storage/transfer media for video editing EDLs are diskettes and printed copies.

MISCELLANEOUS (POWER) KEYS

The following advanced function keys are often found on computer editors. Occasionally they are not readily apparent or are not on dedicated keys, but must be accessed by a series of keystrokes.

BINS—Moves the display into one of several separate files of EDLs, all of which are active within the computer editor.

CONSTANTS—Maintains offsets for reference in a computer file so that commonly used numbers can be recalled and used in list management.

EJECT—Remotely ejects a tape from a machine.

ENABLE/DISABLE—Indicates to the computer editor whether or not an edit has been recorded. Enabling an edit essentially tells the computer that the edit needs to be recorded.

FILL—A calculation key that, when given record and playback durations, computes the speed of the playback needed to fill the record duration.

LEARN (MACRO) KEYS—Saves commonly used keystrokes.

LOOK AHEAD—An option by which the computer looks ahead in the EDL for edits and then precues machines not involved in the current event.

MATCH—Causes the computer to look back in the EDL for a time code match to a previously recorded edit. This facilitates finding an edit in an EDL.

MULTIPLE RECORD OPTION—Allows two tapes to record a program at the same time, producing two same-generation edited masters.

PAGE—Scrolls up or down an EDL a page (one full screen's worth) at a time.

REC START—Tells the computer at what time code on the record tape a program begins. The computer can thus display the running time of the show.

REEDIT—Recalls a previously recorded edit. Changes can be made to the edit, and it can be reinserted into the EDL, or it can be recorded as a new event.

SPLIT EDIT—Allows for starting audio or video later than the IN point of the edit. Some editors allow for both split in and split out edits at the same time.

SYNC ROLL—Rolls numerous VTRs and allows for editing on the fly. Every time you touch a new source machine, the switcher changes sources and an edit is noted in the EDL.

TEXT EDITING—Changes reel assignments, modes, or other information globally within an EDL.

Compatibility

Each editing system is encoding information in separate ways. Sony, CMX, Grass Valley, ETC.℠, Ampex, and other manufacturers are trying to keep up with exploding technology and still stay somewhat compatible. You should investigate the conversion of EDLs if you are going from an off-line to on-line system and changing brands.

SUMMARY

The computer is neither friend nor foe. Learning computer editing is not easy, but using a computer editor can be a very rewarding and remunerative experience.

16

Off-Line Random-Access Editing

The limitation of linearity in videotape editing is an annoying reality. If three video edits are recorded and you want to change the duration of the middle edit, you must rerecord the third or the first edit. In the past, several attempts were made to rectify this problem. The first random-access editor was the CMX 600, described in Chapter 1. The technology at that time was not reliable enough to support a true random-access editor. At its best, the CMX 600 held only thirty-five minutes of video. This is hardly enough to cut a half-hour sitcom. Today's random-access editors are capable of holding hours' worth of video and audio.

Today, random-access editor systems have been totally accepted by the postproduction industry. Hundreds of random-access editors are employed in the film industry, the commercial arena, broadcast television, and the non-broadcast video industry. The speed with which changes can be effected and the easy output of a clean, accurate EDL and/or negative cut list has brought random-access editing from the research and development stages into main-stream postproduction use (see Figure 16-1). Besides making editorial changes quickly, random-access editors virtually eliminate the time consumed by shuttling tapes back and forth.

Let's review exactly what a random-access editor is. We know that editing videotape is a linear process. Each edit is physically recorded onto a record tape. These images occupy a firmly defined space on that tape. To change the length of any edit, and maintain the content of the remainder of the show, the edits following must be recorded one by one. A random-access system is not constrained by this linearity. Because each edit is only a preview, a change in length

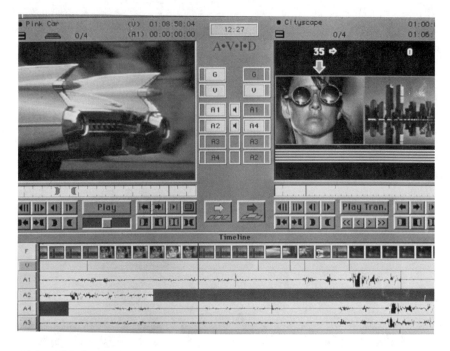

Figure 16-1 The display screen of an Avid random-access editor. Note that the time code is completely absent from the screen. In its place, graphic symbols indicate the edit mode. Photo courtesy of Avid Technologies.

is immediately taken into account by the computer. The edits following are instantaneously adjusted to accommodate the previous edit's change.

A videotape editor is to a random-access editor as a typewriter is to a word processor. The typewritten page needs to be retyped to include new words or to delete words. The word processor, like a random-access editor, just makes room to accommodate the changes. The display of a word processor is only a preview of what the page will look like when printed on paper; similarly, the random-access editor only previews what all the edits of the show will look like when output to videotape. Conventional editing systems can only preview one or two edits at a time.

When a random-access editing session is over, a recording of the show is often made for viewing.

There are three types of random-access editing systems. One type uses multiple videotape playbacks and thus is referred to as a *tape-based* random-access editor. The second type of system uses multiple videodisk copies. This *disk-based* random-access editor requires fewer playback sources than the tape-based system because videodisks can locate a specific frame within seconds. The third system is the most recent (most popular, and most powerful) arrival to the random-access editor group. This type of device uses digitized computer video as its playback source (see Figure 16-2). Videotape or disk images are transferred directly onto a computer hard disk, so these digitized computer images are accessed within the computer itself. All three systems are able to find and review any sequence of edits in real time, eliminating the need to record anything until the segment or show has been completely edited.

TAPE-BASED EDITORS

Consider an editing machine with seven playbacks, each with a copy of the same videotape. You could preview seven edits without having to use any machine twice. That is the concept behind the tape-based, or video-based, random-access editor. By using modified videotape machines that shuttle tape quickly, the editing computer calculates how far it is to the next edit and which machine is closest to that point. Since there are multiple playback decks, the system can preview multiple edits before having to shuttle any tape. If an edit is changed, then the preview of that edit changes, and the edits behind are previewed later or earlier as required. When the show has been edited to everyone's satisfaction, the preview is recorded onto a standard three-quarter-inch tape and saved for viewing or reference. One tape-based editor is the Ediflex®.

Figure 16-2 The Lightworks™ random-access editor, another popular random-access editor. Photo courtesy of Tektronix.

DISK-BASED SYSTEMS

Videodisks are similar to long-playing (LP) records. In disk-based random-access editors, the original footage is transferred to disk, and these disks are used as playbacks. The videodisk can find a particular frame of video extremely quickly. By using multiple disks, the editor can achieve the same effect as with video-based systems. The edits are always previewed and are recorded only when the whole show or segment is finished.

DIGITAL COMPUTER VIDEO EDITING SYSTEMS

The appeal of a digital computer random-access editor is obvious. This device transfers video images onto a computer hard drive, allowing the computer to access the disk-stored images very quickly. Some systems will also create DVE effects (enlarging, reducing, or spinning the image), sepia tone (a wash of color over a scene), and posterization effects (radical changes in the picture's chroma values). Icon-based computer screen interfaces are also employed to eliminate time code manipulation and other cumbersome technology that is involved in linear editing systems. As the cost of memory continues to drop, digital computer editing systems will become more affordable.

Garbage In/ Garbage Out

Though a random-access editor is fast, reliable, and flexible, if erroneous information is put into the system, erroneous information will flow out. Inputting footage with the wrong reel number, or losing the original master footage, is just as inefficient and costly as in a linear videotape system. It is extremely frustrating to have a supposedly immaculate EDL delivered to on-line with incorrect reel assignments. This causes a massive search for the correct reel, costing time and money. Tapes without time code that are input into the random-access editor will create an EDL with inaccurate time code references.

Another problem can arise from not checking the three-quarter-inch source input to the on-line material. If the on-line source is different from the off-line reels, offsets may be required, or a new source reel might have to be located, delaying the delivery of the program. It only takes a little time to double-check off-line material with on-line tapes. It saves hours of on-line time if the discrepancy is found before the session begins.

Organization and attention to detail is a requirement for every edit situation, no matter what system is being used. Any error during the labeling of a reel will cause massive problems later.

Creativity versus Speed

Every year some major motion picture is cited in terms of how fast it was brought from production to the screen. Editors and other postproduction professionals read these press releases and sigh. Hundreds of people worked long hours into the night trying to accomplish the impossible. Random-access editors do not create more time for editing. On the contrary, because more options are available, there are more editorial choices; thus the creative process takes longer. The word processor does not make the creative process of writing any quicker. The creative process is helped by technology, but it does not make the process faster.

THE RANDOM-ACCESS CONFUSION

As with any emerging technology, there are various approaches to a single challenge. There are numerous random-access editing systems being used in the video and feature film postproduction arenas. Each machine has its individual strengths and weaknesses. You should consider each system carefully before using it, just as you would examine any off- or on-line editing bay. There are, as in the early days of videotape editing, two or three companies that are leading the way in this field. However, as with all electronic systems, today's leader can be tomorrow's has-been. It is a good idea to keep abreast of the current leaders in the field.

THE POWER OF RANDOM-ACCESS EDITING

Random-access editing is unlike traditional tape editing. Search and preview times are dramatically reduced or virtually eliminated. Various systems may operate differently, but their goal and ultimate impact are the same: to foster more creative and efficient editing by minimizing obtrusive technology and making the process truly interactive. Random-access systems currently target off-line editing, but this will change as technology continues to evolve.

Most random-access systems do not require extensive time code manipulation. They operate via relatively intuitive icon- and cursor-based computer screen interfaces. Real-time picture displays and dynamic graphic diagrams of the work in progress facilitate visualization and decision-making, as opposed to traditional reliance upon representative time code numbers, creating an editing environment that encourages experimentation. Initial editing decisions can easily be corrected or abandoned.

All successful random-access editing systems maintain accurate, clean EDLs in their memories. Many also convert video footage to film key numbers.

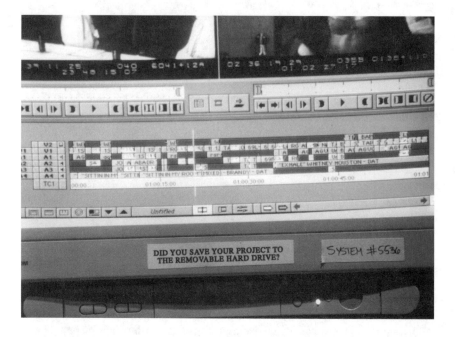

Figure 16-3 A closeup of the Avid Media Composer® time line. Note the two tracks of video and four tracks of audio. Photo by Sean Sterling, courtesy of New Wave Entertainment.

Although early random-access systems were expensive, prices of subsequent generations have dropped dramatically. (Prices range between $20,000 and $100,000.)

The Future Is Here

Random-access editing will do to tape what tape did to film. It will take some time, but eventually videotape will disappear. Avid® is marketing a random-access news system. A large video server holds news footage in memory, and editing stations are used to cut the day's news program. The footage could be sent by microwave from the field, edited, then broadcast while the reporter is doing his live remote.

Hundreds of feature films have already been cut on these random-access machines. By using a 24-frames-per-second image rate, all frames are accessed and not duplicated (as in film-to-tape transfers at 30 frames per second).

Figure 16-4　The Pioneer™ Laser Recorder. This read-many/write-many laser disk recorder may change the video editing market by replacing tape with disks. Individual frames can be recorded or erased. The playback deck can be operated like a video deck and programmed to freeze, dissolve, or play in forward or reverse. With its quick access time, it could also be used as a random-access editing device. Photo courtesy of the Pioneer Corporation.

Computers have made typewriters obsolete, and are probably going to eliminate videotape as well. As long as the cost of computer memory continues to drop, more and more random-access editing systems will replace older linear editing bays.

Figure 16-5 The off-line edit bay—a working random-access edit bay. The three-quarter videotape deck is to load audio, video, and time code into the computer as well as to record the output. A mixer controls the output of the computer to the three-quarter.

An Example of a Random-Access Edit Session

The commercial has to be on the air tomorrow morning. Broadcast air-time has been bought. The client is waiting. The spot has to be created and then on-lined today and dubbed overnight. The production crew has returned from their grueling shoot. A three-quarter-inch window dub has been made of the original material. It is time to edit.

The three-quarter-inch tape is transferred (digitized) into the random-access editor. During this process, time code, picture, and audio are transferred into the computer. The three-quarter-inch tape, the original footage, and now the digitized footage, all contain the same label information. The original footage is sent to the on-line facility. Other footage and support material (graphics, logs, pre-built effects, and character generator material) have also been sent on ahead to the on-line facility. These materials have already been put into the editor. We have digitized the picture in AVR6e (level of digitization). This is an off-line-quality picture. If we were going to use the random-access editor as the on-line editor, we would input the images into the computer at the highest resolution—in the case of this computer, AVR75.

The off-line edit session begins. We create one video track and five sound tracks in the time line (we'll need two tracks for audio because the music is in stereo). Narration and sync sound bites are placed onto tracks one and two, creating the framework of the commercial. Picture is carried along on the video track as sync sound is placed. Several music segments are cut into a music bed that builds to a climax. Since we input the audio at maximum quality, it will be output onto a DAT (digital audio tape) and used in the final commercial mix, so careful attention must be paid to each edit.

Now, picture edits are made. Cutaways are placed over the narrator's lines and the jump cuts that were created by cutting the performers' narration together. The editor works frantically, trying different combinations of edits, saving each version that she likes. Finally, she has two similar, but different versions of the commercial. The in-house producer cannot make up his mind which he likes best. Luckily the facility has a fiber-optic line that feeds directly to the client's office. The two spots are played over the fiber and viewed in the client's office across town. The client makes several minor changes in the second choice. They are accomplished in a matter of fifteen minutes. Remember, so far, no videotape has been used in the editing process, except the three-quarter-inch tape put into the random-access computer.

Another fiber session results in a final approval. Two three-quarter-inch dubs are made of the approved spot. A DAT of all five audio tracks (narrator, dialogue, effects, and both tracks of the stereo music) is made. One of the three-quarter-inch tapes is sent to the sound facility. The second three-quarter-inch tape, an EDL disk, and a printout are sent to the on-line facility. Everything but the temporary (temp) narrator is used in the finished audio commercial. The footage is on-lined. The spot is first finished without titles. A dub of this is sent to the sound facility as a final check for sync. While the audio mix is being finalized, the textless spot is now used as a playback and graphics (prices and disclaimers) are placed.

When completed, the commercial is again fibered to the client in his office across town. Picture is approved. The D2 master is dubbed for protection. The original tape is sent to the audio facility and laid back with final audio. Another fiber session results in final approval. This final version is cloned (a digital copy of the original is created in a digital-to-digital edit). This clone is delivered to an uplink facility and satellitted to a dubbing facility in the midwest. At the dubbing facility the commercial is copied to many delivery formats (one-inch, D2, Betacam, etc.) and overnighted to over 400 stations for broadcast the next morning.

A linear editing system might be able to meet the extreme deadline of the above example, but the ease with which changes can be made, the accurate EDL, and the high-quality audio output all combine to make the off-line technically painless and the on-line as easy as possible.

On-Line Random Access

Dozens of shows have been on-lined within the random-access computer. More will come. The visual quality of the random-access editor approaches that of D2. Random access will be the standard method of video on-line; it is just a matter of when. Again, the tools the editor uses will continue to change, but the task will not. Organization, conceptualization, and selecting shots and audio that serve the show's audience and purpose will continue to be the editor's ultimate goal no matter what machines are used.

SUMMARY

The ability of random-access editing to nearly instantaneously access video and audio has been commercially proven. Existing editing systems will continue to expand and improve along with the technology. However, garbage in, garbage out. Information put into the computer must be accurate. It is of no use to have a perfect EDL in terms of time code, with erroneous reel assignments. Expensive editing systems do not eliminate the need to be precise, accurate, and detail-oriented.

17

The On-Line Edit

An on-line edit session can be as simple as performing a single cut or it can involve thousands of edits. In this chapter, we will look at the on-line edit from an operational standpoint and explain what happens during the session.

A proper on-line edit cannot be performed if the person running the equipment does not know how it works. Trying to learn how a particular controller performs during an edit session obviously detracts from the editing process. Practice is the only way to become familiar with an edit system, but an editor should know how the system operates before attempting to edit a project on it.

If a switcher is being used during the on-line edit, the video inputs must be in the proper phase relationship with each other. In larger facilities, a tape operator or engineer performs this function, but in smaller facilities, editors might be required to do this chore themselves. For more on system timing, see Chapter 4.

BEFORE THE SESSION

Before starting the editing process, the editor must make sure that the audio levels are properly aligned. A 0-dB tone sent from the mixer or playback tape should read 0 dB on the record deck during a test record or when you check the input signal on the record machine in E-to-E mode. The audio test tone should also read 0 dB on the record machine playback VU meter. Finally, audio monitors and mixer should be properly balanced before the session begins.

Another pre-session task is to make sure that all color monitors are set properly. If there are multiple color monitors in the edit bay, they should be set up in the same way to avoid confusion over which monitor is correct. Many edit rooms have only one color monitor, so the question of which one is correct never arises.

The editor should also check that all the necessary equipment is in the editing room and that the editing system can access all those machines. The editor should have a list of what the client needs, to help make sure that all equipment ordered is operating.

THE SESSION

Once the record tape is loaded into the record machine and the room has been properly set up, the on-line session can begin. The first edit is usually bars and tone, the reference for later playback of the tape. A black space is then recorded so that a video slate can be inserted later.

During the on-line session, the editor must attend to many details. The following sections explore common areas of concern for an editor during a typical on-line session.

The Audience

Each program has an intended audience, and the on-line editor must be aware of both the audience and the client's expectations of the finished product from the beginning. A simple show on tax preparation does not have to be a dazzling display of digital effects, but another type of presentation might require careful use of such effects.

Slates

One of an editor's most important tasks is making sure that every videotape created during the on-line session has video identification (a slate) and that paper labels are affixed to each box and reel. This simple attention to organization makes keeping track of jobs much easier.

Audio Levels

As mentioned earlier, audio is a very important aspect of any visual project. Audio levels should be carefully monitored, and each audio edit should flow smoothly into the next. If a show is to be viewed on a television with small speakers, it is a good idea to listen to the edited master through that type of speaker, rather than the large studio speakers often found in on-line rooms.

Smaller speakers often mask annoying hisses and hums that originate at location shooting. If the show will be broadcast over a large speaker system, careful attention should be paid to the audio quality of all edits.

If the show will be sent to a professional sweetening facility (see Chapter 18), audio should be recorded without equalization, at full volume, and with at least one-second heads and tails if possible. This gives the sweetening engineer ample room to cross-fade the audio.

Color Balance

Studio productions require few, if any, adjustments once the color bars have been properly set up. A good way to align color bars on a playback tape is to create a hard-edged horizontal wipe at the switcher between the switcher's color bars and the color bars on the playback tape. The playback bars are then adjusted at the TBC to match the switcher's color bars. Location shoots, however, usually require extensive adjustments because of fluctuations in natural lighting. The on-line editor should pay close attention to the video levels indicated on the scopes. An improperly recorded signal might look great on the video monitor but actually be beyond the recording capability of the videotape machine.

Figure 17-1 A DVW-500 Digital Betacam recorder. Betacam is a popular small-format recording and editing medium.

Each shot should be balanced with the next. Facial tones and the video and chroma values of the sky and background should match as well as possible, allowing for an easy transition for the eye.

List Management

It pays to keep a clean EDL while performing the on-line edit. If a shot must be changed later, a clean EDL makes this change much easier. Having a simple video-only insert erase part of an expensive and time-consuming effect because a record OUT point was not cleaned can be very discouraging, both for the editor and for the client.

To avoid potential trouble, an editor should make sure that the on-line EDL accurately reflects the edits on the record master. Editors working with control track systems often forget that there might be changes, even after the editing session is over. These changes might require that the on-line edit be repeated. Without proper notes about where the original edits came from, reconstructing an editing sequence can be extremely difficult.

Key Levels

Problems can occur in key levels. It is good practice to keep white levels at no more than 95%, and if color is being keyed into small letters, the editor should avoid oversaturating the color. Oversaturation, especially with small letters, causes ringing or buzzing in the letters (see the Glossary).

Spelling

An editor should double-check all titles and credits with either the client or a dictionary. It is frustrating to have to reedit a section of a show because a name was misspelled or a location was keyed in with a typographical error. The editor should check anything that he or she is not absolutely sure is spelled correctly. Editors often create textless portions of programs, which are then used as a playback source. Then changes in graphics do not require extensive reediting.

Those Little Red Buttons

On the bottom of three-quarter-inch cassettes is a little red button, or at least a hole where there used to be one. If this button is removed from the cassette, the cassette is protected from accidental erasure by a record machine. The cassette can still be erased by a strong magnetic field, such as that generated by a bulk eraser. The red button must be in place to record on the cassette and should be removed when the edit session is completed.

Record inhibit tabs can also be found on the back of VHS tapes. There are record inhibit switches on D1, D2, D3, DCT, and Betacam tapes as well.

Time Considerations

Fast editors are always in demand, as the ability to complete a project in a short amount of time is a plus when you consider the cost of an on-line session. But completing a session quickly at the cost of increased errors does not save time or money. Speed comes with experience, but speed for speed's sake is worthless if the product is flawed.

Although many editors are capable of editing efficiently for hours at a stretch, errors can occur when an editor becomes fatigued. Some companies frown on their editors taking regularly scheduled breaks, but a walk around the block or simply getting up for a drink of water can make a big difference in editing quality.

All machines can and will fail. When something goes wrong, a professional editor usually tries to help the engineer in any way possible. The editor might also be able to work on other parts of the show while waiting for a particular piece of equipment to be repaired.

Chroma Levels

When the final product will be distributed on three-quarter-inch tape or consumer-quality half-inch tape, the editor should be careful to keep chroma levels down. Too much chroma can cause electronic tearing (where the chroma appears to smear) on half-inch formats. Red is the first color to show signs of deterioration in multiple tape generations.

Editing into Existing Masters

When you are editing into a video master that was created on a different machine, you must match video and audio levels to the old recording. Some machines are not compatible with others. An engineer should be consulted about using a tape that was originally edited on a different machine.

Glitches

Glitches (see the Glossary), video hits (any abnormal flaw in an image), and bad edits come from a variety of sources, including a large dropout, irregularity in a tape's control track, a power fluctuation during a recording, poorly recorded time code, or a machine that was not locked up when the record machine went into edit. The glitch also could be recorded into the video on the playback material. If an editor spots a glitch during an on-line edit, he or she should stop immediately and find out whether the problem can be corrected before continuing. If the editor spots a glitch during an off-line edit, he or she should check the master footage as soon as possible to see whether the glitch is on the original. If the glitch is on the master and cannot be viewed, a cutaway or other footage might be used in the problem area.

Once a glitch has been recorded onto the record master, the only way to remove it is to replace it with another shot, assuming that the glitch is on the playback. If the glitch is due to a damaged record tape, the editor has two alternatives. He or she can copy the edited master onto a new record tape and reedit the damaged area, or start editing the program from the beginning. The choice often depends on the format used for the record master. One-inch and two-inch formats can afford to lose a generation, but half-inch and three-quarter-inch formats degrade rapidly in the copying process. Digital tape can be duplicated with no signal degradation.

If the glitch is on a source tape, and the record tape is D2, you might be able to freeze the previous frame from the record tape in the switcher, and if the glitch is not too big, in a preread edit, use the frozen frame and damaged frame, combine the two in the switcher, and possibly repair the damage.

Multiple Generations

With the commercial acceptance of D1, D2, and component editing, the number of times a program can be duplicated has increased dramatically, depending on the format and signal path. Generally, the more expensive the format, the greater the number of copies that can be made without noticeable degradation. D1, when contained in a component digital path, can be duplicated hundreds of times, while three-quarter-inch tape can only withstand a few copies. The complexity of a project often determines the format of choice. A 30-second commercial with many effects may be edited for weeks on D1, while a syndicated game show may be recorded only one generation away from the camera original.

Television network video is usually crisp and clear because a great deal of money is spent to keep the equipment in prime condition. The table on page 217 indicates the number of generations an editor can go without seeing too much of a loss, assuming he or she starts out with network-quality video.

	Number of Generations	
Format	*Average*	*Maximum*
One-inch Type C	4–6	5–7
One-inch Type B	7–9	8–10
Two-inch Quad	3–4	7–9
Three-quarter-inch	2–3	4–6
D1*	40–60	250+
DCT*	40–60	250+
D2*	10–20	100–120
D3*	10–20	100–120

*Assume digital-to-digital dub or edit.

Match Frames

Match frames are edits in which video from a previous edit is matched and continued. The computer editor and time code make the match frame possible.

A match frame must be invisible to the eye. If the video, setup, hue, chroma level, and blanking are not exactly the same on both sides of the match frame edit, the change will be visible. Every match frame should be checked both visually and on the scopes. If a shift is recorded onto the master tape, the only way to remove it is to redo the edit.

Audio Sync

Several commonly used video devices can delay the video, which can result in a lip sync problem. Frame stores, for example, are electronic devices that synchronize video signals by storing one or more frames of video. The stored frames are then fed out to a system. This is the result when video is processed through a DVE. A one-frame delay is usually not noticeable, but if several generations are made through these devices, the lip sync should be checked carefully.

AFTER THE SESSION

It is always a good idea to watch a show after the editing process has been completed. While in the throes of an editing session, the editor can easily miss errors in content and technical problems. Duplicating a faultily edited master wastes everyone's time, so an editor should always make a final check of the tape before making copies.

THE EDITOR-CLIENT RELATIONSHIP

The client is often present during the on-line edit, and the editor should do everything possible to establish a good working relationship. The first meeting with the client is probably the most important. How the editor reacts to the client makes a lasting impression. Certainly the editor should not have to baby-sit the client during a session, but a brief description of the bay might be in order before the session begins. If the client understands what is going on, he or she can usually be more helpful during the session.

What if the client insists on making a terrible edit? Some editors try to offer an acceptable compromise, while others either make the edit and then modify it after the client leaves or refuse to go any further. The editor should remember that he or she is being employed by the client and must weigh the consequences of being obstinate.

The client has responsibilities, too. Nothing is more frustrating to an editor than having to search reels for shots that do not exist or not having all the reels at hand. The client should make sure the editor has everything he or she needs for the session.

The client should also watch for dropped edits and watch the master monitor closely for edits that look wrong or off-color. The on-line session is the last chance to correct or improve a show. The client should take this opportunity to do so if a change is warranted.

SUMMARY

The on-line edit is a demanding process that requires the editor's eyes, ears, and brain to be at peak performance. It requires that everyone work together to produce the most entertaining and/or informative program possible.

PART V

Other Editing Processes

18

Audio Postproduction

All too often, the audio portion of a show is limited to what was recorded during production. In this type of program, the only sounds added during postproduction are likely to be laughter, audience reactions, or perhaps a short piece of music to connect scenes (often called a *sting*).

The use of stereo audio for television has emphasized the need for greater care and planning of audio in postproduction. Many people listen to television through their stereo systems. Film producers are keenly aware of the emotional impact that audio can have. Most filmed television programs have extensive music tracks. These shows also add effects in the background sound tracks. Feature films go to even greater lengths to heighten, enhance, and improve a movie's audio.

There are two ways to deal with multitrack audio shows, and the choice generally depends on the budget. The two methods are (1) mixing the audio in the editing bay and (2) sweetening.

MIXING AUDIO DURING THE VIDEO EDIT

The audio portion of some shows is mixed during the video editing session. This mixing process can be simplified if the record tape has two tracks of audio available. By monitoring the two audio channels through one speaker, the editor can get an effective audio mix during the on-line session. The advantage of two-track audio mixing is that music and effects can be recorded on one channel and the production audio on the other. If only one track of audio is available when two audio sources must be heard at once, the two sources must be mixed onto one channel. When this type of mix is recorded, the audio levels of the two sources are married together. This process is complicated further if a long piece of music must be present throughout a series of edits. Each edit now requires the music to be mixed at the same level.

With one-track audio editing, there is a method of gaining another track of audio for music and/or effects without going down another generation of video. However, this method requires going down two generations of audio. Once the show has been edited, a copy is made. This copy is then recorded onto the show master in an audio-only edit. While this is being done, another audio source (a reel-to-reel audio machine or an audio cassette player) is mixed with the copy of the show master. The dub of the original show must be in sync with the original edited master for this process to work correctly.

If two tracks of audio are available on the record tape, effects and music can be edited on one of the available tracks, but this method requires that the playback of the two tracks be set at the same level before attempting a mix. If more than two sources of audio are required on the music and effects track (sometimes called an M&E track), those sources must be mixed onto one track, or a procedure similar to the one described earlier can be followed. First, a dub of the master is made. The effects and music are then edited onto the two audio tracks of the dub (erasing the copy of the edited master's audio). This audio build is then recorded onto the M&E channel of the original edited master, mixing the two sources from the dub as the edit is made. Again, this method requires that the edit be audio-only and in sync with the record master.

Digital formats have four available audio tracks. If you are mixing in the on-line edit, an ideal situation would be to separate the audio into: narration, dialogue, music, and effects (one on each separate track.) This way alterations can be made to one of the elements without affecting the other three.

Each production's audio needs are different, and the manner in which they are dealt with changes with the production. A producer may choose to go to an audio company and create a final mix on quarter-inch audio tape, which is then transferred to the record master. The audio for commercials is often done this way.

SWEETENING

Sweetening is the placement and mixing of audio on an audio multitrack machine or digital audio workstation (DAW).

The first step in sweetening is to edit the program onto a video master in a normal video on-line session. The edited master could be on any standard video format. The digital formats have the added advantage of four available channels for recording audio. These allow for recording overlapping dialogue, music, or effects on different channels, giving the audio mixer handles (additional material at the beginning and end of each edit) for creating audio fades or for multiple audio cues.

All audio is recorded at full level without fades or equalization and with ample heads and tails to allow the sweetening engineer to cross-fade the audio tracks. The audio edited onto the master includes all production sound, as well as other effects that are available on source videotapes. Often dialogue is recorded on one of the audio tracks and effects and music on the other.

The edited master is then brought to the sweetening facility, where the audio from the edited master is transferred to a multitrack audio machine. During this process, called a *layover*, the time code from the edited master is also copied onto the multitrack machine. In addition, a three-quarter-inch videocassette copy of the master is recorded (see Figure 18-1). Some digital audio workstations have the ability to record digital picture as well as audio.

Once these preparations have been made, prerecorded music, prerecorded or live voice-over narration, effects, and background sounds are recorded on the remaining tracks of the multitrack tape. The process of transferring all of the necessary original elements and other audio information onto the multitrack or DAW is called *prelay*. Prelay also includes editing the audio portions to usable lengths when placing them onto the mixing medium (multitrack tape or DAW). When the bulk of the audio has been placed onto the multitrack, the mixing process begins (see Figure 18-2).

There are usually four final tracks in a project: dialogue, effects, narration, and music. Each of these four final tracks is built onto its own discrete track by transferring the prelay information to the specifically designated track. When transferred to its final track, the sound level is adjusted and, if needed, effects such as echo and equalization are added. While the mixing and prelay occur, the three-quarter-inch copy of the program is played in sync with the multitrack or DAW. The three-quarter-inch tape is used to prevent possible damage to the master during the sweetening process.

Once the audio tracks have been recorded on the multitrack tape, a mixed version of the audio is recorded on another track of the multitrack tape. This track, which contains the final sweetened audio, is then transferred to the edited master, erasing the original audio. This process, called a *layback*, is accomplished by locking the time code of the record master and the multitrack together and performing an audio-only edit on the edited master.

DIGITAL AUDIO TAPE (DAT)

Digital audio tape (DAT) stores audio on tape using digital encoding rather than analog encoding. As with other digital recording media, DAT can be copied over multiple generations with little effect on the original recording quality.

Because of DAT's small physical size and high quality, it was quickly accepted in the audio world. DAT is used for recording and transferring material from one audio facility to another. Broadcast-quality DAT machines use time

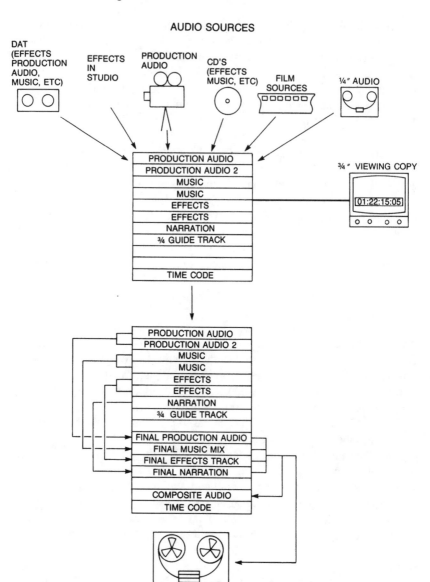

Figure 18-1 The audio path for multitrack audio mixing (sweetening). The original tracks are transferred to final tracks, but not mixed together. This process allows the mixer to return to his or her original audio and make changes. Saving the four separate audio tracks (production dialogue, music, effects, and narration) allows for foreign distribution, as well as other audio functions, such as remixing for syndication or revisions.

Figure 18-2 A video sweetening suite. Note the large mixing console in front of the two men as well as the window dub being projected in the front of the room. Photo by Gil Smith, courtesy of Compact Video Services, Burbank, California.

code and accept input from edit controllers. With this equipment, multiple generations of audio edits can be made without loss of quality. Another digital tape format, besides DAT, is called a "DA88."

THE DIGITAL AUDIO WORKSTATION (DAW)

As random-access editors and digital videotape have revolutionized the video picture-editing process, digital audio has changed the way audio is handled in postproduction.

DAWs store audio information on computer hard disks and are then able to perform mixes within the computer without rolling tape until output is required. The DAW controls equalization, compression, volume, echo, and track slippage (see the Glossary). Some DAWs can generate effects and music. Feature film companies and television producers use DAWs to increase audio postproduction efficiency. The speed of digital mixing is impressive, and as more DAWs are manufactured, the cost of these extraordinary devices will drop.

COMBINING DIGITAL AND ANALOG AUDIO MIXING

With random-access editing stations' output used as a final source of finished audio and with DAT's editing capabilities, the boundaries of mixing and editing are becoming blurred. DAT can be used as an input source to a 24-track tape or

Figure 18-3 A Senaria™ Digital Audio Workstation. Veteran operator David Cantu is sitting in front of the automated faders. Just above his shoulder is the master monitor for the DAW. To the left of the master monitor are the audio controls for EQ (equalization) and compression. David's hand is holding a light pen. Just below the clock (center) is the video monitor. Bottom right is a DAT machine. Photo courtesy of New Wave Entertainment, taken by Sean Sterling.

to a DAW. Some production companies use the audio output of the random-access editor transferred to DAT as a final audio source. Some DAWs are used for prelaying effects and building tracks rather than actual mixing. The combinations are endless, from using multiple three-quarter-inch sources to creating a track on tape, to digitally mixing multiple tracks on DAWs. However, no matter what equipment is used to construct the four basic audio tracks, effective audio mixing depends on the human ear. Subjective and selective combinations of many different sounds create an aural experience that blends with the visual aspect of the program.

AUDIO COMPRESSION, LIMITERS, AND EQUALIZATION

There are three major areas of audio manipulation beyond the obvious adjustments of placement and relative volume. The first area, *equalization*, is the selective alteration of a specific frequency within a given sound. For instance, if a sound had a hiss, proper equalization could isolate, then reduce or eliminate the hiss. At the other end of the audio spectrum, a thin voice could be made stronger by increasing the low-end or bass frequencies.

The other areas of audio manipulation—compression and limiting—are similar, yet different concepts. *Compression* has two elements: the threshold and the ratio of compression. A threshold is a level at which compression is to take place. The ratio is the amount of compression that will take place above the threshold. A 4:1 ratio will reduce a sound that is 4 dB above the threshold to 1 dB above it. The *limiter* also has a threshold, but limiting, unlike compressing, just cuts off any sounds above a certain volume level.

EFFECTS

Audio effects can enhance a program's production value immensely. Watch a television drama. There are literally hundreds of sounds added to the audio track that are not in the picture: sirens, cars passing, medical equipment beeping, police radios talking, etc. There are many types of sounds that can be added to the track to make a program much more believable. Many of the sound effects that are used come from libraries. These are series of tapes or CDs that contain sound effects for an unbelievable number of events. It is often worth the time and cost to purchase these libraries. Thousands of dollars of perceived production value can be added to your program for only a few hundred dollars.

LIP SYNCING

Lip syncing to playback audio can cause problems in the editing bay. The speed of a turntable or reel-to-reel machine will fluctuate unless it is crystal-controlled (the machine's motor is "slaved" to the oscillation of a crystal). If a typical home reel-to-reel machine is used for lip sync audio playback, the speed of the playback will change throughout the session. When matching the action to the one take of the song, it will be almost impossible to keep the picture in sync with the audio.

If lip syncing is planned, you should use a crystal-controlled playback deck. In the editing session, when the song is being recorded onto the edited master, it is best to use the same type of machine used in the lip sync recording session.

If a crystal-controlled machine is not available, the song could be transferred to videotape and the tape used for playback during the production. When the piece is edited, that same videotape could be used for the audio source on the record master.

LACK OF AUDIO EQUIPMENT

Most video editing bays are not fully equipped to deal with audio problems. Video equipment is, as a general rule, more expensive than audio equipment, which means it will cost more to rent time at a video facility than at an audio facility. Although larger video editing companies often have sweetening facilities, many smaller companies do not. Similarly, some audio companies are designed to deal with audio only.

When you are working on a simple show with only a few music selections to lay in under the production audio track, a video facility might be fine to use for the final audio. If, however, extensive equalization is required for the production audio or the production requires numerous sound effects, sweetening might be the most cost-effective way to deal with the audio portion of the show.

USING MULTITRACK FORMATS DURING THE ON-LINE EDIT

The multitrack audio machine is a tape recorder with many audio tracks available. As more productions begin treating audio with the respect it deserves, more on-line editing houses will offer multitrack audio editing or will access the four tracks available in the digital formats. Using video editors to control audio tape machines is not a new idea, but it is not standard practice. More sophisticated audio editing equipment is becoming available as the need for better audio is recognized more widely.

EXTRA AUDIO TRACKS

If an editor is using one-inch or three-quarter-inch tape as a record master and plans on using a sweetening facility, he or she can gain extra audio tracks by making a submaster (an exact copy of the original edited tape, including time code). This frees up two more tracks that can be used for audio. The submaster is brought to the sweetening company, and the two extra tracks are laid over to the multitrack. This method allows more exact placement of original production audio against the edited visuals and can save time and money during the sweetening session.

SUMMARY

Audio is probably the most ignored and/or forgotten aspect of a video production. With a little work, audio can add more excitement and interest to a program than you would have believed possible.

19

Editing Film on Video

OVERVIEW

In the early days of video postproduction, the film industry looked down on electronic devices. Their poor image quality, unreliability, and linearity did not appeal to the movie industry. Now the film industry uses video daily. This includes such technology and methods as *video assist* (an on-set video recording of what the film camera exposes on the negative), cutting on random-access editors, mixing on DAWs, and creating effects on D1 and electronic graphics systems.

VIDEO VERSUS ELECTRONICS

Video is only one type of electronic image. Many other devices in numerous configurations can also store electronic images. This chapter deals with three types of electronic images: video, random-access computer images, and proprietary computer images.

THE GROWING CASE FOR FILM FINISH

Several years ago, television productions shot on film were finished on videotape. The major stumbling block to this process was that to deliver a PAL master for foreign television distribution (a major TV program revenue source), either an electronic conversion had to be made or a separate PAL telecine and editing session had to be performed. The electronic conversion was less than pleasing aesthetically. Duplicate telecine and editing processes were expensive. As a result, random-access editing, which produced an accurate film negative list, was embraced by some film producers. The program was finished on film, including titles and opticals. The finished film was then transferred in a telecine session to video tape (see Figure 19-1).

Figure 19-1 An Ursa® film-to-tape telecine manufactured by the Rank Cintel Corporation™. This high-end transfer machine can feed and color-correct a video signal from a film element. Note that the left side of the film reel, the supply reel, is nearly full. Photo by Sean Sterling.

THE TELECINE PROCESS

Before any film can be edited electronically, the film image and audio must be transferred to an electronic medium. In most applications, this medium is videotape. Even if the footage will end up in a random-access editor, tape is used as an intermediate step. Telecine machines transfer film to tape.

Top-of-the-line telecine machines can perform numerous tasks. They usually employ a CRT to expose the film onto three video pick-up tubes or charged coupled devices (CCDs—see the Glossary). Mirror images, reverse play, zooms, and image reductions are commonly accomplished in the telecine session.

Several considerations within the telecine environment should be addressed. The first is key code. *Key code* is the Kodak™ bar-code system that records key numbers on film. An additional piece of equipment is needed to read key code during the telecine transfer, but it is an ideal way to encode video footage with visual key numbers. If key code is unavailable, key numbers can still be burned into the video picture. Inserting key numbers into the footage enables film negative cutters or other personnel to quickly determine the original source of the visual footage.

Time code is a second consideration. At the time of the telecine transfer, time code is recorded onto the videotape. If a film workprint is being transferred, a log correlates the videotape's time code with the original negative's key numbers. A sync point, usually the closing of the clapboard, is used as a common reference point. These key numbers are then entered into the random-access computers. In addition to key numbers and time code, the final medium is another vital concern. The medium determines the level at which all film-to-tape transfers will be made. If the final product will be film finish, the film-to-tape transfer will not be a critical process because the final film timing and color balance will be determined at the film lab. If the video footage is to be used for a video finish, the color and brightness of the film transfer merit careful attention. The best telecine operators (called *colorists*) maintain an extremely high standard. However, every client has his or her own look. Music videos are transferred with a different eye than a wildlife documentary is.

Other issues also affect the telecine process. On wide-screen footage, which area of the screen should be shown, or should the footage be letter boxed? (See "Television's Four-to-Three Ratio" in Chapter 20.) What type of audio is to be transferred to tape? Does music or dialogue need to be transferred? Should the tracks be mixed or recorded onto separate tracks (narration, dialogue, music, and effects)?

THREE-TWO PULLDOWN

Television runs at 30 frames per second. Film is usually shot at 24 frames. This six-frame difference is resolved by repeating fields of visual information, a process called *three-two pulldown*. For every other frame of film, one *field* of video is repeated. Over the course of one second, the six frames are filled. Some producers, knowing that they will edit and finish on videotape, shoot the film at 30 frames per second to eliminate three-two pulldown (see Figure 19-2).

When you are converting time code back to film key numbers, occasionally the three-two pulldown process creates edits on frames that do not exist in film. In this case, the negative cutter has to adjust the film edits to accommodate the duplicated fields (see Figure 19-3).

Some random-access editors can edit at 24 frames per second, which eliminates the need for three-two pulldown. Other editing systems can calculate the three-two pulldown rate if the operator enters information about the first frame of the telecine transfer, specifically where the three- or two-field transfer occurs. However, the process of transferring material into the computer editor differs for each random-access machine. You should thoroughly examine and test any editing system before committing a project to it.

An error may occur when using 30-frame videotape to edit 24-frame film. For every other film frame, an extra frame of video is created through the three-two pulldown process. If both the beginning and ending frames contain a manufactured field, there are now two video fields of nonexistent footage, the

THREE-TWO PULL DOWN

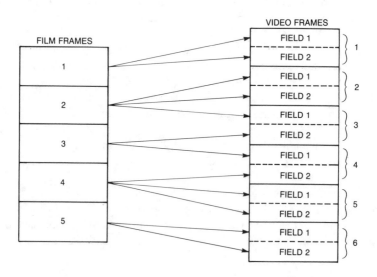

Figure 19-2 In three-two pulldown, the 24-frame-per-second film footage is transferred to 30-frame-per-second videotape. This is accomplished by repeating a field of picture every other film frame. Four frames of film are converted to five frames of video: 24 film frames result in 30 video frames.

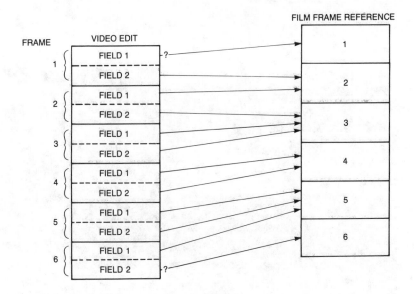

Figure 19-3 Considering the three-two pulldown that occurs during film-to-tape transfer, there is the possibility of missing a frame when conforming the film to the off-line workprint. In the example from Figure 19-2, if key numbers displayed in the window dub are used to cut the film negative without physically checking the edit, the cut negative will be one frame (2 video fields) short. In many video-to-film conversions, a kinescope (video-to-film transfer) is created to ensure that edits follow the video precisely.

equivalent of one frame. In a video finish, these extra frames are of no concern. But in a film finish, the negative cutter will have to add one film frame during the negative process to keep proper sync (see Figures 19-2 and 19-3).

OTHER ADVANTAGES AND DISADVANTAGES OF ELECTRONIC EDITING

Editing a film project on a random-access system is fast and exciting. There are no *trims* (remainders of shots that are not cut into the workprint). Random-access editing is visual rather than character oriented; pictures are cut, not time code numbers. There are some drawbacks to the electronic process, however. For example, feature films require previews in movie houses, yet the electronic image cannot withstand expansion to a full screen. Often, feature film editors have to keep a current film workprint ready for screenings. Yet even with these drawbacks, electronic editing has become a common method of editing feature films.

Figure 19-4 The Montage random-access editor system. The left hand monitor is for editorial work, the right hand for picture viewing. Photo courtesy of the Montage group.

TWO STANDARD PATHS

Several standard paths use electronic editing to finish a project shot on film. The first method finishes the program on video and the second finishes on film. Each of these processes is under constant reevaluation. With nonstop development in all phases of electronics, any of the steps in either path could change in the near future.

FILM-TO-VIDEO FINISH

The first path, in which a program is finished on video, has two generally accepted finishing processes. One uses film-editing equipment; the other employs electronic editors.

Using Film-Editing Equipment

Conforming video to film keeps the creative editing tasks within the film process. Many producers and film companies are comfortable with film editing, and this method retains an established system. The film editor cuts the show on film. The workprint is struck from the original camera negative, and the program is edited. This process is illustrated in Figure 19-5. A final audio mix is completed once the workprint picture has been approved, using either electronic or film-style procedures (see Chapter 18). The combination of film workprint and final audio is often then transferred to video for intermediate reference viewing.

After you finalize the workprint, the film negative still needs to be transferred to video. There are two methods: either only selected takes are telecined, or the negative is cut by a negative cutter, and that final picture is transferred to video.

Cutting the Negative

Cutting the film negative retains the film-finishing aspect of editing, so that only color timing, effects, and titling are added in the video environment. The cut negative is telecined. Image manipulation and chroma keys are generally done during telecine. Titles, fades, wipes, and dissolves are created in an edit bay. If the negative has been cut to conform to the (film) workprint, this film negative is transferred to video and synchronized with the transfer of the video workprint and audio track. The audio portion of the program is finished at a sound facility, once the workprint is approved, in a standard dubbing process (that is, film style).

When there is more than one reel to edit, as with an hour-long drama, the several reels of cut negative are transferred to video and edited together to match the workprint. Titles may be added on a second pass, using the edited video master as a playback to preserve an untitled version of the show for later use in syndication. (The running time of a show is altered for syndication, usually requiring the original show to be shortened. Having an untitled master facilitates this editing process.)

Using Select Shots for On-Line Editing

Instead of cutting the negative, the production staff may choose to edit the program on-line. In this case, an off-line editing session typically precedes the on-line edit. The concept is to take a quick, one-shot run at the film footage, not spending the time to color-correct every shot. This footage is transferred to an off-line format, usually three-quarter-inch. The off-line edit is performed to locate the selected shots and create an EDL, thus saving time and money in the on-line and telecine sessions. If careful notes are taken (see Chapter 6), there are film-to-video computer programs that facilitate the process of finding original film footage. An ideal situation would be that the film footage was key coded,

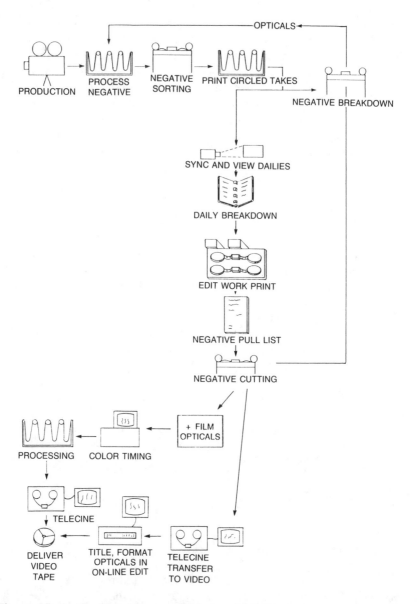

Figure 19-5 The film edit-to-tape finish route. Note that there are two choices once the workprint is approved: pursue the film process all the way through opticals, or alternatively, do the final picture conforming on-line. If there are many edits, an off-line edit is performed to locate all footage before going on-line.

and the footage numbers were burned into the off-line copy along with the time code. These numbers make locating the film much easier.

After you match the selected shots to the film negative, these selections are telecined and then edited on-line. Following the on-line edit, the audio portion of the program is finalized, using either digital or analog procedures at a video sweetening facility.

Once an edited film negative is transferred to NTSC-format video, it can be reproduced in PAL. After completing the NTSC version, a PAL version is recorded to a PAL videotape from the film negative. Then, the same edits that were performed in the NTSC editing session are repeated in the PAL editing environment. There are editing bays and editing machines that can be converted from NTSC to PAL. In this way, the film editing process is kept, yet the edited master can be delivered in excellent NTSC or PAL formats. The alternative has been to take the NTSC video master and convert the image to PAL, an inferior method, as discussed in Chapter 2.

Using Electronic Editing Equipment

Electronic editing produces EDLs, using either random-access systems or standard linear computer editing systems. These EDLs can be auto assembled in an on-line session like the one in Figure 19-6. Audio is usually sweetened in a multitrack environment or a DAW.

With electronic editing, the film footage is transferred to video with the intent to release on video. Thus, once the footage is transferred to the playback format (usually one-inch, DCT, Digital, BetaCam, D1, or D2), window dubs are struck for the off-line or random-access editing systems. Effects may be built in a separate edit session in the same way that opticals are built separately in normal film postproduction. The video effects can then be approved and inserted into the program as it is being built. An alternative is to create the effects during the on-line session. Simple effects such as fades, dissolves, or keys are often created on-line. Complicated effects, including paint box graphics, should be performed in a separate session.

ELECTRONIC EDIT-TO-FILM FINISH

Finishing a program on film allows for projection in movie houses or a return to video in a telecine session. This film-finish process, again, allows for transfers to PAL or other formats through telecine transfer (see Figure 19-7).

The film dailies (daily footage) are transferred to video with key numbers and time code correlation logged at the telecine session. The transfer is edited either linearly on a videotape editing system or, more often, on a random-access editing system. If at all possible, key numbers should be burned into the director's copy of the picture to help when conforming the film negative.

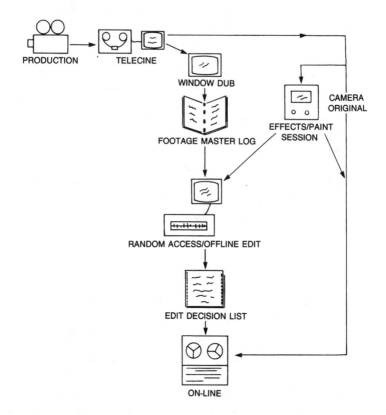

Figure 19-6 Electronic editing with a video finish. The window dubs refer to the telecine original footage for an auto assembly. Any effects created in on-line or graphics sessions are window-dubbed in the off-line session.

It should be noted at this point that, for single-camera productions, production footage should be organized in scenes. This approach ensures a logical place to record each new day's footage as it is brought to be transferred. If the transfers are made randomly, it becomes difficult to locate scenes during the editing process. Changing reels in the transfer process takes only a short amount of time, but it can save hours later when trying to locate a shot that was transferred, but not placed logically on the tape.

Once the program is cut and locked (approved), the editing system can produce an EDL and viewing copy. Some random-access editing systems can produce both a time code edit list and a key number list for conforming the film negative. A kinescope (see the Glossary) is often created for the negative cutter so he or she can have a film reference of the program.

Audio can be finished in either film (dubbing) or video (sweetening) style. Audio for most projects edited in a film style is completed by dubbing, but the DAW has been gaining favor in the film postproduction world, especially in

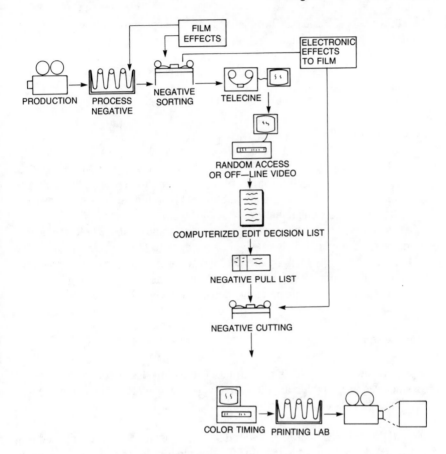

Figure 19-7 Electronic editing with a film finish. With a properly maintained key-number to time-code reference, film can be edited on video. The time code listing is then converted to key numbers for conforming.

trailer (the "coming attraction" promotion seen before the feature presentation in a movie) and commercial finishing.

ELECTRONIC FILM EFFECTS

In the past, the only way to create effects for movies was with optical printers. Video effects did not have the image quality for movie projection. Now D1 is being used for movie effects. There are several proprietary systems that expose D1 images onto film. In addition, effects can be created on large computers, then transferred to film. Early uses of electronics were seen in the movies *Ghost* and *Terminator 2*. Optically created effects are on the way out; electronic effects are here. Morphing (the changing of one shape into another) and everything from simple elimination of effects wires and telephone poles to building entire cities within the computer are commonplace. Examples of these types of effects exist in almost every movie released today, especially action/adventure movies.

THE FUTURE

With D1 and electronic effects systems, the merging of film and electronic technologies is an accepted fact. Film will continue to be the production medium of choice; however, the manipulation of these film images will more and more become electronic in nature.

A major portion of film effects are designed and executed electronically. Electronic editing is already of equal importance to film cutting. In the fall of 1995, the first totally digitally created film was released. Perhaps entire productions will be built in the computer, with actors merely performing in front of blue screens for later insertion into the electronic image.

SUMMARY

There are several ways to use electronics in the film postproduction process, all of which require transferring the film to video or to another electronic storage medium:

1. VIDEO FINISH—Film is edited and cut using traditional film-editing methods. Cut negative is transferred to video. Effects and titles are added during a video on-line edit session or in an optical printer.
2. VIDEO FINISH—Camera-original film negative is transferred to video for editing on an electronic system (linear or random-access). The resulting EDL is used to edit the program in a video on-line edit session. Effects and titling are created on-line.
3. FILM FINISH—In this process, film dailies are transferred to video for editing on an electronic system (linear or random-access). The resulting EDL is given to a negative cutter and the program is finished on film. Effects are created electronically or in an optical house.

In any of these situations, audio postproduction can be accomplished by sweetening (video-type audio finishing) or dubbing (film-style audio finishing).

20

Special Circumstances

This chapter addresses some special circumstances and explores some editing procedures not discussed thus far.

TELEVISION'S FOUR-TO-THREE RATIO

The television picture is in a four-to-three ratio. Transferring feature films to video often requires special care because movies are usually shot in a wide-screen format. That is why movies shown on television often have a mask at the top and bottom of the frame during the title sequences. A technique called *pan-and-scan* (see Figure 20-1) is used in the body of the film to keep the essential portion in the center of the screen.

Adjustments must also be made when still pictures are transferred to video. A tall, narrow picture or a thin, wide one will not fit properly in the television format. One method used to make the picture look right is to pan up or down. Another method is to shoot the whole picture and make a box wipe around the edge. This second method will show the whole picture but not fill the frame. A background color generated by a switcher is often used in this instance to enhance the presentation of the picture.

DUPLICATION

Misunderstandings in the video duplication process can be very costly. When making dubs of master material, the editor must make sure that there is a *submaster* (also called a *protection* or *safety* master) to back up the edited master

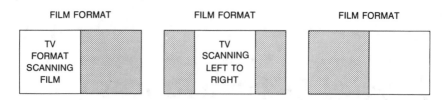

Figure 20-1   Diagram of the pan-and-scan concept used in transferring wide-format film to videotape. Because the television screen ratio differs from most feature film screens, the essential portions of the picture are scanned by the film-to-tape machine.

in the event something happens to the duplication master. In addition, the editor or producer must provide explicit instructions for the duplication company.

Making a submaster for duplication or protection is common practice. Too much money is spent on the production and editing to risk damage to the master, either in duplication or in additional editing. A protection copy is very inexpensive insurance.

Duplication runs of 100, 1,000 or even 2,500 copies of videotape projects are not unheard of, but heaven help the person who orders 100,000 copies of the wrong tape. To avoid such disasters, every aspect of the duplication process must be clearly explained to the duplication facility in writing.

PROTECTION

Making a photocopy of all EDLs is an important follow-up to any off-line edit, whether it is a computer, random-access, or control track process. The rates for off-line editing can be as low as $25 an hour or as high as $200 an hour. Whatever the cost, it is silly not to protect the list. A handwritten EDL can be photocopied in minutes, while a printout and disk can be easily duplicated.

It is also a good idea to photocopy the production notes. You should put the originals and copies of the notes and the EDLs in different places, which gives added protection from theft and accidents.

TAPE CONSIDERATIONS

What happens when a shot is on a tape that has no code or is at the head of the tape and there is not enough preroll to edit the shot? Or what if the tape just in front of the shot is damaged and cannot be played? You can transfer the section to another time-coded tape. In this way, enough code can be recorded at the head of the shot to allow for editing, every frame of the good portion can be accessed, and any damaged tape will be played only once.

BAD BLANKING

Bad (wide) blanking can occur in several ways. Blanking is created by the original transfer source, such as a film-to-tape telecine or video camera. Even if the original blanking is perfectly acceptable, a poorly adjusted playback machine can play back the video improperly, resulting in wide or unacceptable blanking.

Blanking problems can also occur when a shot is taken from VHS or from some other source over which the editor has no control. In these cases, if the blanking is wide (unacceptable according to FCC guidelines), the video must be expanded with a digital effects device.

HOME COMPUTERS

Home computers have permeated video postproduction. Computer-controlled effects devices, editing systems, and animation programs can create or edit material on videotape.

Logging/List Manipulation Programs

These computer programs can manipulate simple VTR functions and mark time code locations for logging and building EDLs. Such off-line screening can result in a rough EDL that can be brought to off-line or on-line editing sessions. Log creation is simplified, and with detailed logging, a word processor or log program can search for specific lines or locations. Data bases and word processors can be designed as logging tools for preedit lists. Data bases can be extremely helpful in documentary shows because a single shot can be logged for a variety of aspects, such as dialogue, audio effects, characters, location, and reel number.

This editor uses a data base to keep track of the numerous projects that are kept in storage, as well as titles of various programs stored on long video tapes. Sorting this list alphabetically makes finding a program much easier.

DIGITAL EFFECTS

Some digital effects generators have more capabilities than others. As a rule, the more a machine can do, the more expensive it is to rent or buy. It is best to become familiar with the tools available and the price of each tool before booking time and beginning to edit.

The most recent industry trend is to create noticeable or visually stunning effects, often by using paint box devices. Effects are used less and less as transitional devices and more as carefully planned multiple images, composited in digital editing suites. Bumpers and show opens can cost tens of thousands of dollars and take weeks to create. Digital effects machines that can animate three dimensions with motion are used for these complicated, usually short, visual pieces. Original video can be input into the device, then effected. Occasionally the effect is created completely within the computer.

Digital effects can be exciting and innovative when the footage is already moving within the frame (a pan, tilt, zoom, or dolly heightens the look of an effect) or when the effect is used in an especially creative way.

GRAPHICS

Although programs do not usually consist entirely of graphics, these elements are used in almost every type of production. Most graphics come from one of several sources: an art card, computer output, or a paint box creation.

An art card comes from an artist or graphics company. Sometimes it is as simple as a block-lettered card, or it can be a color drawing. These elements are placed under a video camera and then recorded on tape. Computer-originated elements must be recorded onto a compatible format. Proper computer-to-video conversion must take place for the graphic to be included in a typical editing situation. Occasionally, computer output can be converted to a film slide, which is then either telecined or placed on a light box and shot by a video camera.

The paint box system can output to tape and can also output a hold-out matte, an important element when trying to key the image over a picture. Often an art card or other image is captured by the paint box through the use of a videotape playback or video camera. For creating movie commercials, advertising agencies often take static, white-on-black title cards, shoot them with a video camera, and then color and animate them in the video paint device.

Some motion and combining of numerous graphic elements can be accomplished through the use of digital video effects devices or in video paint systems. Zooms, reveals, and slides, as well as ripples and page turns, are often added after the graphic is created. Newscasts use paint box graphics and place them in the frame through the use of a DVE.

Complicated animated images that have many elements and seem to be three-dimensional are often created through a combination of extremely powerful computers, DVE devices, and digital editing bays. Movies-of-the-week openings and some prime-time news shows have elaborate graphics openings. Most of these are created in the rarefied environment of high-end digital editing video, or graphics computers.

There is no doubt that over the years, graphics have become an incredibly important part of any visual program. Simple flat art has become passé. The graphics requirements of any program should be seriously considered. A classy open and close will always make the internal portion of the program seem equally classy.

THE EDITING ROOM

You should always examine any editing system that you plan to use to make sure it has all the needed equipment. Perhaps the bay has only a black-and-white camera when you need a color camera. Some character generators have a limited range of type styles, and some cannot store information on disk. Some switchers can do only one key at a time, while others cannot wipe on a key.

You should list what you will need in postproduction, then check the editing room with someone who is familiar with it. Limitations might make a difference in how the director shoots the show or where the on-line takes place.

In addition, you must keep track of the time spent in the room, along with the equipment used and how long you used it. If you need only three playback machines, you should not pay for four. Although comfortable editing bays often lull producers into complacency, this is no time to let your guard down.

SYNCING AUDIO IN THE BAY

There are several instances when original playback audio may not be in sync with the playback picture. These situations occur when narration is recorded on audio tape, when film audio is telecined separately from picture, or when off-line voice-over has no visual time code because other pictures cover the off-line window code of the voice-over reel.

If there is picture to sync to sound, backtiming is a commonly used method. First, you mark the beginning of the edit. Then, by reading the performer's lips or choosing a specific sound, you mark OUT on the record tape. This produces a duration. Next, you play the source and mark IN at the area of that sound or word. Finally, you subtract the duration of the record from the IN point on the source. A preview allows you to fine-tune this edit.

You may also need to put sound in sync when off-line audio exists, but there is no EDL. This situation can be corrected by backtiming, too. If two audio channels are available, it is easy to preview the off-line audio against the incoming audio. If this capability does not exist, you should preview half of the edit, to ensure that the right IN and OUT marks were located.

Film is *double system*, meaning that the audio is recorded on a separate medium from the picture. On occasion you have to sync up the audio with the picture, and record the audio onto the picture reel. Syncing film sound to picture is made easier by reading slates and matching audible slates. Once the proper takes are established, the clap of the closing slate is synchronized with the picture of the slate closing.

SYNC MODE

To understand *sync mode* editing, imagine a concert recorded with six cameras, each with its own record machine. When the concert is over, the tapes are brought to an editing facility. Using sync mode (called *real time* in some systems), all source tapes are run in sync during each edit. While the six playback machines are rolling, the editor can switch from one tape to another as if the show were being cut live. This method of editing is also described as *on-the-fly editing*. (Some of the more advanced random-access editors are also capable of editing in sync mode.)

The advantage of this type of editing is the ability to edit using all sources at once, yet still having the option to make corrections and changes. If a mistake is made or sections of the show must be deleted, normal editing is performed until the correction or pull-up has been made, and then all playbacks are put back into sync and editing resumes in sync mode.

The disadvantages of this method are that (1) more edits tend to be made and (2) more playback machines mean higher costs for the edit session.

ADDING VIDEO

An editor finishes the on-line editing of an hour-long show. Now someone (the star, the director, the network, the editor's mother) wants to add a shot in the middle of it. This presents a challenge with tape because, unlike film, you cannot just cut the tape in half to insert a new slot.

The show has been on-line edited but not sweetened. There are three ways to add this new shot to the existing show:

1. *Go down one generation of video on the whole show, except the new shot.* The easiest way to approach this problem is to rerecord the show in an editing session. The edited master is now the playback. A new piece of record stock is placed on the record machine. A (very long) edit is made until the scene change. The new shot is added and another edit performed, copying the rest of the show onto the new master video stock.
2. *Do another on-line edit of the show, adding the new shot.* This option is not usually considered. On-line editing of a video show is costly to begin with, so doing it again is almost unheard of. Nevertheless, this might be an option for shorter shows or commercials.

3. *Save the longest portion of the show and go down two generations on the shortest part.* This approach is used to fix credits or when the change is in the first or last few minutes of a program. It saves money without degrading the longer portion of the project.

The first step is to copy the shortest portion of the show, either from the beginning of the show to the new shot or from the new shot to the end. The new shot is then added, which erases a portion of the original show; however, that section has been preserved on the dub.

If the end of the show was the shortest section, the dub of that portion is added to the end of the tape after the new shot. If the front end of the show has been dubbed, it is backtimed to end at the same point as the beginning of the added video.

The editor must make sure that there is enough videotape to make this correction. Adding ten minutes to a 60-minute show on a one-hour tape cannot be accomplished.

This procedure must be approached cautiously. Editing a show takes time and patience. Erasing a portion of the video is a big move and must be done only when the editor has backed up the video and protected the tape as much as possible.

Digital tape formats have helped improve this situation. Digital copies of the program can be made with little or no signal degradation. However, digital tape formats are expensive and may not be an economical alternative for all productions.

PERSONNEL

Any piece of equipment, from an expensive film-to-tape transfer machine to an inexpensive off-line system or character generator, is only as good as its operator. Good equipment in bad hands is worthless. A good editor, a clever machine operator, and a reputable on-line facility can make the difference between a high-quality, profitable venture and a dud. Unqualified or sloppy personnel can do irreparable damage to a production.

Bad Editors

Several years ago, a producer made his first television movie-of-the-week. The show included a well-known cast and was given a considerable budget. The production went smoothly, and when the film was brought to the film editor, the producer went home thinking everything was fine.

A week later, he drove to the editing room to screen the first cut of his movie. He could not believe his eyes. The film was a disaster. None of the nuances and wonderful performances were there, the pacing was all wrong, and not one scene worked.

For the next month, the producer stood over the editor's shoulder and viewed each take, instructing the cutter how to put the show together. The movie went on to be one of the top-rated shows of the season, in spite of the editor's shoddy performance.

The editor determines the pacing of the show, the timing between lines, the expansion or compression of time, and the juxtaposition of images. Editing is one of the more powerful tools of the visual media because an editor can enhance or destroy a production.

SUMMARY

The professional use of video facilities and their equipment can be a pleasant experience or a nightmare. To get the most out of a commercial company, an editor must be familiar with the editing requirements of the show and the company's capabilities. Then the editor must be aware of the special circumstances discussed in this chapter.

21

Examples of Professional Video Editing

With any show, there are probably a half dozen correct ways to cut the program, five other methods that could be considered acceptable, and a million methods that are just plain wrong. Each show tends to find its own path through the postproduction maze, depending on its technical and political (whose brother owns the editing company) needs. The following examples reflect the varied approaches to video postproduction in the real world.

NEWS

News editing is accomplished at an incredibly fast pace. This rush has been exacerbated by the competition between cable news stations, independent television stations, the networks, and local broadcasters. Before the widespread use of video, the news was shot on film, which had to be developed in the lab and then edited. The introduction of videotape quickened the pace of the news process tremendously.

Television news is broadcast from a studio or a remote truck, but much of the show consists of *news clips*, stories that are shot in the field, edited, then played back during the broadcast. Most of these clips are shot with a single camera, with one record machine. The footage is edited very quickly on a control track editor, a simple cuts-only computer system, or, most commonly, through a machine-to-machine editing configuration.

Most news stories are edited on-line. There is no time to experiment. The editor, along with the producer or on-camera talent, views the original camera footage, records the narration, then starts cutting. In some cases, the editing system is transported with the camera crew, and the clip is edited and broadcast from the location.

Most news editors tell a similar story: They perform preediting preparation (coding tapes, organizing labels, recording bars and tone, and making sure that the equipment is operating properly) for the first part of the shift. Then, one or two hours before the broadcast, the reporters show up with their footage and there is a mad rush to edit the stories before airtime. Editing the news is not for the faint of heart. It is a pressure-filled job, and the bigger the news operation, the greater the pressure.

If the production crew and reporter have done their job, the heart of the story will appear at the front and middle of the reel, often with the reporter talking on camera. Action footage available on location should be cutaway footage that can be used to cover jump cuts. The editor often works in conjunction with the producer or on-air talent, madly throwing cassettes into the machines, hoping there is enough time to go back and cover the jump cuts and perhaps include that special shot.

There is a very funny, and somewhat accurate, news editing scene in the movie *Broadcast News*.

Larger news operations spend time and money on the production of feature news stories. These edited pieces take longer to put together because they use computer-generated graphics and digital video effects. Many news specials are off-line edited on a computer editing system before the on-line session.

MULTIPLE-CAMERA VIDEO PRODUCTION

Many television shows are shot with multiple cameras. The director sits in a control room and gives instructions to a technical director who, through the use of a switcher, preselects which camera shots will be recorded on the master production tape. Often there are several other camera feeds sent to isolation (*iso*) record reels. Ideally, these iso reels contain camera shots that differ from those on the master reel. The iso shots are used for additional coverage during the edit session.

When production is complete, window dubs are made of all the original tapes (occasionally the window dubs are recorded simultaneously with the camera originals). In the off-line editing suite, the editor and the director choose the best angles and takes for each performance from the show master and iso reels. Also, it is common practice to record two performances of the show. The first is usually called the dress rehearsal, the second, the air taping. During the off-line session, the show is edited to a specific running time. Once the off-line cut has been approved, the show is on-line edited. A sweetening process follows, and the show is delivered to the network or station for broadcast.

MULTIPLE-CAMERA ISOLATION VIDEO PRODUCTION

Multiple-camera isolation production usually does not have a master record tape. Instead of having a tape that has camera selections already made, the end result of the production is a videotape of each camera's output. Some directors record an additional three-quarter-inch tape. An extra camera shoots a group of monitors, showing all available camera angles. This tape is then referred to in the off-line session to see every shot that is available at that moment.

When editing this type of show, the editor makes every change of angle. Unlike the previous example, the director does not preselect shots through the switcher. However, at any point in the performance, there are multiple angles to choose from.

Some producers who use multiple-camera isolation choose to edit in sync mode, cutting on the fly. (See the "Sync Mode" section in Chapter 20.) Once the off-line is complete, the show is on-lined and sweetened. Filmed sit-coms use multiple film cameras. When the film is transferred to video tape, three or four separate angles of the action are available.

SEGMENT SHOWS

With the demand for less expensive programming, more and more reality shows are broadcast. The-best-of and real-life programs, including the home video shows, rescue, and police programs are particularly common. These shows use preedited segments that can be combined with studio footage. The segments are usually shot on location using single-camera techniques. Most often, the recording medium is professional half-inch videotape. The segments are off-lined using window dubs. Once the segments are completed, the remainder of the show is recorded. These *wraparounds* are combined with the segments in an on-line session. The final master is sweetened before being broadcast. Figure 21-1 illustrates the steps of a segment show.

COMMERCIALS

Commercials are one of the most challenging and creative types of program. Telling a story in thirty seconds can be extremely challenging. Any commercial goes through many revisions. The product people, director, and agency people all are involved in the postproduction process. Obviously this becomes a political

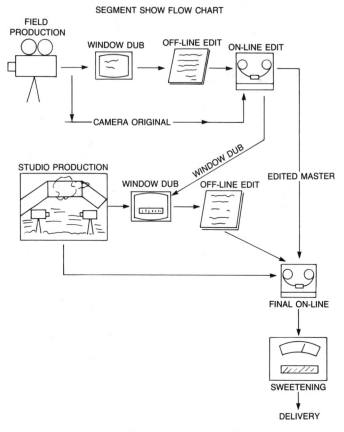

Figure 21-1 A segment show flow chart.

juggling act as each of the players tries to take creative control. However, there is a great deal of money to be made in editing commercials and the people in demand live very well. A combination of graphics and editorial sense is most important in commercial editing. There are a number of ways that the spot can be cut. It can be edited to a sound track, or created in the bay. However, most large commercial editing companies use random-access editors to the exclusion of all other types of editing.

INFOMERCIALS

Infomercials have invaded the broadcast arena. These staged shows must be edited. Like a multiple-camera sit-com, they are shot either with isolated cameras, or with a director's cut and one or two isolated camera feeds. Again, the editor must keep in mind the purpose of the program: to entertain and sell a product.

LIVE SHOWS

Live shows, such as sporting events or award ceremonies, often have edited segments played back during the broadcast. These segments may include interviews, promotional pieces on specific colleges, a brief biography of an individual, a clip from a music video, or a scene from a motion picture.

SUMMARY

There is no ideal editing process. Each show has its own requirements in terms of look, speed of completion, equipment, budget, and personal preferences. With the tremendous flexibility of video, there are usually several right (and many wrong) ways to fulfill a show's postproduction needs.

22

Finding a Job in Postproduction

Video editing provides a challenging and enjoyable career. Every show is different, the footage is never the same, and the demands of editing each program vary. Video editing is also creative. Given identical footage, 10 editors will come up with 10 different versions of the same show.

The video editing job market is still growing and career opportunities in postproduction can be found in many industries. Hospitals have extensive video departments, as do department stores, and car and electronics manufacturers. Large corporations and smaller companies offer management jobs overseeing video productions. In addition, small video producers, larger network production companies, cable companies, local television stations, and nationwide television networks offer thousands of editing opportunities. Although off-line and on-line editing facilities hire numerous editors, some people choose to go it alone, earning some or all of their living taping Little League baseball games and weddings.

NARROWING DOWN THE FIELD

The first step in finding a job in postproduction is deciding where you want to work and what type of program you want to edit. Should you work in a big city or small town? Which is preferable: working with home videos, corporate videos, or television programs? How about a career in editing instructional programs or documentaries?

Competition and Cash

Video has become a popular field, and more and more schools are offering video courses. As people graduate from these schools and enter the video marketplace, competition increases in all areas of the industry. Landing a good job requires talent, expertise, and a certain degree of politicking. Résumés and reels demonstrating your talent and experience are important tools to use in the search for employment.

As a general rule, you should begin a career in the type of company that reflects your ultimate goals. Starting out in a small town and hoping to someday move to New York does not work as well as going to the city, getting a feel for the environment, and meeting the people who can help advance your career. Knowing the right people is often half the battle of getting a job, and the people in that small town cannot always help you land a job in the big city.

The pay scale for well-trained, professional video editors, tape operators, film transfer technicians, and postproduction coordinators is wide. One point to remember is that more money usually means more responsibility. In addition, jobs in larger cities usually pay more, but the cost of living is higher and the competition tougher. Corporate video editing usually does not pay as well as editing network television programs. However, the pay scale is rising at some of the larger corporations, especially as the powers-that-be recognize the vast influence a video department can have.

Figure 22-1 An S-VHS hi-fi playback editing deck. The introduction of S-VHS was quickly accepted as an industrial production and postproduction medium. Decks such as the Panasonic AG-1960 are used to provide inexpensive editing on this versatile format.

Employment Opportunities

More and more companies are installing their own video equipment (see Figure 22-1). Some corporate installations have only two video machines, while others have as many as three on-line editing bays that run 24 hours a day (see Figure 22-2). With the cost of video production and postproduction still dropping, the video boom has crept into every conceivable type of company.

Some of the ways in which individuals earn income from video editing are not always readily apparent. Artists have received grants for video projects as well as video documentaries. There are also internships available in many postproduction companies. Certain educational facilities hire videotape editors, as do companies that teach professional editing.

Real estate companies show houses on videotape in the office, saving both the agent and the prospective buyer the time and expense of traveling to a location. Point-of-purchase advertising (tapes played in stores to promote a special item of sale) is often edited by a store's in-house video department, and corporate video newsletters are sent through a video network.

One company makes videotapes that play at a well-known resort hotel and describe the surrounding places of interest. These tapes are hour-long commercials for nearby tourist attractions and are set up so that segments can be easily added or deleted. Other enterprising individuals traveled to Hawaii to

Figure 22-2 An on-line studio editing room.

shoot exotic footage. After editing, the tapes were sold to distributors for home video rental or were marketed directly to consumers by mail. One individual shot large bulldozers and earthmovers. That home videotape made the producer a millionaire.

Editing for television is also a growing field. If network and local broadcasting seem voracious in their demands for programming, cable is insatiable. All these shows must be edited somewhere (usually at a well-known editing company in a large city), and editors are needed to staff these facilities (see Figures 22-3 and 22-4).

PLAN OF ACTION

Once you have determined an area of employment, it is probably best to move close to a facility that offers those specific opportunities. For instance, if you wish to work on hospital-type programs, you should contact some of the leading hospitals in your location of choice and find out what types of positions are available.

If you want to edit network shows, then New York and Los Angeles are the places to go. You should seek an entry-level position at a production company if you are interested in the management aspect of postproduction or an entry-level position at an editing company if that is your area of interest. As with any job, there is no one way to secure the perfect position. But no matter what your ultimate goal may be, it is best to go right to the production source and get some kind of job inside the business. Making personal contacts is an excellent way to move up the professional ladder.

Editor
  Effects
  Cuts only
  Show specific (sit-com, news, etc.)
  Off-line/On-line
Assistant editor
Paint box/graphics operator
Scheduling
Character generator operator
Sales

Postproduction supervision
Audio mixer
Telecine operator
Telecine assistant
Producer
Assistant director
Production assistant
Accountant/payroll
Facilities owner

Figure 22-3 Jobs in video postproduction.

Sit-coms	Reality/clip shows
Movies of the week	Game shows
Music videos	Cartoons
Informational programs	Local news
Corporate video	Daily network news
How-to videos	Network news specials
Public service announcements	"Home video" shows
National commercials	Movie commercials
Regional commercials	Movie behind the scenes
Sports	Television promotion

Figure 22-4   Some types of shows edited on tape.

THE POLITICAL ARENA

This discussion is not about electoral politics, but the politics of acquiring a job. People hire people they know, especially in the entertainment industry. Even in corporate situations, if a person knows one applicant and does not know another, with all things being equal, the known individual will be hired. If you decide to pursue a network editing job, contacts are vital. The best method in any industry is to become known to those in power or those who do the hiring.

Being the best editor in the world is a good calling card, but unless the people hiring know who is the best and who is available, the editor probably will not be hired. One way to be known to those who hire editors is to freelance. Rather than being a staff editor, the freelancer works one job at a time for a variety of clients. In this way, the editor finds out about the facilities as well as the people in each location. It also allows the people at the facilities to get to know the freelance editor.

The premise always remains the same: The editor needs clients and a facility. The only way to meet these people is to get close to the individuals wh work in your chosen field and make friends with them. Friends will hire a fr d before they hire a stranger; it is as simple as that.

THE EXPANDING NUMBER OF JOBS IN POSTPRODUCTION

There are more and more jobs in video postproduction, ᵃalization of the more editing controllers, tape formats, and types of editing jobs. This types of editing. market requires more training and more knowledge of their experience. A good editor can cut any type of show, but editors a

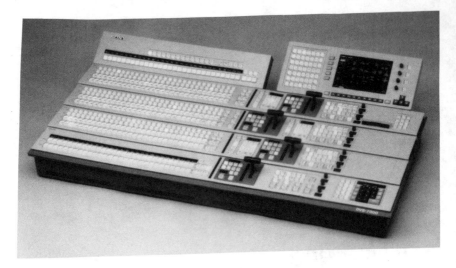

Figure 22-5 The Sony DVS 7000, a master switcher found in broadcast control centers. This on-air switcher is operated by a quick-moving technical director (TD) who controls which signal is going to be broadcast from the network.

The previously mentioned plan of action should always be in the editor's mind. For example, if you want to cut sit-coms, random-access editors and program formats are items that you should thoroughly understand.

SUMMARY

The video revolution has invaded the home and the corporate world, opening new avenues of employment and offering new challenges. Whatever aspect of video postproduction appeals to the new editor, employment opportunities are here to stay and will undoubtedly continue to grow as the video field expands even further.

23

A Look into the Future

Video is an electronic medium, and the electronic world is changing daily. What is on the horizon in the video world? One thing is certain: The video reality that exists today will change. The video signal itself is under assault. Consumers want a large, high-quality picture and high-fidelity stereo audio in their television sets. NTSC video is limited in its resolution and aural qualities, and thus its life span is limited.

CONTINUING FORMAT CHANGES

There seems to be no end to new format introductions. HDTV will be one of many newcomers, although its arrival has been delayed for economic and technical reasons. Digital video continues to change the configuration of the videotape editing bay and the types of edits being performed.

As these technological improvements are implemented, more sophisticated, high-paying jobs will be created. Random-access off-line editing is already commonplace. Random-access on-line is already a reality. Films will continue to be shot on celluloid, but most of the postproduction chores will enter the domain of electronic editing. Already, many effects are being created on D1 or other electronic effects devices, and then re-exposed onto film.

The boundaries between audio mixing and editing will disappear as well. Machines capable of both functions will exist within the same computer. Originally high, costs involved in computer editing will continue to decline, and the ability to edit, add effects, mix, and deliver a program all from one powerful workstation will become cost-effective. It will remain the human factor that keeps the jobs separate. The best audio mixer will not always be the best picture editor. The system may be all in one box, but the people operating that box will be different personalities with different strengths.

DESKTOP EDITING SYSTEMS

One of the fastest growing areas of editing will continue to be desktop editing systems. These systems will eventually make three-quarter-inch editing obsolete. IBM-compatible clones and Macintosh systems are able to perform wipes, dissolves, keys, chroma keys, and digital effects. Also, the divisions between character generator, switcher, and edit controller may disappear in the late 1990s. Which of these new equipment manufacturers will be setting the standards is yet to be determined.

RANDOM-ACCESS NEWS EDITING

Random-access invaded the television and motion picture world. Now it is headed for the newsroom. Special cameras will record digital images that can then be transmitted to the station, or loaded directly into memory at the station when the crew returns. The day's footage will be immediately available, and editing will be incredibly fast. There will be no dubs because the station can air the finished piece from the same footage from which it was cut. Archived footage will be available from huge computer storage.

RANDOM-ACCESS ON-LINE

The on-line process will move from linear, tape-based editing to random-access. But do not be fooled into thinking that this will be cheap, easy, or quick. Much editorial time is spent making decisions. That time will not shorten. Actually, with more choices, the editorial time should lengthen. Random-access on-line will become an every day occurrence, but reloading of original footage may be a pre-edit step. Storing hours of footage in broadcast formats requires massive amounts of memory. A more efficient method would be a hybrid of today's systems and random-access. The specific sections of tape would be loaded into the on-line computer for completion. The off-line editing chores would be handled as they are now, in compressed video formats that allow large amounts of footage to be stored within cost-effective disk space.

HIGH-DEFINITION TELEVISION

High-definition video exists in several technological forms. It is only a matter of time before one of these systems is chosen to be the United States' broadcast standard. Direct-to-home satellite signals, which already are being marketed as an alternative to cable, could be the delivery vehicle. Or high definition might be delivered to the home by the phone company through fiber-optic cable. Digital effects generators already convert the video signal to digital video in order to produce complex movements. Digital audio is available commercially in the compact disk player and DAT. Digital video is used on a daily basis in random-access editors. It is only a matter of time before someone invents a camera that can convert video images into an extremely high-quality signal that can be viewed at home on a large screen. A television screen that covers an entire wall could become a standard fixture in the home.

VIDEO PROJECTION AND EDITING

Theaters might be converted to accommodate huge video screens that accept satellite transmission based on one print of a film. This would eliminate the thousands of prints that are now physically transported to theaters around the world. As for editing, random-access editors will become less expensive and more common in small editing companies where control track editors are now used.

The family den could become a high-tech room with a computer, HDTV set, VCR, editor, and stereo system tied together. Control track editors might be a standard piece of equipment in this home entertainment center. Even today, total audio and standard video systems, enclosed in one unit, are available for home use, and the use of such systems will no doubt expand.

SUMMARY

No matter what changes, editors will still be cutting pictures and making edits. The machines might change and the editing process might be radically different, but people will still be required to choose the right shots and place them in a logical, creative order. And if all these amazing changes do come about, there will only be more employment opportunities in the postproduction world.

Appendix: Compatibility

The video editing environment comprises many types of computers and machines. Each machine has its limitations in addition to its compatibility with other, similar machines.

VIDEO RECORD MACHINE COMPATIBILITY

Any video machine can, if not properly maintained, make a recording that only it can play back. To avoid this situation, a videotape record machine must be regularly checked and maintained.

Editing into a tape that was created on another video machine will often require some adjustment. You should pay careful attention to the chroma and video record levels, tension, and skew, and should also look for potential whips (see the Glossary).

COMPUTER EDIT DECISION LIST COMPATIBILITY

In the early days of editing, there was neither a standard format of EDL nor a standard technical method for recording an EDL on a computer diskette or paper punch tape. Today, although the CMX and SMPTE formats have been recognized as the industry standards, a number of editing systems have been marketed, and there is no guarantee that floppy disks will be compatible.

Most disks created by editing systems of the same company are compatible, but when planning to use the floppy disk of an EDL from one type of computer editor on another, you should first check their compatibility. Also, most linear editing systems are on IBM compatible or RT11 hardware. Avid random-access editors run on Macintosh computers. Dvision runs on IBM-compatible machines. It is a good idea to have your EDLs put on both a Mac-formatted disk and an IBM-type disk to save any confusion during the on-line session. Many computer editing companies will either convert or accept other machines' EDLs. You should test the diskette(s) before starting an on-line session by reading a short list from the first computer onto the second. This simple test may save hours of frustration and prevent the need to handload an EDL. There are also programs that can convert EDLs from one format to another.

ADDRESS TRACK TIME CODE

As in the examples of record machines and diskettes, not all systems are totally compatible with each other. A general rule is that the machines in a particular series will be compatible, but there are exceptions. Testing is the only method of ensuring compatibility.

In three-quarter-inch computerized editing, time code is often recorded on one of the two audio tracks. However, using different brands of machines can cause a discrepancy in reading the code. Because three-quarter-inch machines do not normally read time code on the audio tracks, they are often modified by placing audio read/record heads in the tape path. The placement of these audio read heads can affect how the time code is recorded and read. For instance, the difference between a Sony three-quarter-inch tape machine and a JVC™ one reading the same coded tape can be as much as fourteen frames. So if an off-line session used a JVC machine for playbacks, and then the on-line session used a Sony machine, all the source numbers in the EDL would have to be adjusted to reflect this difference. It is a good idea to check for this potential compatibility problem when editing with three-quarter-inch track one or track two time code.

VIDEOTAPE

Within the United States, VHS is a standard video format, as are quad and three-quarter-inch tape. One-inch Type C tape is generally transferable, although older Sony machines (model 1000s) usually need a modification to play an Ampex recording, and only Type C recordings can be played on Type C machines. Similarly, D1 recordings can be played only on D1 machines, and Betacam can be played only on Betacam decks.

CHARACTER GENERATOR FLOPPY DISKS

Generally speaking, each type of character generator writes its storage diskettes in a different format. There is no industry standard for character generators.

INTERNATIONAL STANDARDS

Each country has its own broadcast standard. The NTSC recommendations were accepted by the FCC as a national standard for the United States. This standard consists of a 525-line, 29.97-frames-per-second scanning system, which is also used in Japan and South America (countries using alternating current of 60 cycles per second).

PAL is another standard, which is a modified form of NTSC. PAL uses 625 lines and 25-frames-per-second scanning.

A third major video standard, SECAM, varies significantly from NTSC and PAL. Though incompatible, SECAM also uses 625 lines, scanned at 25 frames per second.

None of these systems is compatible; an NTSC recording cannot be played back on a SECAM tape machine. Following is a list of the different formats and the countries that use them:

- **NTSC** North America, Greenland, Burma, South Korea, Japan, Taiwan, Philippines, Dominica, Guyana, Venezuela, Puerto Rico, Peru, Chile, Trinidad, Curacao, Cuba, Panama, Costa Rica, Nicaragua, Honduras, El Salvador, Guatemala, Cayman Islands, Mexico
- **SECAM** Soviet Union, Poland, Germany, Czechoslovakia, Hungary, Romania, Bulgaria, Greece, Albania, France, Luxembourg, Tunisia, Morocco, Senegal, Ivory Coast, Gabon, Congo, Zaire, Egypt, Iraq, Iran, Mongolia, North Korea, New Caledonia, French Guiana, Haiti
- **PAL** Bolivia, Paraguay, Uruguay, Argentina, Iceland, Ireland, United Kingdom, Norway, Sweden, Finland, Denmark, Germany, Netherlands, Belgium, Switzerland, Austria, Italy, Spain, Portugal, Malta, Andorra, Turkey, Cyprus, Israel, Jordan, Kuwait, Algeria, Libya, Sudan, Uganda, Kenya, Tanzania, Zambia, Zimbabwe, Swaziland, Nigeria, Ghana, Liberia, Sierra Leone, Afghanistan, Pakistan, India, Sri Lanka, People's Republic of China, Tibet, Bangladesh, Thailand, Malaysia, Singapore, Borneo, Sabah, Australia, New Zealand, Hong Kong, Macao
- **PAL-M** Brazil
- **PAL and SECAM** Saudi Arabia
- **Black and white** Jamaica, Falkland Islands, Syria, People's Democratic Republic of Yemen, Solomon Islands, Vietnam, Cambodia, Laos, Nepal, Ethiopia, Somalia, Madagascar, Malawi, Mozambique, Lesotho, Botswana, Angola, Burundi, Rwanda, Central African Republic, Cameroon, Equatorial Guinea, Chad, Niger, Guinea, Gambia, Fiji Islands

Bibliography

Anderson, Gary H. *Video Editing.* 2d ed. White Plains, NY: Knowledge Industry Publications, Inc., 1988.

Anderson, Gary H. *Electronic Post-Production: The Film-to-Video Guide.* White Plains, NY: Knowledge Industry Publications, Inc., 1986.

Avid Media Composer User's Guide. Avid Technologies, Inc., 1994.

Browne, Steven E. *Film-Video Terms and Concepts.* Boston: Focal Press, 1992.

Browne, Steven E. *The The Video Tape Post-Production Primer.* Burbank, CA: Wilton Place Communications, 1982.

EECO. *The Time Code Book.* Santa Ana, CA: EECO Inc., 1984.

Fuller, Barry J., Steve Kanaba, and Janyce Kanaba-Brisch. *Single Camera Video Production.* Englewood Cliffs, NJ: Prentice-Hall, Inc., 1982.

Harwood, Don. *Everything You Always Wanted to Know About Videotape Recording.* Syosset, NY: VTR Publishing, 1983.

Millerson, Gerald. *Video Production Handbook.* 2d ed. Boston: Focal Press, 1992.

Ohanian, Thomas. *Digital Nonlinear Editing: New Approaches to Editing Film and Video.* Boston: Focal Press, 1993.

Paulson, C. Robert. *BM/E's ENG/EFP/EPP Handbook.* New York: Broadband Information Services, Inc., 1981.

Roberts, Kenneth H., and Win Sharples, Jr. *A Primer for Filmmaking.* New York: Pegasus, 1972.

Schetter, Michael D. *Videotape Editing.* Elk Grove, IL: Swderski Electronics, 1982.

Weise, Marcus. *Videotape Operations.* Woodland Hills, CA: Weynand and Associates, 1984.

Weynand, Diana. *Computerized Videotape Editing.* Woodland Hills, CA: Weynand and Associates, 1983.

Glossary

A   The letter in an EDL indicating that the edit is an audio-only edit. In the newer EDL listings, *A* indicates an audio-only edit to tracks 1 and 2. *A1* indicates an audio-only edit to track 1; *A2* indicates an audio-only edit to track 2.

A & B rolls   Two separate reels of video or film on which scenes are alternately placed to perform special effects.

A copy   Either an original playback reel when a B copy has been made to create an effect, or the first of several preedited masters created to be combined in a final version of a complicated effects sequence.

A mode   A description of a computer on-line procedure in which the edits are recorded sequentially starting with the first edit, then the second, and so on. Also referred to as an *A mode assembly* or *assemble 1*. See **B mode**.

Address track time code   Time code that has been recorded onto the address track of a video cassette. Address track time code must be recorded at the same time as the video signal. Only certain machines can record this type of time code, and not all brands or models are compatible.

ADO®   The brand name of a digital video generator manufactured by the Ampex® Corporation.

ADR   The abbreviation for *automatic dialogue replacement.* Process in which a loop of video or film is created so that a performer can repeatedly deliver a line while watching the footage.

AGC   The abbreviation for *automatic gain control.*

All stop   The abort command on a computer editor, usually activated by pressing the space bar.

Ambient audio   See **Room tone.**

Ampex   The company that invented the quad videotape machine and markets many video products, from videotape to one-inch machines to editors.

Analog   The storage or encoding of a signal through the use of continuously varying voltages representing signal characteristics. See **Digital.**

Animatic   A test of a commercial. By using several drawings and a video camera with a zoom lens, a commercial is simulated using the artwork, the camera work, and the editing (including simple effects) to demonstrate how the spot might look.

Animation   The drawing (either electronically or in a physical medium) of motion. Usually animation is completed in a frame-by-frame process.

Assemble recording   A technical method of recording video. An assemble recording replaces all existing video, audio, and control track with new signals. See **Insert recording**.

Assemble 1   See **A mode**.

Assemble 2   See **B mode**.

Audio   The sound portion of any show.

Audio-only   An edit that records only audio, not affecting the picture portion of the record tape. The only way that an audio-only edit can be performed is by making an insert recording.

Audio/video keys   The keys or switches on editing keyboards that designate whether an edit will record audio, video, or both.

Auto-assembly   An automatic on-line edit in which an EDL is loaded into the computer editor and the computer performs edits as the human editor watches for technical problems in the video. In almost all cases, these assemblies use an insert recording, not an assemble recording.

Automatic gain control (AGC)   An electronic device in an audio circuit that automatically raises and lowers the record volume. This type of circuit should be used with caution because of its tendency to raise and lower background sounds between words or other sounds that are meant to be recorded.

   Video cameras also have an AGC circuit. This device opens and closes the aperture on the camera depending on the amount of light available. Most professional camera operators do not use the AGC.

AVRXX   The designation of digital recording level used in Avid® random-access editors. AVR1 is the lowest quality level of picture representation; AVR27 is one of the highest. AVR27 is on-line picture quality.

Avid®   One of the established random-access editing systems using digitized video and audio to store information.

B   The Letter in an EDL indicating that the edit is both an audio and a video edit. *B* indicates that audio is recorded on tracks 1 and 2. A both edit to just track 1 is listed as *B1*; a both edit to just track 2 is listed as *B2*.

B copy   Also called a *B roll* or a *B reel*. This is a video and/or audio copy of original footage, with identical time code, usually made to move an effect from one area on the playback tape to another area on the same tape.

B mode   Also called a *checkerboard assembly*. An on-line procedure in which all edits from the available playback reel are performed, skipping edits that require different reels. Then another group of playback reels is loaded, and the edits from those reels are performed, until the show is completed. This method requires that the entire EDL be loaded into the computer editor and that the EDL be perfect, with no overrecords or false edits (see **List cleaning**). This method also requires that the off-line (human) editor be very familiar with B mode assemblies as well as list cleaning. If the EDL is not perfect, the mistakes are usually discovered only after most of the show has been on-line edited. (See **C mode.**)

B wind   The direction of tape wind used on a Type B machine (usually a Bosch-Fernseh℠ one-inch machine). This is in the direction opposite the wind used on a Type C machine. Although Type B generally delivers a better picture than Type C, most one-inch video recording in the United States is done on Type C machines.

Background   (1) The source of video over which other video sources are keyed. See **Key cut.** (2) The area behind the main action in a visual frame.

Backtiming   The process of placing a particular point in an edit by calculating the distance from the designated point to the end of the edit.

Back porch   That portion of the blanking interval from the end of the color burst to the beginning of the picture signal.

Backspace editor   Another name for a *control track editor,* so called because it counts control track as it backs up to perform an edit. It backspaces tape a certain amount, then rolls the tape forward to the edit point.

Bars   A reference signal recorded on the beginning of a video tape for the purpose of aligning the playback of that tape. Most often, an audio reference (tone) is recorded at the same time as the bars.

Bay   Another word for an *editing room.*

Betacam℠   The brand name of Sony℠ broadcast-quality half-inch videotape and re-corders. A standard in news and low- to medium-budget video productions, the camera and recorder are contained in one lightweight unit. The recorder also has a Dolby℠ encoder, an audio limiter, and the ability to record address track time code. Even slow-motion playback of this format is available. This format is also available in a metal tape format (Betacam SP®) and a digital format that can play back analog or digital recordings.

Betamax®   The brand name for a Sony home-use half-inch videotape. Though not intended for broadcast, with proper care, it can be used for this purpose. Generally speaking, the quality of the video is inferior to that of any other broadcast tape. Betamax® produces a slightly better video signal than the more popular VHS half-inch home video.

Bins   (1) Electronic storage areas where edit decision lists are kept. (2) Metal contain-ers with hanging devices where strips of film are stored during the film editing process.

Black   In video, this level of white is also called *pedestal* or *setup level.* On a waveform monitor, black is measured at 7.5 IRE units (see Chapter 4 on time base correctors and video scopes). Anything below this level is considered part of the horizontal blanking and is unacceptable as part of the video broadcast signal according to FCC definitions. Blank tape is not black tape. Blank tape is blank, devoid of any video signal. Consider video black as a video signal. In the early days of videotape, a black signal was also called *crystal black.* In some editing systems, *black* (BLK) is used in the EDL to indicate that the source of the edit is black.

Black and coded tape A videotape onto which a video signal of black (7.5 IRE units) and time code has been recorded.

Black-video-black preview See **BVB**.

Blanking A portion of the video signal that is undetected by normal television sets. The technical information for making the picture (the horizontal blanking) and information such as automatic color tuning and vertical interval time code (the vertical blanking) are recorded in this area. During the blanking interval, the electron beam that scans the picture tube is blanked to retrace to the beginning of the next line of video or to the start of the next video field.

Blanking is created by the original video source, which can be a camera or a film-to-tape transfer. Each generation of video (each transfer from one tape to another) usually makes the horizontal blanking slightly larger. If a tape has wide blanking to start with, blanking will be a concern later on.

When a television signal is broadcast over the air, the FCC has jurisdiction over the technical requirements of the video signal and has issued regulations concerning horizontal and vertical blanking. These requirements are often regulated by editing houses, duplication companies, and the television stations themselves. If the video blanking on any particular tape does not meet FCC specifications, it may be rejected by the duplication house or the station. Editing houses will usually warn a client about a blanking problem but will edit the tape if the client agrees to take responsibility for it. In-house demonstrations, shows for home viewing, and other programs that will not be broadcast usually do not have a problem with blanking because they are not seen on normal television sets. The FCC requirements for vertical blanking are 20 to 21.5 lines, and for horizontal blanking, 10.3 to 11.4 microseconds.

The only way to correct blanking is to run the video through a digital effects device, expanding the original video until the blanking is corrected. There are three potential problems with this process: (1) the video portion might be delayed a frame, (2) a poorly maintained effects device might degrade the video, and (3) the process can be expensive.

Bleed-through The bleeding through of the high-pitched whine of time code onto the production track of three-quarter-inch tape. This can occur when time code is recorded onto one of the audio tracks of the three-quarter-inch tape during production. There are three ways to avoid bleed-through: (1) use address track time code, (2) use VITC, and (3) record the time code onto the other audio track after production. The third method is the most expensive in the long run, and there is still a chance that the time code will bleed through to the other channel if the time code level is too hot (loud).

BLK In an EDL, an indication that the source of the edit is black.

Blocking The planned movement of performers or the camera.

Bosch-Fernseh The inventors and manufacturers of the Type B videotape format.

Both cut A cut that records both audio and video.

Breezeway That portion of the horizontal blanking interval from the end of the sync pulse to the beginning of the color burst.

Broadcast To modulate a signal onto a radio frequency and beam that signal into the atmosphere for the purpose of being received and decoded (demodulated).

Broadcast quality   This term refers to the technical specifications of the video signal and the actual look of that signal. A technically perfect video signal might look terrible. For instance, a VHS tape, properly doctored through a digital effects generator, might meet a station's technical requirements but be rejected because it is not a broadcast-quality picture. Each broadcast company, network, or station has its own level of quality.

Bulk   To erase a videotape with a bulk eraser.

Bulk eraser   A machine that creates a limited but very strong magnetic field. Placing a videotape on this machine will disorganize the magnetic particles on the tape, effectively erasing any signal on that tape. There is no protection for any tape placed on a bulk eraser once the machine is turned on.

Bump   A term used in reference to transferring video from one format to another. For instance, three-quarter-inch tape could be bumped to one-inch, or a two-inch tape to Betacam.

Burned-in time code   Another way to describe the window in a window dub.

Burst   See **Color burst**.

Buzzing   See **Ringing**.

BVB   An acronym for *black-video-black*. A preview that shows black, the incoming edit portion, then black again.

C   In an EDL, an indication that the edit is a cut (as opposed to a dissolve, wipe, or key).

C copy   Also called a *C roll* or *C reel*. This is a video and/or audio copy of original footage, with identical time code, usually made to produce a complicated effect when a B copy has already been made. A C copy indicates that three images from one playback reel will be on the screen at the same time. A C copy might also be made if three preedited tapes were to be combined to make a final version of a complicated effects sequence.

C mode   Another form of checkerboard assembly. An on-line procedure in which all edits from the available playback reel are performed in ascending order. All edits from one reel are accomplished first, shuffling the record machine back and forth, while the playback reel only moves forward to the next edit, saving shuttle time and therefore edit time. This method requires that the EDL be clean and accurate, because the entire show cannot be viewed until the on-line is completed. See **B mode**.

Camera   See **Video camera** and **Film camera**.

Camera original   The first-generation videotape that has the original camera signal recorded on it. If there were two tape machines recording a signal from one particular camera, there would be two camera originals of that footage.

Cartridge machine   Also known as a *cart machine*. A machine used at television stations to roll commercials automatically. For instance, 20 commercials in separate quad cartridges might be loaded into a tractor-like mechanism. A master computer would then tell each cartridge when to play. An audio cart machine performs a similar function at automated ratio stations.

Cassette A videotape or audio tape contained in its own housing. Videocassettes are sold in the following formats: VHS, 8mm Betamax®, MII® Betacam, and three-quarter-inch. Quad cassettes are designed for the automated broadcasting of television commercials.

CCD The abbreviation for *charged coupled device*, an electronic chip that converts light into electrical impulses. The CCD has replaced pick-up tubes in most video cameras.

Character generator An electronic typewriter that creates letters and symbols in video, usually available for rent in editing bays. The less expensive models have no memory and few type choices. The more expensive models offer many type styles and have the ability to store information on diskettes. The top-of-the-line models can store video frames and create effects similar to wipes, dissolves, and digital effects.

Checkerboard assembly See **B mode, C mode, D mode,** and **E mode.**

Chroma key A key that electronically cuts a specific color out of a background picture and inserts another video source in that hole.

Client The person directly responsible for booking, paying for, and/or supervising a session.

Clip (1) A short segment of a program. (2) To crop or eliminate a portion of a picture. Key clipping circuitry will cut off a certain white (luminance) value of a picture.

Clock number A term occasionally used instead of *time code number.*

Close-up The camera framing of an object or person. A close-up shows a person from approximately the shoulders up, leaving headroom at the top of the frame.

Closed caption A signal that carries subtitling information in a broadcast signal. This encoded signal is inserted into the vertical interval. Devices can be purchased that decode the information and display the text on the screen.

CMX® The company created by CBS Labs and Memorex® to develop videotape editing systems. CMX was the first company to market a random-access editor and the first industry-accepted frame-accurate videotape editing system. CMX is still a leader in videotape and random-access editing systems.

Coding (1) To record time code onto a video tape. (2) To print identical numbers onto film mag (magnetic tape in the shape of film used to edit, mix, and store audio) and film workprint to facilitate keeping the audio and picture in sync with each other.

Color burst A reference signal transmitted with each line of video between the end of the line's sync and the picture signal. The burst consists of a few cycles of chroma signal of known phase.

Color correction The changing of color shadings in a video picture. The process of color correction is time-consuming, so it is much wiser to get the color balance right during the production. Color correction can be as simple as changing the hue on a time base corrector or as complicated as using a machine that breaks down the video signal into its original components and then adjusts certain elements of those components. A video signal might require color correction for various reasons: (1) the camera was not white-balanced (see **White-balance**); (2) one of the camera's color pickup tubes was not working correctly; (3) a playback was not properly set up to bars during an original edit, requiring the shot be fixed to balance the color of one or several shots; (4) a color shot must be made black-and-white (see **Color burst**).

Color corrector A machine that is capable of drastically altering the color levels of a video signal.

Component video recording A technical method of recording a color picture on videotape that separates the black-and-white portion of the signal from the chroma. This method is used in half-inch professional video formats such as Betacam, Beta SP, MII, and D1.

Composite The encoding of complete video information into one signal. Originally designed for broadcasting, this process was used extensively in postproduction until the late 1980s when component switchers, recorders, and other devices allowed for the creation of totally component signal paths. Component is a more accurate signal.

Compositing The process of combining numerous visual elements in the frame. Compositing can consist of still or action footage. With the advent of D1 and D2, along with the digital switchers and other digital devices, compositing has become a common practice in commercial and high-end postproduction projects.

Compression To proportionally lower the volume of a signal that crosses a predetermined threshold.

Computer edit Either an edit performed by a computerized editing machine or the generic term for a computer on-line edit.

Computer editing system An editing system that is capable of storing more than one edit and has the ability to manipulate the EDL for list cleaning. A computer editing system uses time code to locate specific positions on the playback and record tapes.

Computer In/Out keys A group of keys that initiate the output of a computer EDL. Input and output can be in the form of punch tape, a printout, or a diskette.

Computer memory Each computer editing system has a finite amount of memory for EDL storage. Some editors hold up to 100 edits, while others can hold several thousand. When the memory is full, it is time to save the EDL to punch tape, a printout, or a diskette.
  There is also a difference in the way that computer memory works. In some editing systems, the computer will remember the EDL even if the power is turned off. In others, the information in memory is erased when the power is turned off. Both types of computers can protect the EDL by backup to a printout or a diskette.

Continuity The smooth flow of action and content during a program. This flow is controlled by careful attention to detail during the production.

Control track An electronic signal recorded on videotape at each head revolution and each field that tells the next machine how to play back that particular video signal. It is similar in concept to the sprocket holes in film. Some editing machines, called control track, backspace, or pulse editors, use these pulses for editing.

Control track editor   A simple videotape controller, usually cuts-only, that edits from a playback machine to a record machine. Easy to operate, this type of editor is great for viewing footage and window dubs as well as performing inexpensive off-line edits and simple on-line edits (for animatics and demo reels).

Countdown   A leader at the head of a program, which counts backward until two seconds before the show. At two seconds, a brief audio beep is recorded as part of the countdown. See **Two pop**.

Cross-pulse monitor   A television monitor capable of putting the horizontal and/or vertical blanking in the center of the screen so that these signals can be more closely examined.

CRT   The acronym for *cathode-ray tube*. This electronic device is the screen in televisions and computer displays. In most cases in this book, CRT refers to the computer display on an editing system.

Crystal black   A term formerly used to refer to the black recorded on a videotape before an editing session using insert recordings. See **Black**.

Crystal-controlled playback   The audio playback to which a performer lip syncs during a videotaped performance. This playback must run at a perfectly constant speed. A variable-speed playback will cause each take of the performance to be slightly different. Because a normal reel-to-reel machine does not run at a perfectly constant speed, an editor must use a crystal-controlled machine, such as a quarter-inch Nagra™ audio deck, or a video deck.

CU   The abbreviation for *close-up*.

Cut   The complete and immediate change from one image or sound to another in video, film, or audio. This was the first effect used in editing and is often the most effective.

Cutaway   A shot, edited in a scene, that cuts away from the main action.

Cuts-only editor   An editor that performs only cuts.

D   In an EDL, an indication that the edit is a dissolve (as opposed to a cut, wipe, or key).

D mode   An EDL list which is organized in such a way that a playback reel is used in its entirety, as in the B mode assembly, but with all effects listed at the bottom of the EDL.

DAT   The acronym for *digital audio tape*. A cassette format featuring qualitatively superior sound, referring to either a recorder or a tape. It has two tracks as well as the ability to record time code.

DAW   The abbreviation for *digital audio workstation*. This computerized mixing device can be used to create effects, edit audio, or mix programs—replacing or augmenting analog multitrack audio mixing.

Demo reel   A videotape that shows a production company's or editor's best work, usually made to sell that individual's talent or that company's services.

Demodulate   To decode a signal that has been impressed onto a carrier frequency.

Digital A signal that is encoded in ones and zeros (binary code) rather than by modulating a carrier wave's signal.

Digital effect A generic term for the effect(s) generated by a digital effects generator.

Digital effects generator A device that produces digital effects. Each device has different capabilities and limitations and may have one or more channels. Each channel can manipulate one video signal. A multibox effect would require multiple channels or multiple video generations. In a very complicated sequence, both multiple channels and multiple generations might be used.

Digital video A video picture that is recorded digitally. Some machines can store single frames and short segments of video digitally on disks. There are also tape machines that can store large amounts of video digitally. Multiple generations of digital video look exactly like the camera original because the picture is recreated by digital signals rather than by copying the signal.

Disk drive The machine that reads and writes information on computer disks.

Diskette A computer disk with a magnetic coating that can record computer information. In video production and editing, these disks are used to store EDLs, character generator information, switcher information, and digital effects.

Dissolve The fading of one image into another. A dissolve from black or to black is called a *fade*. The dissolve or fade is made either in a film lab or through a video switcher.

Dolly A shot created by movement of a camera (toward or away from a performer or object) that is usually on a set of tracks.

Downtime The time when equipment is unavailable due to malfunction or maintenance.

Drop frame time code Time-accurate time code. Drop frame time code is time accurate because it drops two numbers every minute to make up for the small error that results from assuming that video runs at exactly 30 frames per second. Because video actually runs at 29.97 frames per second, the numbers 00:00:00:00 and 00:00:00:01 are dropped every minute except at the 10-minute marks (01:10:00:00, 04:50:00:00, etc.)

Dropout Physically, a lack of oxide on the videotape that looks like a silver bullet shooting across the screen. Some time base correctors will correct for this lack of picture by repeating the previous scan line.

Dropout compensator An electronic portion of a time base corrector that senses the lack of oxide on a videotape and repeats the scan line above it.

DT The abbreviation for *dynamic tracking.*

Dub (1) A copy of another videotape or the process of making a copy of a tape. (2) To mix a final version of a film.

DVE The brand name of a digital effects generator manufactured and marketed by NEC℠.

Dynamic tracking   A process of reading videotape that locks to the video frame line rather than the control track and tends to help unstable video recordings play back correctly. It is especially effective in eliminating playback errors due to control track hits. Most of the newer one-inch machines offer this mode of playing back tapes.

E mode   A method of organizing an EDL for minimal source shuttle time as in a C mode list, but all effects are listed at the bottom of the EDL.

ECU   The abbreviation for *extreme close-up*.

Ediflex®   The brand name of a random-access editing system that uses tape or laser disks to store information.

EditDROID™   The brand name of a random-access editing system that uses tape or laser disks to store information.

Edit decision list (EDL)   A computer-generated or handwritten list of the edits performed in either an on-line or an off-line editing session.

Editec®   One of the first editing systems developed by Ampex and first sold in 1963.

Editing   The process of creating a structure from the pictures and/or audio in a visual program.

Editing bay   An editing room.

Editing on the fly   See **Sync mode**.

Editing session   The time spent in an editing facility during which the visual and audio portions are placed in order, creating a portion of a program or a completed program.

Editing suite   An editing room.

Editor   (1) A person who creatively and/or technically assists the owners of a visual show in creating a structure from pictures and audio. (2) A videotape controller that is capable of making edits.

EDL   The abbreviation for *edit decision list*.

EECO   The corporate developer of time code.

Effect   Any transition or combination of images other than a cut.

EIAJ   The abbreviation for *Electronic Industries Association of Japan*.

Element   A portion of a show, graphics, audio, videotape, or film; especially used in describing materials for creating effects.

Electron beam   A stream of electrons aimed at a particular target. In television, the electron beam is aimed at a phosphorus tube. As the beam hits the phosphors, they glow, creating a picture.

EMC²®   The brand name of a random-access editing system that uses computer digital processing to store information.

E-MEM® Effects memory, trademarked function created by the Grass Valley Group™, which stores switcher setups and/or effects. An E-MEM can be stored in an EDL or on a computer disk.

ENG The abbreviation for *electronic news gathering*, the shooting and editing of news on video. The production process of ENG usually occurs on location.

E-PIX® The brand name of a random-access editing system that uses computer digital processing to store information.

Equalization The changing of sound frequencies to alter the original sound, making it more pleasing to the ear.

ESS The brand name of a slow-motion machine that uses a metal disk to store and play back video.

Extreme close-up A camera framing of an object or person that is very close to that person or object and usually does not allow for any headroom. An ECU can also be of any part of a person's body.

F mode A method of organizing an EDL according to source and record times so that the reel can be edited with the minimum amount of shuttling from either machine.

Fade A dissolve to or from black, a dissolve to or from a key, or the raising or lowering of audio levels. See **Dissolve** and **Black**.

Field (of video) Each frame of video in the NTSC signal (the United States' television format) consists of two fields. Television creates a picture through vertical lines, and each field has 262.5 lines of video. The lines are displayed on the television tube in an interlace pattern. The odd lines of each frame are scanned, producing one field, then the even lines are scanned, producing the other field. Together, the two fields create a frame.

Field dominance The field at which an editing system begins an edit. Field 1 dominance begins the edit at the first field of a frame of video. Field 2 dominance begins an edit in the middle of the frame, on the second field.

Film A strip of silver-coated acetate or polyester base, coated with a light-sensitive material, and perforated with sprocket holes on the side. The silver reacts when exposed to light. This was the first visual recording medium that could be projected. Also see **Videotape**.

Film camera The machine that exposes a controlled amount of light to film.

Film lab The place where all film is developed and where film effects are incorporated into a project.

Film-to-tape The process of transferring images from film positive or negative onto a videotape.

Foley The process of creating sounds that will eventually be edited into a sound track while viewing footage of a project.

Foreground   That portion of a key signal that appears over the picture (which is called the background). In a key using a title over a newscaster, the words are considered the foreground and the newscaster the background.

Frame (of video)   A frame of video consists of two fields (see **Field**). Each second of video consists of 29.97 frames, which is usually rounded off to 30 frames a second. See **Drop frame time code** and **Non-drop frame time code**.

Frame accurate   An adjective describing an editor's ability to make accurate, color-framed, quality edits. Until the coming of time code, frame accuracy was only a dream. Most computer-based editing systems are field accurate, meaning that an edit is performed on a specific field and can be repeated accurately.

Frame store   An electronic device that stores multiple frames of video.

Frame synchronizer   A device that accepts nonsynchronized video, stores it for a full frame, then sends the signal back out, properly timed with the rest of the video system.

Freelance   An editor, stage manager, director, or other professional who is self-employed and works for numerous employers.

Freeze frame   A frame of video that has been frozen. A freeze frame can be accomplished through the use of several electronic devices, including a video machine with dynamic tracking, a digital effects device, a frame synchronizer, a slow-motion disk, a videodisk, a frame store device, a paint box, or a high-end character generator.

Front porch   The portion of the horizontal blanking from the end of a picture to the leading edge of the sync.

Generation   One copy of a videotape. An edited master is usually one generation away from the camera original. A submaster is two generations away from the camera original.

Glitches   Any oddity in a video signal. The causes of glitches run the gamut from power surges during recording to poor tape stock, control track hits, and gremlins in an editing system.

GPI   General-purpose interface. Many devices can be triggered by an electronic pulse. This trigger device is a GPI. GPIs are used to put digital video devices and other peripheral equipment into a predetermined function (play, rewind, record, or freeze).

Half-inch video   Two types of half-inch video are available: video for home use and broadcast-quality video. VHS and Betamax are the two home-use formats. They have been used for broadcast video, but they have very poor resolution and usually wide blanking. Home-use half-inch tape makes an excellent screening medium, however, and is used as an off-line format. Betacam and MII are the two major broadcast-quality half-inch video formats. See **Blanking, Broadcast quality, Betacam,** and **MII**.

Handles   An additional length of audio and/or video. Handles are the extra heads and tails recorded when dubbing sections of footage. The extra material ensures that there is more than enough program material for editing purposes.

HDTV The abbreviation for *high-definition television,* a wide-screen format with greatly improved resolution. HDTV is a catchall for a group of proposed, standard, wide-screen video formats. See **High-definition television.**

Headroom The area above a person's head in the camera framing. Every shot of a person, except an extreme close-up, should have headroom.

Helical scan A method of recording video on tape at an angle to the tape's travel, also called *slant track recording.* All videotape recordings are helical scan, with the exception of quad recordings.

Heterodyne A method of viewing the unstable video signal from a videotape without the use of a time base corrector. The picture appears stable to the eye, but cannot be used as a signal for direct switcher input.

High-definition television A new technology developed for home and professional use. This method of recording and playback, with more than 1,000 scan lines, will be shown on wide screens both commercially and at home.

Hiss Unwanted background noise in an audio recording.

Horizontal blanking The time during which the electron beam is shut off, or blanked, to allow the beam to retrace to the beginning of the next horizontal scan line. See **Blanking.**

House A word used in place of *facility.* For example, there are editing houses, dubbing houses, production houses, and sweetening houses.

Hue The shade of a particular color.

IEEE The abbreviation for *Institute of Electrical and Electronics Engineers.*

Image enhancement The digital process of sharpening the image of a video picture. Often noise reduction is performed at the same time as image enhancement.

Industry standard A term applied to a machine or format that is commonly used within a certain area of production. For instance, one-inch Type C tape is a broadcast industry standard.

In-frame A video edit in which the previous picture is continued by making a cut. This type of edit is used to create dissolves and other types of effects. A dissolve usually follows immediately after the in-frame. If all the technical parameters of the previous video are not exactly the same, this in-frame edit is very noticeable. The most frequent error that occurs when making this type of edit is a shift, which is a vertical or horizontal movement. Most bad in-frame edits shift left or right (a horizontal, or H, shift).

In-house A term meaning *within the company.* For instance, if a show was totally edited by a corporation's video department, you would say that the show was edited in-house. If all or part of the show was edited at another facility, you would say that the show was edited out-of-house.

IN point The beginning of a video edit. Each edit has two IN points: the IN point of the playback tape and the IN point of the record tape. Two IN points and an OUT point define a video cut.

Insert editing   The process of putting a shot between two other shots.

Insert recording   A method of video recording that does not affect the tape's control track. To make a proper insert recording, an editor must first record unbroken video and the control track on the tape in an assemble recording to ensure a continuous signal. This is the only type of video recording that can perform an audio-only or video-only edit. See **Assemble recording.**

Interface   The electronic component that receives computer command signals and translates those signals into a command that another machine can understand.

IRE   A measure of video devised by the Institute of Radio Engineers, now called the Institute of Electrical and Electronics Engineers (IEEE).

Joystick   A device used as a variable-speed control of a videotape machine, or a device that manipulates any electronic device. Joysticks are found on digital effects generators, switchers, and home computers.

Jump cut   A cut to a similar shot, resulting in one or more objects in the frame appearing to jump into position. The most obvious example is when an edit of a person is made using the same camera angle, but the person has moved. This gives the illusion that the person, or even just the person's head, has jumped from one spot to another. Often a cutaway is used to cover jump cuts. Occasionally, jump cuts are used as an effect to make objects or people disappear. See **Cutaway.**

Kaleidoscope   The brand name of the Grass Valley Group's digital effects device.

Key cut   A signal from a video device to the switcher that indicates the specific area in the background where the key is to be cut. See **Background.**

Key frame   In an electronic device, an event in a series of events that represents one step in the sequence. Key frames are used in random-access editors effects, DVE devices to define moves, and switchers to define a series of events.

Kinescope   A video-to-film transfer, often used for archiving or as a picture reference for negative cutting.

L cut   Also referred to as a *split edit,* this cut has either the audio or the video preceding or extending beyond a both cut.

Lay back   A sweetening term that means to record the audio mix from a multitrack recording on the original edited master. This process erases the edited production audio and replaces it with the final audio.

Lay over   A sweetening term that means to copy an edit master's audio and time code to a multitrack tape.

Layering   The building of effects, one layer at a time, that can encompass from one to hundreds of layers.

Lightworks™   The brand name of a random-access editor used primarily in the editing of feature films.

Limiter   An audio circuit that stops loud noises at a predetermined level. Some video record machines have built-in limiter options.

List cleaning   EDLs can become full of unwanted and unneeded edits as more and more changes occur in the off-line workprint. The process of cleaning these false and inaccurate listings is part of list management. There are two methods of cleaning an EDL. The first is to go through the list on a computer and manually correct the EDL, using the rough cut or workprint as a guide. The second method is to have the computer do this cleaning with a computer program. Three cleaning programs that can be used for this purpose are 409® from the Grass Valley Group, EDL Optimizer™ from CMX, and Edit Lister™ from Comprehensive Video Supply or EDL Xpress®.
   Cleaning a list by hand is tedious, but saves time and expense during an on-line edit. The obvious advantage of using a computer cleaning program is the time saved. The disadvantage is the cost and availability of computer equipment. The 409 cleaning program requires a Grass Valley editing system, Edit Lister requires an Apple® II or IBM®-compatible computer, and EDL Optimizer is a self-contained unit. See **Trace**.

List management   The cleaning and tracing of an EDL before an on-line edit. See **List cleaning** and **Trace**.

Lock   Video must be locked in several ways before a good edit can be made. Time code lock occurs when the computer has moved the record and playback tapes into their proper positions during the preroll. The tape machines must also be locked vertically and horizontally before a proper edit can be made. Most computer editing systems check these three areas before going into edit mode, and if anything is not locked up, the edit is aborted. Occasionally, an edit is performed even though one of these variables is not locked. If this occurs, the edit may have to be performed again.

Lower thirds   Graphics keyed over an image that describe a location or state a person's name and title.

Luminance   The white value of a video signal.

Luminance key   This key senses the dark or light portion of a signal and cuts an electronic hole in the background in the shape of that signal. The hole is then filled with another source of video. See **Key cut** and **Background**.

M&E   The abbreviation for music and effects tracks. Often shows that are prepared for international distribution require M&E tracks because the dialogue and narration will be translated, but the music and effects will remain in the show.

MII   A half-inch broadcast format devised by Panasonic®. MII uses helical scan component recordings, is capable of using address track time code, and has four audio channels.

Master log   The record of a particular show that contains the reel numbers and the footage on those reels, production notes, the show's script, the EDL, where the off-line and camera original masters are stored, the time code start and stop times of each reel, credit notes and spellings, and any other information pertaining to the program.

Match cut edit   See **In-frame**.

Matte (1) A colorized key. (2) A high-contrast image used to cut a hole in the background in a shot. Mattes are used in video and film.

Matte camera A video camera whose purpose is to turn art cards into a video signal, allowing the switcher to combine these graphics with other video. Matte cameras can be color cameras but are usually capable of producing only black-and-white images. The black-and-white signals can be colorized in the switcher by making a matte key.

Matte key A key cut made from a luminance key, key cut, or chroma key and filled with a switcher color.

Medium shot A camera framing of a person or object. A medium shot of a person is usually from the waist to the head, with headroom at the top of the frame. See **Headroom**.

Mixer (1) A device used to combine various audio sources. (2) A person who operates an audio mixing device.

Mixing The process of gathering and combining audio elements for a visual production.

Modulate To encode an audio or video signal onto a carrier frequency by altering its amplitude or frequency.

Modulated wipe A wipe is electronically bent out of its regular shape. Modulation of a wipe can curve, bend, or oscillate straight lines. A vertical wipe could be modulated into a wavy line or a circle into an oval shape. The amount of modulation available varies from switcher to switcher, and some switchers cannot modulate wipes at all.

Montage™ (1) An established random-access editing system that uses disks or tape as a storage medium, manufactured by the Montage Group. (2) A series of relatively quick edits, often made to a music track.

MS The abbreviation for *medium shot.*

Multitrack An audio recorder/player that has more than one audio track. A multitrack machine usually has four or more tracks.

Mylar® A strong, flexible base used for the manufacture of videotape.

Network In television, a company that delivers programs to a group of stations. There are cable networks and loosely knit station networks (sometimes called ad hoc networks), but the three major networks are NBC, ABC, and CBS. There is a fourth broadcast network, the Fox network; however, it does not broadcast as many hours as the other three.

Nonadditive mix A combining of two video sources, with each source having a 100%-video level. In a dissolve, the highest level that two video sources can reach is 50% of each signal.

Non-drop frame time code The original time code, calculated at 30 frames per second. Since television runs at 29.97 frames per second, an error in timing builds up. The other type of time code is *drop frame time code*, which is time accurate.

Nonsegmented video recording   A video recording in which each revolution of the video heads records a complete field of video information. Many nonsegmented video playback machines are capable of still-frame and slow-motion effects without additional modification.

Nonsynchronous time code   Time code that is out of sync with the video with which it was recorded. Time code is recorded in the middle of the video frame. If the code is not recorded in its proper place, the computer editor will think that the video frame is in one place and the video playback deck will think that it is in another. The two will then fight for control of the deck, rendering the code unusable. If this happens, the reel should be rerecorded. See **Time code generator, Regenerated time code**, and **Lock**.

NTSC   The abbreviation for *National Television Standards Committee*, which created the standards for American television. This acronym also refers to the standard formulated by the committee. See the Appendix.

Off-line edit   The decision-making editing session. Not all of the edits recorded during the off-line session will end up in the final version of a program. Off-line editing can be done on a computer editing system or a control track editing system.

One-inch   A videotape format that is one-inch wide. The two subformats of one-inch videotape are Type B and Type C, which use different recording processes and different types of videotape.

Offset   A time code duration used to calculate split edits or to find specific locations on a reel with time code different from the original.

Omni®   A powerful edit controller from the CMX Corporation.

On-line edit   Any video editing session that produces a master that will be used in the final product. This edit session might be a prebuild session that is designed to create portions of the final show or the assembly of various elements to build the final show.

Open-ended edit   An edit that is performed without a defined OUT point. The OUT point is determined during the edit.

Opticals   The film term for *effects*. Opticals can be anything from titles to complex computerized animation.

Original master   A first-generation audio, video, or film recording. See **Camera original**.

Oscilloscope   A device that displays electronic signals on a screen. Waveform monitors and vectorscopes are two types of oscilloscope.

OUT point   The end of an edit on either the playback or the record side. The OUT point is found by adding the edit duration to the time code of the IN point.

Overrecord   In an off-line editing session, an edit is often made longer than it will be in the final show. The following edit will usually erase the tail of such an edit. The erased portion of the edit is called an overrecord. The listing of the partially erased edit in a computer EDL should be modified before the on-line session. If the overrecords are not removed from the EDL, valuable time will be wasted during the on-line edit because the overrecord will only be erased. See **List cleaning**.

Oxide   In videotape, the easily magnetized, brown, ferrous oxide material onto which the video and audio signals are recorded. Usually the oxide is on a strong, flexible backing such as Mylar. Oxide is also used on diskettes and audiotape.

PAL   The acronym for *phase alternate line*. A recording format used in Europe and Great Britain that derives its name from the fact that the burst phase inverts every scan line. See the Appendix.

Pan   A shot created by swiveling a camera horizontally. See **Tilt**.

Paper list   A handwritten EDL, usually the result of a control track off-line edit session.

Pedestal   The lowest IRE portion of the video signal. Also called the *setup*. In standard broadcast signals, the pedestal should not be below 7.5 IRE units. See **Blanking** and **Black**.

Phasing   Phasing occurs when frequencies of the the audio recorded on two different tracks of a tape are not syncronized. The symptoms of the problem are heard when the two tracks are played back together. If the tracks are out of phase, or slightly out of sync, the common frequencies will cancel each other out. If phasing occurs, the phase of the audio on one of the tracks must be reversed. Many audio mixers have phase reversals, that, at the press of a button, can reverse the phase of one of the sources to eliminate the phasing problem.

Phosphor   A substance that will exhibit luminescence when struck by light of certain wavelengths.

Pick-up tube   A device in a video camera that converts light into electrical impulses. The pick-up tube has generally been replaced by a newer device called a *charged coupled device* (CCD), which does the same task but is a computer chip rather than a vacuum tube.

Ping-ponging   The process of transferring the production audio from one track of a three-quarter-inch tape to the other. This transfer is done when the production audio has been recorded on the audio track that the editing system needs for time code. Once a ping-pong has been accomplished, the time code can be recorded on the audio track that the production track originally occupied. To avoid this one-generation loss of audio, you should determine before production begins which audio track the intended editing system uses for time code. This problem is slowly disappearing with the advent of address track time code, which does not require that time code be recorded on an audio track.

Playback IN   The first frame of material that will be copied onto the record tape. See **IN point**.

Playback OUT   The frame after the last frame of a playback reel that will be recorded onto the record tape. See **OUT point** and Chapter 14 on logging control track edits.

Postproduction   All tasks required to finish a program after the body of the show has been shot. This includes, but is not limited to, scoring, dubbing, automatic dialogue replacement, Foley, editing, conforming, creating effects, mixing, off-line editing, on-line editing, and negative cutting.

Prebuild   A videotape built to be used in an on-line session. Prebuild sessions are on-line, but usually take place before the show's on-line session to create complicated effects.

Preproduction   All tasks required to create a program before the body of the show is shot. This includes, but is not limited to, writing the script, booking talent, scouting locations, locating funds, analyzing the script breakdown, reviewing the storyboard, and renting equipment.

Prelay   Locating, transferring, and editing the audio portion of a production and placing those elements onto a two-track or other mixing medium.

Preread   The ability to read a video and/or audio signal and record that signal onto the same tape at the time that the signal is being read. The digital video format D2 is capable of prereading.

Prereader®   A computer program that organizes an EDL so that the preread function is optimized in the EDL.

Preview   To rehearse an edit without actually recording it. See **VVV**, **BVB**, and **VBV**.

Preview keys   The keys on an editing machine that instruct the machine to perform a preview.

Producer   The person responsible for the final version of a visual production. Often the producer is also responsible for paying the bills.

Production   The recording of a show's picture and audio on film, videotape, audio tape, or all three.

Production audio   The audio that is recorded during the production of a show. Most often, pictures are being recorded simultaneously with the audio.

Production company   A company that makes audio and/or video shows.

Pulse cross monitor   See **Cross-pulse monitor**.

Pulse editor   See **Control track editor**.

Quad   Short for *quadruplex*. Another name for *two-inch videotape*. It is called quad because the machines that record the quad signal have four video heads, each recording or playing back one-quarter of the tape.

Random-access   An editing system that can preview multiple events and immediately change any of them.

Random-access editor   An editing system that has instant access to playbacks and has the ability to adjust any edit IN or OUT point immediately, then play back the results of these changes at once.

Rank Cintel™ A well-known, high-quality, film-to-tape equipment manufacturer.

RAM Random-access memory, the amount of memory a computer has available for volatile and unsaved memory. RAM information is lost when the computer is shut off.

Reality programming Usually segment programs that employ historical footage, reenactments, or on-location footage that deal with human-interest stories. *Sightings*, by definition, is a reality program.

Record To make a copy of video or audio on a video or audio machine. A recording could be from a camera original, a transfer of a camera original, or any other source of picture or sound.

Record IN The first frame on which an edit is to start on the record (copying) side.

Record master The record tape that is used in an editing session. See **Record stock**.

Record OUT The OUT point of an edit on the record machine. See Chapter 14 on logging control track edits.

Record stock The tape on which the edited master will be built. For best results, fresh (new) videotape should be used for this purpose. Ideally, it should be coded with the same time code used by the majority of the playback systems.

Reel number The number assigned to a source reel of videotape. Only one number should be assigned to each reel, and that should be the only number used in the show.

Reel summary A sheet of paper in the master log that lists all the reels in a show and briefly describes what is on them.

Regenerated time code Time code is a digitally encoded signal that should be not just transferred but should be fed into a time code generator and regenerated, ensuring a fresh signal. A time code generator locks to the original code and sends out new time code identical to the original. If time code is merely copied, without regeneration, extraneous noise on the tape might render the code useless.

Ringing The apparent crawling of color at the edges of colorized letters due to the inability of the NTSC signal to rapidly change from one frequency to another.

Room tone The natural sounds that are present at any location. Thirty to sixty seconds of room tone should be recorded at each location.

Rough cut See **Workprint**.

Safe title area The area of the screen in which graphics can be seen by most television viewers.

Safety See **Submaster**.

Sampling Measuring a signals strength at regular intervals. The samples are used to created a digital representation of that original signal.

Saturation The amount of color.

Screen direction   The direction of action across the screen. A specific real-life direction of action does not always translate to the same direction on the screen. Screen direction depends on camera placement.

Screening   The viewing of tape or film. There are many reasons to screen a show, from viewing the original footage to considering the purchase of a finished show.

Script   The written plan, both audio and visual, of a program.

SECAM   A foreign standard for television broadcasting. See the Appendix.

Second track   Track two of a two-track audio system.

Segmented video recording   A method of recording video in which more than one revolution of the video head is required to record a field. Segmented video recordings need special equipment to play back in slow motion or freeze frames. Quad and Type B one-inch tape use the segmented video recording method.

Setup   See **Pedestal.**

Shifts   See **In-frame.**

Shuttle time   The actual clock time that it takes a particular videotape to go from where it is sitting to where it is supposed to be, at full speed. Most often, shuttle time refers to the time it takes to go from the head of the tape to the tail at full speed.

Single-camera production   The shooting of a program with one camera (as opposed to using multiple cameras).

Sit-com   Short for *situation comedy.*

Skew   The adjustment on a video machine that corrects the tension on the tape. Many newer tape machines automatically adjust the skew. Misadjusted skew results in a bend at the top of the video picture.

Slate   The audio or video identification of the take and location of a particular show or shot. Slates on the edited master usually include audio information (mixed or unmixed, sweetened or unsweetened) and running time.

Slaved time code   See **Regenerated time code.**

Slow-motion   The effect of slowing down the playback speed of a videotape. Slow-motion can be accomplished using a machine with dynamic tracking or a video slow-motion disk. Also called *slo-mo.*

SMPTE   The abbreviation for *Society of Motion Picture and Television Engineers,* a group of people dedicated to the improvement and standardization of the visual industry.

Snow   Video noise seen when playing a blank videotape.

Source select keys   Keys on the editing keyboard that select auxiliary sources or videotape machines. Once a machine is selected, other keys may be used to control that machine.

Splice   To physically cut a piece of film or video and add another section to it.

Split edit   An edit with sync sound that begins with only picture or only audio before becoming a both edit.

Spotlight   A video effect that darkens a portion of the frame, usually through the use of a switcher wipe pattern.

Sprocket holes   Holes in film that allow it to be physically pulled a certain distance.

Staff   A company's permanent employees.

Steadicam®   Trade name for a hand-held steadying device for cameras, usually bracing the camera to a person's body.

Storyboard   An illustrated plan for a film or video project.

Stripe   To record time code onto a videotape.

Submaster   An exact copy of an edited master, usually made as a backup in case the master is damaged.

Subcarrier   A group of frequencies that is impressed onto a main carrier frequency. In composite video, chroma is transmitted by encoding a subcarrier, which is impressed onto the luminance carrier frequency.

S-VHS®   An improvement over the popular VHS video format that utilizes metal tape.

Sweetening   The audio portion of video postproduction that is done on a multitrack audio machine. See Chapter 18.

Switcher   The switcher takes all the video sources and combines them to make a composite picture that is either broadcast (live television) or recorded on tape. (Both the subcarrier and horizontal signals must be timed with the switcher for it to work properly. Each video source has its own adjustments. See Chapter 4 for more information about switcher timing.) Most computer editing systems have some sort of switcher.

Sync   This term is used in several ways:

1. *Audio sync* is when the picture and audio are in sync with each other. Audio could become out of sync with the picture through repeated dubbing, using a frame synchronizer, or as a result of a poorly planned audio-only edit.
2. The *video signal* is composed of horizontal and vertical sync pulses. If these pulses are not properly recorded or played back, the picture can lose sync, resulting in a glitch, picture roll, or other video abnormality.
3. The *time code* must be synched with the video that is being recorded. If the time code is not in sync with the video, the time code is useless for editing.
4. All *inputs to a switcher* must be timed to each other. If a signal is out of time (out of sync) with the other inputs to the switcher, effects will not be possible.

Sync mode   The rolling of two or more playback machines and editing on the fly. It is much like cutting a show live, except that you can stop to make corrections.

Syndication   When a television show is not carried by a network, it is often sold on a station-by-station basis. This process is called syndication. The people and companies who sell these shows are called *syndicators*.

Take (1) A word meaning *attempt* at the beginning of a scene or shot. "Take One" would be the first attempt to get everything (camera, audio, lighting, effects, acting, and background actors) just right. (2) To select another camera or source in a program through the use of a switcher. "Take Two" the director will shout to the technical director, who will select camera number two to be on the air, or be recorded.

Tape delay The practice of taping a broadcast, then replaying it at a later date.

Tape operator In most on-line facilities, the editor works with a tape operator in the editing bay. The tape operator loads and unloads tapes and is responsible for the technical setup of the video. The tape operator is vital to the on-line edit and is invaluable to the editor.

TBC The abbreviation for *time base corrector.*

Telecine A type of editing bay or the process of transferring film images to video tape.

Three-quarter-inch A video format that is widely used for both broadcast and industrial productions.

Three-two pulldown The method of transferring four film frames to five video frames by repeating a field of visual information every other frame. Thus, three fields of information are recorded, then two, then three.

Tilt A shot created by pivoting a camera vertically. See **Pan**.

Time base corrector (TBC) A TBC synchronizes video signals, allowing the signals to be locked into switcher timing. TBCs usually contain a dropout compensator (DOC), which senses the lack of oxide on the videotape and replaces that scan line with the line above it.

Time code A digitally encoded signal that is recorded on videotape in the format of hours:minutes:seconds:frames. The purpose of time code is to label each frame of video. An example of a time code signal would be 05:15:18:23.

Time code generator A machine that creates time code.

Time code keys Keys used in an editing system to enter time code into the computer.

Time-of-day time code Time code that is generated by a time code generator set to the actual clock at the time of production.

Toaster™ A visual effects device platformed on an Amiga™ computer that can perform switcher effects and create digital video effects.

Tone An audio reference signal that is recorded at the head of any audio recording and is used to calibrate the playback of that signal. On a video recording, bars are usually recorded at the same time as tone.

Trace® A computer program marketed by the Grass Valley Group that searches back multiple generations of workprints to locate original edits.

Tracing powder A very fine powder that was used in the early days of tape editing when tape was physically cut. The powder was sprinkled on the videotape to make the frame line visible.

Tracking   The adjustment of the videotape playback position to phase the video tracks against the video read heads. This is usually an adjustable function of all helical-scan recordings (half-inch, three-quarter-inch, and one-inch videotape). The best tracking will produce the best picture.

Tracking edit   In CMX systems, the two lines that constitute a dissolve. The first line defines the *from* edit, and the second defines the *to* edit. A zero-length first line is called a tracking edit.

Track slippage   A method of moving a digital audio track out of its originally recorded sync relationship. This might be used to place audio in a different location (off camera) or to slip a music track a few frames to make a more pleasing sound edit.

Transport keys   Keys on an editing system that, when used with the source keys, command the videotape machines to stop, fast-forward, play, or fast-rewind.

Trim   (1) The process of altering time code that has been entered into an editor. (2) The remainder of a shot after the chosen portion has been edited into a film project. A trim can be many feet long and stored in a box, or consist of a few frames and kept in an envelope.

Two-inch   See **Quad**.

Two pop   An audible beep placed on a film or video countdown two seconds before the start of a picture or show.

Type A   The original one-inch format created by Ampex. Type A is no longer used.

Type B   A segmented format of one-inch videotape recordings created by the Bosch-Fernseh company. See Chapter 3 on video formats.

Type C   The Sony/Ampex compromise one-inch video format. Most television recording and editing use this format. See Chapter 3 on video formats.

Ultimatte®   The brand name of a highly refined chroma keying device.

User bits   An area in time code set aside for client use. Numbers or selective alphanumeric characters (A through F) can be recorded along with time code and subsequently read back. User bits require additional equipment to encode and decode the information.

VBV   The abbreviation for *video-black-video*. A preview that shows a portion of the outgoing record picture, then black, then the portion of the record tape that will follow the planned edit.

VCR   The abbreviation for *videocassette recorder*, used to indicate any video player or recorder. Most often it is used to describe home-use machines.

Vector scope   An oscilloscope used in video to display color values and phase relationship.

Vertical interval   The frame line between fields and frames of video, also called the *vertical blanking*. Information such as time code and instructions for automatic color tuning can be recorded in the vertical interval.

Vertical interval switcher   A switcher that will perform a cut only during the vertical interval. All professional switchers are vertical interval switchers.

Vertical interval time code (VITC)   Time code that is recorded in a visual, digital form in the vertical interval.

VHS   A popular home-use half-inch format.

Video   An electronic signal created by a camera or signal generator that can be broadcast over the air or recorded in various ways with different record machines.

Video assist   A video recording of the output of the film camera so that a take can be viewed as it is being shot or immediately after shooting.

Video-black-video preview   See **VBV**.

Video camera   The machine that changes a light source to a video image. The video camera also creates blanking. Any camera to be used on a production should be registered and tested before the actual production begins.

Videodisk   A circular disk that has video etched on it. A videodisk can be read only by a videodisk player.

Videotape   A strip of Mylar with an oxide coating that reacts to electrical impulses.

Video-video-video preview   See **VVV**.

VITC   The acronym for *vertical interval time code.*

VTR   The abbreviation for *videotape recorder.* Occasionally, VTR also refers to a videotape player.

VU meter   A meter that measures the volume units of audio.

VVV   The abbreviation for *video-video-video.* The most-used preview, this shows a portion of the outgoing shot on the record tape, the incoming shot, and a portion of what will appear on the record tape after the edit.

Waveform monitor   An oscilloscope that measures the white and chroma levels of videotape.

Whip   An instability at the top of a video frame occurring when mismatched machines are used to edit a single record tape.

White-balance   The process of shooting a white card with a video camera and pressing a button labeled "White Balance." This activates the camera circuit that adjusts the internal settings of the black level, white level, and the three colors (red, green, and blue) to the white card. See **Color correction** and **Video camera**.

Wide shot   A shot that includes a wide area of a scene.

Window dub   An exact copy of original audio and video, usually on three-quarter-inch or half-inch videotape, with a visual representation of the time code burned into the picture. See **Burned-in time code** and **Off-line edit**.

Wipe   A transition from one picture to another through the use of some sort of design (such as a straight line, diamond, or circle).

Workprint   The rough draft of a television show or film, created through an editing process.

Zoom   (1) A lens with movable elements that allows the operator to change the focal length of the lens. (2) A shot where a zoom lens is used to change the focal length within the shot.

Index

299